2500
80X

Southern Literary Studies
Fred Hobson, Editor

Gothic Traditions and Narrative
Techniques in the Fiction of
EUDORA WELTY

Gothic Traditions and Narrative Techniques in the Fiction of EUDORA WELTY

Ruth D. Weston

Louisiana State University Press
Baton Rouge and London

Copyright © 1994 by Louisiana State University Press
All rights reserved
Manufactured in the United States of America
First printing
03 02 01 00 99 98 97 96 95 94   5 4 3 2 1

Designer: Amanda McDonald Key
Typeface: ITC Garamond Book
Typesetter: G & S Typesetters, Inc.
Printer and binder: Thomson-Shore, Inc.

Library of Congress Cataloging-in-Publication Data
Weston, Ruth D., 1934–
    Gothic traditions and narrative techniques in the fiction of
Eudora Welty / Ruth D. Weston.
        p.   cm. — (Southern literary studies)
    ISBN 0-8071-1897-4 (cl)
    , 1. Welty, Eudora, 1909– —Technique. Gothic revival
(Literature)—Southern States. 3. Southern States—In literature.
4. Narration (Rhetoric) I. Title. II. Series.
PS3545.E6Z97 1994
813'.52—dc20   94-6067
                                                   CIP

The author offers grateful acknowledgment to Russell & Volkening, Inc., literary agents of Eudora Welty, for permission to quote from Welty's unpublished letters; to Curtis Brown, Ltd., Executors of the Estate of Elizabeth Bowen, for permission to quote from unpublished manuscripts held in the Bowen Collection, Harry Ransom Humanities Research Center, the University of Texas at Austin; and to the State of Mississippi Department of Archives and History for permission to publish excerpts from letters held in the Eudora Welty Collection in Jackson. The author also thanks the editors of the following publications for permission to quote from her own work: *South Central Review,* for excerpts from "The Feminine and Feminist Texts of Eudora Welty's *The Optimist's Daughter,*" IV (1987); the Kent State University Press, for a version of "American Folk Art, Fine Art, and Eudora Welty: Aesthetic Precedents for 'Lily Daw and the Three Ladies'" that appeared in *Eudora Welty: Eye of the Storyteller,* ed. Dawn Trouard (1989); and *Short Story,* for a version of "The Optimist in Hawthorne's Shadow: Eudora Welty's Gothic as Lyric Technique," I (1991). Excerpts from the following are reprinted by permission of Random House, Inc.: *The Eye of the Story* by Eudora Welty copyright © 1942, 1943, 1944, 1949, 1955, 1956, 1957, 1963, 1966, 1969, 1971, 1973, 1974, 1975, 1977, 1978 and renewed 1970, 1971, 1972, 1977 by Eudora Welty; *Losing Battles* by Eudora Welty copyright © 1970 by Eudora Welty; *The Optimist's Daughter* by Eudora Welty copyright © 1969, 1972 by Eudora Welty. Excerpts from the following are reprinted by permission of Harcourt Brace & Company: "The Purple Hat" in *The Wide Net and Other Stories,* copyright 1941 and renewed 1969 by Eudora Welty; "First Love" and "A Still Moment" in *The Wide Net and Other Stories,* copyright 1942 and renewed 1970 by Eudora Welty; "At the Landing" in *The Wide Net and Other Stories,* copyright 1943 and renewed 1971 by Eudora Welty; *Delta Wedding,* copyright 1946, 1945 and renewed 1974, 1973 by Eudora Welty; *The Robber Bridegroom,* copyright 1942 and renewed 1970 by Eudora Welty; "June Recital" and "The Whole World Knows" in *The Golden Apples,* copyright 1947 and renewed 1975 by Eudora Welty; "Shower of Gold" in *The Golden Apples,* copyright 1948 and renewed 1976 by Eudora Welty; "The Wanderers," "Moon Lake," and "Music from Spain," in *The Golden Apples,* copyright 1949 and renewed 1977 by Eudora Welty; "Lily Daw and the Three Ladies" and "A Memory" in *A Curtain of Green and Other Stories,* copyright 1937 and renewed 1965 by Eudora Welty; "A Curtain of Green" and "Old Mr. Marblehall" in *A Curtain of Green and Other Stories,* copyright 1938 and renewed 1966 by Eudora Welty; "The Hitch-Hikers" in *A Curtain of Green and Other Stories,* copyright 1939 and renewed 1967 by Eudora Welty; "Death of a Traveling Salesman," "A Worn Path," "Clytie," and "A Visit of Charity" in *A Curtain of Green and Other Stories,* copyright 1941 and renewed 1969 by Eudora Welty; "The Burning" in *The Bride of Innisfallen and Other Stories,* copyright 1951 and renewed 1979 by Eudora Welty; "No Place for You, My Love," in *The Bride of Innisfallen and Other Stories,* copyright 1952 and renewed 1980 by Eudora Welty; "Going to Naples" and "The Bride of Innisfallen" in *The Bride of Innisfallen and Other Stories,* copyright © 1955 and renewed 1983 by Eudora Welty.

In memoriam
Ruth Marguerite Vande Kieft
September 12, 1925–October 27, 1992

Contents

Acknowledgments xi

Abbreviations xiii

Introduction
Nothing So Mundane as Ghosts
Plotting the Gothic Connection 1

I
Settings Between Time and Space
The Gothic Space as Narrative Technique 15

II
Spatiality and the Short Story
The Lyric Technique 48

III
Texts and Contexts of the Self
Patterns of Enclosure, Exposure, and Escape 90

IV
Character Role Reversals and Confluent Genres
The Female Hero 133

Conclusion
Psyche, the Great Mother, and Marriages of Death
A Structural Coda for Female Liberations 173

Bibliography 185

Index 195

Acknowledgments

First thanks go to Katherine P. Scully, who introduced me to Eudora Welty's "A Worn Path" twenty years ago, when I was a novice instructor and Kay was my mentor-teacher at Tulsa Junior College. I am grateful also to the Graduate Faculty of English at the University of Tulsa: to Professors James Gray Watson, Gordon Taylor, and Norman Grabo, who guided this study in its early stages. I am especially grateful for the professional and moral support of Professor Watson, who continues to be for me a model of excellence in scholarship and teaching. Thanks also to Professor Shari Benstock and to the staff of *Tulsa Studies in Women's Literature,* then and now. I gratefully acknowledge the efficient and cheerful assistance of the staffs of several libraries and archives: the McFarlin Library at the University of Tulsa; the Inter-Library Loan staff of the Cadet Library, United States Military Academy at West Point, New York; Elbert R. Hilliard, Forrest Galey, and the staff of the State of Mississippi Department of Archives and History in Jackson; Dr. Thomas Staley, Cathy Henderson, and the staff of the Harry Ransom Humanities Research Center, the University of Texas at Austin. I also thank the Fenimore House Gallery, Cooperstown, New York.

I am especially grateful to Oral Roberts University. The faculty, staff, and students constitute a faithful family who have been a blessing to me during the past five years: the best of times and the worst of times. My deep appreciation goes to a supportive ORU administration for two summer research grants and travel money that was hard to come by, especially to my chairman, Professor William R. Epperson, my other colleagues in the English Department, and to Loretta Williams, who typed the entire manuscript early on.

Welty scholars and other lovers of southern literature are generous folk, and many have befriended, aided, advised, and encouraged me throughout this project: Professors William Bedford Clark, Dawn Trouard, Robert H. Brinkmeyer, Jr., Colby Kullman, Gail Mortimer, Rebecca Mark, and my good editors at Louisiana State University Press, especially

Acknowledgments

John Easterly and Julie Schorfheide, to mention a very few. For their gracious hospitality during my two summers of research in Jackson and one expedition on the Natchez Trace, I thank Professor and Mrs. William V. Brewer. I am deeply grateful to Professor Suzanne Marrs for her friendship and scholarship, and for making me personally acquainted with Eudora Welty one summer evening down in Natchez. Apparent throughout this book will be my profound indebtedness to Professors Louis D. Rubin, Jr., Ruth M. Vande Kieft, Peggy Whitman Prenshaw, and Michael Kreyling, whose invaluable contributions to southern studies have informed and enabled my own, even more than citations can reveal. My profound regret is that Professor Vande Kieft, my friend and the mother of us all in Welty studies, who took an early draft of this book, line by line, through her own refiner's fire, did not live to see it published. I hope the book does honor to her memory.

My family has sustained me greatly: my mother, Mary Seale McLain of the "Staggers Point" Texas Irish; my husband, Professor Kenneth C. Weston, of the University of Tulsa; our daughters, Patricia L. Alexander, June A. Alexander, and Marla R. Weston; and my sister, Betty Lynch. They have provided encouragement, sympathy, and/or a reality check, whatever the moment's need.

My greatest appreciation must go to Miss Welty, even beyond her kind permissions to quote from her writing, published and unpublished. I am grateful to her for several gracious responses to my inquiries, beginning with a 1975 note of encouragement that she has no doubt forgotten, but most of all for her stories, for their wisdom and radiance, their gravity and joy, which continue to give me and my students so much pleasure.

Abbreviations

C	*Conversations with Eudora Welty* (1985)
CS	*The Collected Stories of Eudora Welty* (1980)
DW	*Delta Wedding* (1946)
ES	*The Eye of the Story: Selected Essays and Reviews* (1978)
GA	*The Golden Apples* (1949)
LB	*Losing Battles* (1970)
OD	*The Optimist's Daughter* (1972)
OWB	*One Writer's Beginnings* (1984)
RB	*The Robber Bridegroom* (1942)
TP	*Three Papers on Fiction* (1962)

Introduction

Nothing So Mundane as Ghosts
Plotting the Gothic Connection

I have never seen, in this small section of old Mississippi River country . . . ,
anything so mundane as ghosts, but I have felt many times there a sense of place
as powerful as if it were visible and walking and could touch me.
—Eudora Welty, "Some Notes on River Country"

In the thirty years since Ruth Vande Kieft first discussed Eudora Welty's
use of classical mythology, many Welty scholars have contributed to our
understanding of the intertextuality of her fiction. Welty herself has acknowledged that she makes use of themes and patterns from Greek, Roman, and Irish myth and legend, or "whatever is about that I think truly
expresses what I see in life" (*ES,* 119). Critics have often remarked on
the ways that Welty's interest in mystery has informed her work, but it
has not been generally recognized that a classic source of mystery, the
Gothic, is instrumental in discussing the extraordinary effects that she
achieves. And yet Eudora Welty's relation to the Gothic romance is a
subject that has been on the periphery of critical studies since she began
to publish her stories. From the beginning, commentators have found
gothic overtones in her work, but she has strongly and persistently ob-
jected to being labeled a Gothic writer; and when the "Gothic" suggestion is made now, she is likely to be defended against it, as in William
McDonald's recent comments.[1] And, in fact, she utilizes the tradition not
as the popular Gothic (upper case) genre of "escape" fiction but as a
core of gothic (lower case) materials—plots, settings, characters, image

1. W. U. McDonald, Jr., "Postscript," *Eudora Welty Newsletter,* XII (1988), 15.

patterns, and vocabulary—that operate in her stories in concert with many other literary conventions. Her connection to the Gothic tradition is far from tenuous, however; and in its nature lie answers to some of the most puzzling, and most intriguing, aspects of a fiction that she herself described, especially in its relation to myth, in terms of its "mystery and magic" (*C,* 343).

Welty's adaptation of gothic conventions owes much to both her American and European, especially British, literary forebears. American writers from James Fenimore Cooper forward adapted gothic characteristics such as enclosed settings, pervasive dread, the themes of imprisonment and isolation, the mysterious powers and energies of authority figures, double or disguised characters that represent the unknowable, and numinous phenomena based in the psychological. Washington Irving's "sportive Gothic," though essentially humorous, not only provided the American equivalent of Jane Austen's burlesque of the classic Gothic of the late eighteenth-century British novelist Anne Radcliffe, but also, according to Michael Davitt Bell, forced readers to come to terms with their own romanticizing of human violence and evil.[2] Charles Brockden Brown and Cooper used gothic atmosphere and machinery in ways that suggested the dark side of the human psyche, as did Nathaniel Hawthorne, who established American romantic fiction as a serious investigation into essential human mystery. In Hawthorne, the deep Massachusetts woods became the ambivalent metaphoric equivalent of internal psychic enigmas, on the one hand, and the exhilarating but dangerous freedom from civilized society, on the other.

Eudora Welty, often using strikingly Hawthornian symbols in her fiction and Hawthornian theoretical terminology in her critical essays, has in many ways continued in that tradition. Welty's gothic adaptations take two complementary general forms that follow the lead of writers of the Gothic romance: in settings that create a sense of mystery, and in the theme of enclosure and escape of the "female Gothic"—a generic misnomer, I believe, since all forms of the Gothic offer "deep revelations about gender, ego, and power."[3] Welty's link to the Gothic tradition, then, is her employment of this theme, along with its characteristic settings and conventions, in the creation of the narrative patterns of her fiction. But never does Welty explain away life's mysteries, as did Mrs. Radcliffe, for example. Rather, she tries to suggest "the sense of mystery in

2. Michael Davitt Bell, *The Development of American Romance: The Sacrifice of Relation* (Chicago, 1980), 78–79.

3. Judith Wilt, *Ghosts of the Gothic: Austen, Eliot and Lawrence* (Princeton, 1980), 3.

life we do well to be aware of" (*C,* 62). More than that; she honors—indeed celebrates—the "absolute mystery of the universe" (*C,* 68) as essentially unexplainable.

Welty's earliest and most basic use of gothic convention is in her landscapes, where her well-known affinity for place lends itself to special gothic effects. Judith Wilt, a modern commentator on the Gothic, asserts that "no single aspect of plot, image, or mood says 'Gothic' to us so clearly as the aspect of place," and that "an important part of the Gothic setting is the region of *approach* to the place of mystery, the area in which the land begins to change, or seems to begin to change . . . [, suggesting] the extreme instability of the material world as perceived . . . [, perhaps] as it exists in itself."[4]

Such a setting is the history-haunted Natchez Trace wilderness of Mississippi, which Eudora Welty transforms into her own gothic space: a portentous "neutral territory," recalling the space that Hawthorne described as "somewhere between the real world and fairy-land where the Actual and Imaginary may meet." In this context, "neutral" is not a featureless terrain but rather an ambivalent, indeterminate, but atmospherically supercharged, and sometimes lawless, borderland, a place where "the land begins to change, or seems to begin to change." Welty's literary "neutral grounds" align her work with other American visionary writing: what Alfred Kazin calls the middle ground in Emerson's "infinitude of the private mind" (from *Nature*) and the "undisclosed territory" between capitalized nouns, dashes, gaps, and great silences in the poems of Emily Dickinson; and what Clarence Gohdes has described as the "no-man's land of art" in Poe and James.[5] She often relies upon actual historic borderland settings similar to Hawthorne's forests and to the "neutral ground" between armies in the Hudson Highlands area of New York that is the setting for Cooper's novel *The Spy: A Tale of the Neutral Ground.* In her twentieth-century tales of the neutral ground, through the creation of gothic spaces and functionally active atmospheres, Welty continues the tradition of adapting conventions of the European Gothic for American fiction.

Given the emphasis on the supernatural in the historical literary Gothic, perhaps gothic landscapes are to be expected from a writer who

4. *Ibid.,* 136.
5. Nathaniel Hawthorne, *The Scarlet Letter,* ed. Sculley Bradley *et al.* (1850; rpr. New York, 1962), 31; Alfred Kazin, *An American Procession: The Major Writers from 1830–1930—The Crucial Century* (New York, 1985), 165; Clarence Gohdes, "An American Author as Democrat," in *Literary Romanticism in America,* ed. William L. Andrews (Baton Rouge, 1981), 6.

came to maturity in a land that Walter Hines Page described as haunted, since the Civil War, by the ghosts of the Negro, religious orthodoxy, and the Confederate dead, or as Flannery O'Connor explained it, in a "Christ-haunted" region whose "ghosts cast strange shadows in our literature." Although Welty employs the devices of grotesque characters like O'Connor's and prisonlike, "claustrophobic" houses like those Louise Westling describes in the fiction of Carson McCullers, Welty does not follow those writers into the so-called Southern Gothic; nor does she create the overlay of "gothic sauce to spice up the history of American society" that Cleanth Brooks claims for William Faulkner's *Absalom, Absalom!* She also maintains a wary distance from the importunate ghosts of a moribund aristocracy that trouble Faulkner and so many other Southern writers.[6]

British and American Gothic traditions are generally recognized as comprising several major periods of development, beginning with the classic Gothic romances that were marked by sensationalism: those of Horace Walpole, C. R. Maturin, Matthew G. "Monk" Lewis, and Anne Radcliffe, and their American counterpart, Charles Brockden Brown, in the latter half of the eighteenth century. In the nineteenth century, what Robert Heilman has called the "new" psychological Gothic novel (as opposed to the Gothic romance) was developed by Scott, Austen, Brontë, Eliot, and Dickens, whose American counterparts were Poe and Hawthorne. In the twentieth century, following D. H. Lawrence in Britain and Faulkner, O'Connor, McCullers, and Capote in America, came the proliferation of Gothic subgenres that resulted in a veritable American Gothic revival in the 1970s.

The most famous exponent of the American "school" of Southern Gothic is Faulkner, mainly because of *Absalom, Absalom!*, with its Byronic villain and haunted house, and such macabre shorter works as "A Rose for Emily" and *As I Lay Dying.* O'Connor's fiction is best known for characters whose physical deformities symbolize spiritual deformities, as does Hulga's wooden leg in "Good Country People." The tradition is ex-

6. Fred Hobson, "The Rise of the Critical Temper," in *The History of Southern Literature,* ed. Louis D. Rubin, Jr., *et al.* (Baton Rouge, 1985), 253, summarizing a major theme in *The Southerner* (New York, 1909), the autobiographical novel Walter Hines Page published under the pseudonym of Nicholas Worth at the publishing company he founded, Doubleday; Flannery O'Connor, *Mystery and Manners: Occasional Prose,* ed. Sally and Robert Fitzgerald (New York, 1969), 44–45; Louise Westling, *Sacred Groves and Ravaged Gardens: The Fiction of Eudora Welty, Carson McCullers, and Flannery O'Connor* (Athens, Ga., 1985), 181; Cleanth Brooks, *William Faulkner: The Yoknapatawpha Country* (New Haven, 1966), 295.

emplified in McCullers by nightmarish, near-surreal spaces on the margins of life, like the southern army post during peacetime in *Reflections in a Golden Eye* and the bizarre living quarters of the grotesque characters in *The Ballad of the Sad Cafe.* The appellation *gothic grotesque* usually accompanies any discussion of the characters of McCullers and O'Connor. McCullers denies the tag *gothic* in favor of what she calls a "peculiar and intense realism," and she prefers the term *freakish* to *grotesque* in describing the sexually aberrant self perceived by her female adolescents when they are forced to identify themselves as females at puberty. For example, Mick in *The Heart Is a Lonely Hunter* and Frankie in *Member of the Wedding* are young female protagonists who grow up, as does Miss Amelia in *The Ballad of the Sad Cafe,* without parents or other nurturing role models. They exist in a sort of void, experiencing a freedom that is portrayed as horrifying when seen against the background of the prejudices of the family-oriented southern culture.[7] But the devices of character and structure employed by these major writers began earlier in southern literature with novelists such as Evelyn Scott in *The Narrow Room,* and continued with contemporary writers such as Truman Capote in *Other Voices, Other Rooms.* Ellen Moers's *Literary Women,* which tracks the development of the characteristics of the Gothic, the grotesque, and especially the female Gothic, is helpful in untangling the confusion of these terms in modern southern fiction.

Black writers also work in the Gothic tradition. Perhaps the southern literature that most nearly produces the sensations once caused by the classic Gothic—unrelieved fear and surreal dread—is that of Richard Wright in *Native Son* and Ralph Ellison in *The Invisible Man.* And such sensations are also produced in Gloria Naylor's *Linden Hills,* which, with its grotesque villain and victim and its contemporary gothic dungeon, is only a northern cousin to the Southern Gothic, since its Luther Nedeed family has roots in the South.

Although Welty cannot be placed in the category of Southern Gothic, she *is* a "southern" writer in the sense that the South, as her home, provides a natural source of place in her fiction, and in the sense that she shares in what Heilman calls "the Southern temper": "the coincidence of a sense of the concrete, a sense of the elemental, a sense of the ornamental, a sense of the representative, and a sense of totality." The "ornamental" in Welty includes patterns and images of entangling complexity that heighten the concrete reality of the natural wilderness; and thus it expresses the elemental mystery that is at the heart of her fiction. Still, it is

7. Carson McCullers, *The Mortgaged Heart,* ed. Margarita G. Smith (Boston, 1971), 252.

not the *southernness* of her wildernesses that make them gothic spaces but rather their function as settings for the kind of experiences that penetrate the world of ordinary life, experiences that Martin Buber has called "queer lyric-dramatic episodes or uncanny moments." And, though she follows in the tradition of the Faulkner who wrote that "memory believes before knowing remembers," it is not the *southernness* of that phenomenon of memory and knowing but rather its legitimacy as a universal mode of human understanding that makes its use a powerful component of her narrative technique. The patterns that emerge from Welty's stories, and that derive from many sources, form the link between place and theme. These patterns constitute a vital element in what Welty, in discussing the problem of adapting *The Ponder Heart* for the stage without sacrificing the source of motivation provided by the novella's narration, called a story's "thick, insulating texture of background . . . that [does] the necessary work of making credible the motives for . . . behavior."[8]

A concomitant element in a story's texture is that of plot, not as the "mere" vehicle on which the theme rides, but as Peter Brooks has described it: as the story's vital sense of "boundedness, demarcation, the drawing of lines to mark off and order." Plot indicates where a protagonist psychologically and physically begins and ends; and plot reveals the shape, that is to say, the significance, of the experiences between the beginning and the end. Brooks's concept of plot, based in Aristotle's *Poetics* and influenced by the theories of Paul Ricoeur, is useful in describing Welty's fiction, especially the more complex works of her maturity. Proceeding from the Aristotelian concept of tragedy as "an imitation not of men but of a life, an action, and [the idea that people] are happy or unhappy in accordance with their actions," Brooks emphasizes the constructive role of plot as "the dynamic shaping force of the narrative discourse." The emphasis on the active role of plot, Brooks believes, "offers a useful corrective to the structural narratologists' neglect of the dynamics of narrative and points us toward the reader's vital role in the understanding of plot." The energy for such a dynamic comes largely from the fact that plot, as Ricoeur asserts, "places us at the crossing point of temporality and narrativity," where the sensitive reader will feel the impact of the forces acting on a character who is caught between time(s) and space(s), but who, we must not forget, experiences narrative time, a fic-

8. Robert B. Heilman, "The Southern Temper," in *South: Modern Southern Literature in Its Cultural Setting*, ed. Louis D. Rubin, Jr., and Robert D. Jacobs (Garden City, 1961), 48, 52; Martin Buber, *I and Thou*, trans. Walter Kaufman (New York, 1970), 84; William Faulkner, *Light in August* (1932; rpr. New York, 1968), 111; Eudora Welty to Joe Fields and Jerry Chodorov, March 28, 1955, in Eudora Welty Collection, Mississippi Department of Archives and History, Jackson, Miss., hereinafter cited as Welty Collection.

tional time that is a more complex phenomenon than historical, linear time. The plot, which takes place in narrative time, is not simply the series of episodes that the reader interprets; plot, as Brooks makes clear, is itself "the interpretive activity" of the story. It is what Ricoeur calls the "configural dimension [which] *elicit*[s] a pattern from a succession" of episodes.[9]

Part of the mystery of Welty's genius is her ability to construct plots that serve as signifying patterns corresponding to cognitive processes; and one of the most basic of these processes (and thus of narrative patterns) is that involving the recognition of similarity and difference—a process that, in fiction as in life, is accomplished through experience, or narrative repetition. In other words, we learn through perceiving likeness or change between a new experience and life as we have lived it, or heard tell of it, before. So with narrative. According to Peter Brooks, a narrative pattern that reveals that "the beginning presupposes the end . . . , [that, in fact,] beginnings are chosen by and for ends," and thus a pattern that constitutes an image in the reader's mind of a same-but-different "double operation upon time," is one specifically designed to shape the reader's imagination to fit the writer's.

The stories of Eudora Welty rely again and again upon patterns such as that of the double spiral that converges upon a still center before opening out again, constituting a narrative transformation that is meaningful because of its formal mirror-image repetition. For the attentive reader, the chaotic forces that bear in upon a character at the beginning of a story are interpreted, as cognitive content, by such spiral patterns and by their reflections in a same-but-different, perhaps also chaotic, expansion at an unresolved ending. The "recognition" available to the reader of such fiction resides not so much in a traditional "recognition scene," or epiphany, as in a subtle, cumulative awareness in the reading consciousness of the convergence of the parts of the pattern. One succinct approach to understanding the concept is through the familiar passage of Faulkner's to which I have already alluded, the theoretical implications of which link Welty's imagination with his in a more profound way than has been recognized:

> Memory believes before knowing remembers. Believes longer than recollects, longer than knowing even wonders. Knows remembers believes a corridor in a big long garbled cold echoing building of dark red brick soot-

9. Peter Brooks, *Reading for the Plot: Design and Intention in Narrative* (New York, 1984), 12–14; Paul Ricoeur, "Narrative Time," in *On Narrative*, ed. W. J. T. Mitchell (Chicago, 1981), 167, 174; Aristotle, *Poetics*, trans. Gerald F. Else (Ann Arbor, 1967), 27 [1450a 16–20, 23–25].

bleakened by more chimneys than its own, set in a grassless cinderstrewn-packed compound surrounded by smoking factory purlieus and enclosed by a ten foot steel-and-wire fence like a penitentiary or a zoo, where in random erratic surges, with sparrowlike childtrebling, orphans in identical and uniform blue denim in and out of remembering but in knowing constant as the bleak walls, the bleak windows where in rain soot from the yearly adjacenting chimneys streaked like black tears.

The narrative/cognitive connection suggested, and briefly demonstrated here in Faulkner, consists of the mysterious "long garbled . . . echoing . . . random erratic . . . [and] adjacenting" words of his long stream-of-consciousness "corridor," a verbal pattern that serves as an interpretive link to the gothic setting of the enclosure in which young Joe Christmas grew up. Like the adult Joe who struggles to remember what he somehow knows, the reader of the passage is "trapped" in labyrinthine "purlieus . . . [of words, of images] like a penitentiary" where, in spite of being "in and out of remembering," he or she is, by virtue of the total impact of the piece, "in knowing constant as the bleak walls." The pattern derives its power as a signifier from the fact that the memory is able to recognize the *shape* of the emotion as it is played out in the narrative; for in this passage Faulkner validates a form of knowing about fictional texts as he suggests a form of knowing for his fictional character. The reader accepts its legitimacy when he or she recognizes that it corresponds to a mode of human understanding about life: in the terms of these images of Faulkner's, about the dread of life's myriad "penetentiar[ies]," both physical and psychological, that confine the human spirit and haunt the winding passages of the memory in spite of the very human tendency to repress their painful traces. The narrative strategies of Welty's fiction rely on such correspondences and on their relation to the cognitive operations of a fictional character and a fiction reader. And they also rely on codes, according to Robert Scholes, including "genres [that] persist like any codification of cultural behavior" and that are recognized by writer and reader from their lifetimes of reading in many literary traditions—traditions which, in Welty's case, include the heroic epic, the mythic, the fairy tale, and several forms of the Gothic. Indeed, Welty's "conflation of meanings . . . and her use of mythic tales . . . [serve to] revive our cultural memories," as Gail Mortimer has shown.[10]

10. Brooks, *Reading for the Plot,* 91–93; Faulkner, *Light in August,* 111; Robert Scholes, Introduction to *The Fantastic: A Structural Approach to a Literary Genre,* by Tzvetan Todorov, trans. Richard Howard (Ithaca, N.Y., 1975), viii–ix; Gail L. Mortimer, "Image and Myth in Eudora Welty's *The Optimist's Daughter,*" *American Literature,* LXII (1990), 633.

Although Welty's central themes are characteristically developed by allusions to the inherent intimacy that she senses between people and places, she is always primarily concerned with human experience. Thus, settings like the intimidating wilderness of "A Still Moment" and the disorienting, hypnotic atmosphere of "No Place For You, My Love" suggest the limitations inherent in being human and in suffering the bondages that love can cause. By means of such dramatic natural landscapes and by analogous spatial patterns in the fiction, Welty communicates the mysterious and disconcerting qualities of life that result from cultural labyrinths that "twine a man [or woman] in," causing such problems as Eugene MacLain's gothic dread of the female in "Music from Spain." Against such complex settings and equally complex human entanglements, Welty's characters contend; some, like Eugene, are defeated, but some, like Dr. Strickland in "The Demonstrators," are visited by what may seem to be unreasonable "assault[s] of hope" (*CS,* 618).

In writing about such enclosures and such hopes of escape, Welty's aim is not stories with "Gothic effect" but rather gothic effects that function organically as tools in the formal shaping of fictional space. She writes about physical and psychological confinement in family and culture, not only through the concrete images of the forest, which are basic to her narratives, but also through her concern with space instead of time, or with spatial representations of time, or with space as it intersects time, and always with spatial more than causal continuity. Like Hawthorne, she intellectualizes her landscapes through symbolic mindscapes. Through the illusion of dramatic motions, she creates the sense of forces converging upon a victim, or the equally frightening sense that a character's ordered world is dissolving in chaos. Especially in "The Burning" and in "The Wanderers," her technique recalls that of Faulkner's "memory believes" passage from *Light in August.*

Yet her fiction achieves intellectual complexity without Faulknerian syntactic fragmentation. She constructs a story that is, she says, "steadily visible from its outside" (*ES,* 120), externalizing inner emotions by the use of the spatial components of painting, drama, dance, and even the geometric shapes of mathematics and physics. By combining a powerful sense of physical space with a knowledge of the many human ways of knowing, she allows us not only to "see" a Welty story but also to "feel" the pull of powerful forces that surround and affect her characters.

Welty characteristically writes comedy; yet, like Washington Irving, she forces the recognition of human complicity in the romanticizing of the violence that has historically accompanied the American experience. Thus, even while we enjoy the fun of *The Robber Bridegroom,* we are

9

horrified by the crimes of its bandits and Indians, as Welty, in discussing its adaptation for the stage, said we should be. She refused to exonerate Jamie, even though he, "as hero," is "detached" from the rape, mutilation, and murder of the Indian maiden. She insisted that, in the adaptation, "the actual horror should be given—simply and quickly, but no mistake." In fact, though Welty's "most direct" sources for *The Robber Bridegroom* may be the tales of Apuleius and the Grimms, the tale also bears a striking resemblance to Irving's "Story of the Young Robber," in which a young member of a robber band helps to capture his beloved. Even the unfortunate girl's name, Rosetta, resembles that of Welty's heroine, Rosamond. Rosetta is abducted for love by the young robber, as is Welty's Rosamond; but because Irving's robbers have shared an oath that "all spoils of the band were determined by lot," and because Rosetta is declared by the band's captain to be "a prize" and thus to be shared jointly, she is repeatedly raped by the robbers. Her lover is unhappy about this, but he is, alas, bound by his oath. His only recourse is to dispatch the girl himself to save her honor, so he murders her with his poignard. In the Grimms' version, the worst violence is vented upon a girl other than the heroine. The victim in Welty's story is also displaced, in this instance by an Indian girl whom Little Harp mistakes for Rosamond and who is drugged, mutilated, raped, and murdered. Nevertheless, the parallels in the stories, including the dirk that, in Welty's *The Robber Bridegroom,* kills an innocent girl who is mistaken for the beloved of a member of the band, constitute an uncanny link between Welty and the early American Gothic tradition. An interesting "modern" emendation in both Irving and Welty is the rape of the victims; the Grimms' robbers chopped up their victims in little pieces, salted them, and ate them.[11]

The language of the literary Gothic—a language of seduction, betrayal, and captivity—is appropriate to Welty's portrayal of the closed-in quality of life in a carceral society and to the more specific theme of female enclosure and escape. The prominent role that Welty ascribes to family and culture, as society's (carceral) guardians of binding myth and memory, constitutes Welty's nearest recognized literary link with her southern contemporaries William Faulkner and Katherine Anne Porter. In Welty's fiction, such bonds are often depicted as both realistic and symbolic representations of all the cultural binds and boundaries that have limited individual, and especially female, development. However, Welty's

11. Eudora Welty to John Robinson, December, 1948, in Welty Collection; Kenneth D. Chamlee, "Grimm and Apuleius: Myth-blending in Eudora Welty's *The Robber Bridegroom,*" *Notes on Mississippi Writers,* XXIII (1991), 38; Washington Irving, "Story of the Young Robber," in *The Works of Washington Irving* (1824; rpr. Philadelphia, n.d.), 411.

protagonists either oppose the tyrannies of ordered culture or penetrate and infuse that culture with new life; and increasingly throughout the Welty canon, these catalytic characters are female.

A progressive development throughout Welty's career has been that of the female protagonist who envisions a wider latitude in self-determination. From Rosamond's insistence in *The Robber Bridegroom* that she be loved as an equal and not used as a romantic heroine caught in love's thralldom, to Virgie's tacit acceptance in *The Golden Apples* that her rebellious independence makes her an outcast, to Laurel's qualified victory in *The Optimist's Daughter* over the hold of memory and tradition, Welty has followed a subtly feminist track. Her approach is related to the classical, "first-wave" feminism of the nineteenth century and specifically to that of Virginia Woolf, as Woolf articulates it in *A Room of One's Own,* which assumes the writer as androgyne (neither male nor female in voice), and which emphasizes a woman's right of access to the wide world of experience and culture. It also includes identification with the cultural feminism of Woolf's *Three Guineas,* which describes a female moral vision that is "anti-facist" and thus more humane. Welty cannot be identified with radical feminists who espouse female separatism; nevertheless, her stories rely on matrilineal cultural traditions even as they appropriate the techniques of the patrilineal canon. Instead of passive heroines who figure in masculine quests, her most interesting characters are female heroes intent upon their own quests for selfhood. Welty does not soften the harsh reality that, as Julia in *Losing Battles* demonstrates, the cost to the female of individuation often is a self-imposed isolation from life that is merely different in kind from isolation imposed from without. The pervasive patterns of enclosure and escape that, as I have argued elsewhere, emerge from the study of Welty's relation to the Gothic in its many forms complement her equally pervasive use of the mythic and other primitive and classic traditions; and together they represent the most basic longings of the male and female, familiar to readers since Oedipus. In Welty, they can be characterized in terms of paired opposites: holding on and letting go, order and freedom, convergence and dispersion.[12]

But though Welty's texts are deeply informed by the conventions of romance, one of the most telling aspects of her stories of enclosure and

12. Virginia Woolf, *A Room of One's Own* (New York, 1929); Virginia Woolf, *Three Guineas* (New York, 1938); Josephine Donovan, *Feminist Theory: The Intellectual Traditions of American Feminism* (New York, 1990), 31–63, 171–86; Ruth D. Weston, "The Optimist in Hawthorne's Shadow: Eudora Welty's Gothic as Lyric Technique," *Short Story,* I (1991), 74–91.

escape is that her narratives themselves "escape" from the thralldom of the romance plot, which is a literary analogy of the prevailing culture's ideas about gendered roles and options. "Romance plots of various kinds," as Rachel Blau DuPlessis has shown, such as "the iconography of love, the postures of yearning, pleasing, choosing, slipping, falling, and failing are, evidently, some of the deep, shared structures of our culture." And since the point of resolution in romance plots is a place where "trans-individual assumptions and values are most clearly visible, and where the word 'convention' is found resonating between its literary and social meanings," a primary component of Eudora Welty's narrative techniques is her replacement of the marriage-or-death closure with what DuPlessis calls "writing beyond the ending." DuPlessis views "story" as itself "a symbol of ideology," and "any literary convention . . . [,] as an instrument that claims to depict experience, [as one that] interprets it." She examines a number of ways in which twentieth-century female writers "delegitimize" romance plots, including the Gothic, by conceiving alternate narrative strategies that constitute critiques of culture. In eighteenth- and nineteenth-century narratives, the female quest was always subordinated to the romantic ending, DuPlessis asserts; thus what began as a female hero became, in the end, a heroine. Because "the *Bildung* and romance could not coexist and be integrated for the heroine at the resolution, . . . any plot of [female] self-realization was at the service of the marriage plot. . . . Writing beyond the ending begins," DuPlessis says, "when authors, or their close surrogates, discover that they are in fact outside the terms of this [romance] novel's script, marginal to it." [13]

DuPlessis shows how modern novelists disrupt this script, how they critique the narrative and thus the culture: for example, by rupturing and reimagining traditional sequences; by establishing points of view from what have been the margins of narrative (and culture); and by creating choral (collective) characters, which may represent aspects of women's lives or may stand for cities or countries. One key chapter in *Writing Beyond the Ending* is entitled "Beyond the Hard Visible Horizon," based on a quotation from Dorothy Richardson's 1921 novel *Deadlock*, Volume III of the four-volume *Pilgrimage*. Two epigraphs refer to *Deadlock* and to Zora Neale Hurston's *Their Eyes Were Watching God* (1937), both of which look to powerful "maternal spirit[s]" who lived at times when there were brief breakthroughs in social integration of genders and who "offered . . . elements of symbolic protest . . . , [such as] expressed energy,

13. Rachel Blau DuPlessis, *Writing Beyond the Ending: Narrative Strategies of Twentieth-Century Women Writers* (Bloomington, 1985), xi, 2–6.

and personal triumph." This passage from the Richardson epilogue could, in many respects, be written about Eudora Welty's most important female protagonists: "The open scene, that seemed at once without her and within, beckoned and claimed her, extending for ever, without horizons. . . . Here was the path of advance. But, pursuing it, she must be always alone; supported in the turmoil of life that drove the haunting scene [of conventional romance and beauty] away, hidden beyond the hard visible horizon, by the remembered signs and smiles of these far-off lonely women."[14]

Most of Welty's short stories and all her major novels have no real sense of closure; rather, except in a few brief tragedies like "Clytie," "Flowers for Marjorie," and "At the Landing," they move to a point of new openness for her protagonists. Welty has never considered herself a feminist, and she attempts to deal evenhandedly with male and female human limitations and possibilities; yet she has developed into a writer with a decidedly contemporary female literary imagination, one who has continually called upon codes and conventions of many genres, but especially myth, fairy tale, and Gothic, as building blocks in the design of fictional liberations of the female psyche. In fact, the myth of Psyche can be seen as a sort of coda that informs the structure of much of her fiction, since the myth's components appear again and again. Chief among these are the Psyche and Eros figures: the female who experiences psychic growth and the godlike male; but they also include the Aphrodite figure, sometimes known as the Great Mother or the Terrible Mother, who may empower the Psyche character to achieve individuation, as well as various evil-sister figures who complicate the problem.

If, as it seems in Welty's fiction, these mythic figures converge with surprising ease with fairytale characters like sleeping beauties, handsome princes, and evil stepmothers, as well as with the sentimental heroines, chivalric but errant gentlemen, and dominating matriarchs of American southern culture, it is because Welty draws from the aesthetic traditions of many artistic media, blending the most affective narrative techniques of these forms, and because she conceives plots that appeal to basic ways of human understanding. She combines and transforms her raw materials in ways that allow us to recognize patterns that reveal meaning, from tales like "Why I Live at the P.O.," rendered in Welty's most homely

14. *Ibid.,* 142 (DuPlessis' ellipses and gloss). Her epigraphs are from Dorothy Richardson, *Deadlock* (1921; rpr. New York, 1976), 198, Vol. III of Richardson, *Pilgrimage,* 4 vols.; and from Zora Neale Hurston, *Their Eyes Were Watching God,* ed. Henry Louis Gates, Jr. (1937; rpr. New York, 1990), 85.

manner, to *The Golden Apples, The Bride of the Innisfallen,* and *The Optimist's Daughter,* which showcase her most dazzling virtuosity.

Welty's place in the larger traditions of the American romance and of the American lyric short story has been neglected by literary historians in general and by Welty scholars also, the latter usually emphasizing her relation either to Europeans or to a selected few American women writers. This study is meant to extend the scope of Welty studies to a wider range of literary history, as Peter Schmidt's recent work has done with respect to Welty and nineteenth-century American women's fiction. Welty's thematic approaches and narrative strategies have been empowered by an even greater diversity than has been realized, especially by short-story writers of the American mainstream; her relation to important acknowledged sources such as Austen and Faulkner has not been adequately understood; and a recognition that her imagination makes use of many aspects of the Gothic not only will help to remedy those two lapses but also will teach us to read her with more intelligence and pleasure. Imagination, Welty has remarked, "is the shortest route to anything." If we follow the shapes of that imagination, we will recognize gothic influence in many of her narrative techniques.[15] Sometimes the gothic provides a primary structuring device, sometimes a very subtle atmospheric touch; but whether great or small, the "ghosts of the gothic" are always perceptible to those who are able to adjust their reading eyes to see, in the rarefied light, the significant routes through the stories that Welty has marked with such gothic traces.

15. Eudora Welty to Elizabeth Bowen, 1951, in Elizabeth Bowen Collection, Harry Ransom Humanities Research Center, University of Texas, Austin, hereinafter cited as Bowen Collection. Welty is writing from the *Ile de France* after having made an extended visit to the Irish writer at Bowen's Court, County Cork, Ireland. It was during this visit that she wrote "The Bride of the Innisfallen."

I

Settings Between Time and Space
The Gothic Space as Narrative Technique

Eudora Welty's commitment to her native "place" began with her first real introduction to the diverse regions of Mississippi as she traveled about by bus as a Junior Publicity Agent for the Works Progress Administration (WPA) during the Great Depression in 1930. Her fiction rests, she says, upon the foundation of its setting as both a stage and a test of the validity of the characters she places there. For, as she told Bill Ferris, she is convinced that the many aspects of a place—its geography and climate as well as the folkways that develop in and around it—constitute the "fountainhead of [a person's] knowledge and experience." Welty's dependence upon the actual geography of place, and especially the ways in which its felt mysteries inform her fiction, has affected even the language of the critical commentary on her work. For example, in the first book-length treatment of Welty's fiction, Ruth Vande Kieft claims to have used what she calls (from Welty's "Circe") "instruments of air" as the most appropriate critical tools. Indeed, Vande Kieft's commentaries all demonstrate her agreement with what she says is Robert Heilman's "fine summation of Welty": that the "penumbra of mystery" in her works is "a mystery to be accepted, not solved." [1]

Welty's relation to the Gothic has been hinted at since Louise Bogan's early review of *A Curtain of Green* in 1941. The fullest consideration of gothic elements in Welty criticism to date is that of Alfred Appel, Jr., in *A Season of Dreams.* Appel concludes—rightly but for the wrong reasons—that the term *Gothic,* the capitalized word designating the Euro-

1. Bill Ferris, *Images of the South: Visits with Eudora Welty and Walker Evans* (Memphis, 1977), 15; Ruth M. Vande Kieft, "Eudora Welty: Visited and Revisited," *Mississippi Quarterly,* XXXIX (1986), 459, 457.

15

pean genres of terror and horror fictions, is misapplied to Welty. He only superficially analyzes gothic application to Welty: first, in terms of grotesque character used to show monstrous humanity, and second, for what he calls special effects. His only recognition of the gothic landscape is a sentence on the "convoluted foliage" of "A Curtain of Green" and mention of what he terms the "middle ground" between nature and urban society in "Death of a Traveling Salesman."[2]

The conventional setting of the European literary Gothic was in medieval castles or cathedrals characterized by vaulted arches and elaborately carved gargoyles and floral tangles. That just such Gothic architecture is suggested to Welty by the landscape of her region is evident from her description of the Natchez country about which she so often writes:

> There is something Gothic about the vines, in their structure in the trees—there are arches, flying buttresses, towers of vines, with trumpet flowers swinging in them for bells and staining their walls. And there is something of a warmer grandeur in their very abundance—stairways and terraces and whole hanging gardens of green and flowering vines, with a Babylonian babel of hundreds of creature voices that make up the silence of Rodney's Landing. Here are nests for birds and thrones for owls and trapezes for snakes, every kind of bower in the world. . . . Perhaps the live oaks are the most wonderful trees in this land. Their great girth and their great spread give far more feeling of history than any house or ruin left by man. Vast, very dark, proportioned as beautifully as a church, they stand majestically in the wild or line old sites, old academy grounds. The live oaks under which Aaron Burr was tried at Washington, Mississippi, in this section, must have been old and impressive then, to have been chosen for such a drama. (*ES,* 295–97)

Even though her use of gothic convention does not constitute what has historically been known as Gothic fiction, by such statements Welty consciously appeals to the Gothic and its images, suggesting her awareness that, in the writer's hand, the confluence of such images with the aura of place implies aesthetic potential for the sense of life's mystery that she strives to communicate in her fiction (*ES,* 114; *C,* 62, 211). The ghost town of Rodney's Landing on the old Natchez Trace is the setting for many of her stories, and it is the primary example that Welty herself uses to describe the energizing spirit of place. Maps no longer mark the town, and only plantation ruins remain. Welty recalls once having seen a

---

2. Louise Bogan, "The Gothic South" (Review of Eudora Welty's *A Curtain of Green*), *Nation,* December 6, 1941, p. 572; Alfred Appel, Jr., *A Season of Dreams: The Fiction of Eudora Welty* (Baton Rouge, 1965), 99.

ghost when she took Elizabeth Bowen to see the Longwood ruin in Mississippi, where they were given a guided tour by a caretaker they later heard had been killed several months before their visit.[3] In this densely forested area the river has receded, leaving a once-thriving port city to stagnate and decay. But the spirit of the place remains, Welty believes, and perhaps is heightened by the recession of ordinary reality.

The opening passage of "Some Notes on River Country" is one of Welty's most self-conscious statements about her artistic vision, and one that aligns her with what T. S. Eliot called Hawthorne's "ghost sense" of the present's being haunted by the past—a "ghost sense" that Welty shares not only with Hawthorne but also with Faulkner, for whom, in the words of his protagonist Gavin Stephens, in *Requiem for a Nun,* the past is "not even past."[4] In Welty's words,

> A place that ever was lived in is like a fire that never goes out. It flares up, it smolders for a time, it is fanned or smothered by circumstance, but its being is intact, forever fluttering within it, the result of some original ignition. . . . I have never seen, in this small section of old Mississippi River country and its little chain of lost towns between Vicksburg and Natchez, anything so mundane as ghosts, but I have felt many times there a sense of place as powerful as if it were visible and walking and could touch me. (*ES,* 286)

Perhaps what is most to the point here is that Welty's critical vocabulary recalls a genre that has close ties to the Gothic: the ghost story. In that context, one aspect of Welty's relationship to her friend Elizabeth Bowen becomes apparent. Bowen's influence on Welty's theoretical writings was noticed early on by Vande Kieft, but it has yet to be fully appreciated, as Peggy Prenshaw has recognized. But whether because they are kindred spirits as writers and literary theorists, or because of direct influence, Welty's idea that a lived-in place has its "being . . . intact, forever fluttering within it" has a remarkable likeness to Bowen's statement, in her introduction to a volume of ghost stories, that "obsessions stay in the air which knew them, as a corpse stays nailed down under a floor."[5]

One has only to read through Welty's letters to Bowen to see evidence

3. Albert J. Devlin and Peggy Whitman Prenshaw, "A Conversation with Eudora Welty, Jackson, 1986," *Mississippi Quarterly,* XXXIX (1986), 431–54.

4. William Faulkner, *Requiem for a Nun* (1951; rpr. New York, 1975), 80.

5. Ruth M. Vande Kieft, *Eudora Welty* (Boston, 1962), 179–83; Peggy Whitman Prenshaw, "The Antiphonies of Eudora Welty's *One Writer's Beginnings* and Elizabeth Bowen's *Pictures and Conversations,*" *Mississippi Quarterly,* XXXIX (1986), 639–50; Elizabeth Bowen, Introduction to *The Second Ghost Book,* ed. Cynthia Asquith (London, 1952).

of the two women's similar philosophies of writing. Compare, for example, Welty's well-known assertions in "Place in Fiction": that feelings "are bound up in place" (*ES,* 118); that "place has a good deal to do with making the characters real, that is themselves, and keeping them so" (121); that place, "by confining character . . . defines it" (122); that it is "the named, identified, concrete, exact and exacting, and therefore credible gathering spot of all that has been felt, is about to be experienced, in the novel's progress" (122); that it is "the ground conductor of all the currents of emotion and belief and moral conviction that charge out from the story in its course" (128); and, about Hemingway, that the "response to place has the added intensity that comes with the place's not being native or taken for granted, but found, chosen" (131). In an unpublished manuscript about the Mississippi stories of Eudora Welty, Elizabeth Bowen compared Welty's characters with the Wessex people of Thomas Hardy. "Locality," Bowen asserts, "is the root of character—if today there are fewer 'characters,' that is because we live in a fluid and de-localised world. And locality can be more, it can be destiny. Nothing more shows fatality than the returns of natives."[6]

Part of the felt mystery of the Rodney's Landing area is evoked by the remembered sound of the river in the ominous present silence. In this land, Welty says,

> heat moves. Its ripples can be seen, like the ripples in some vertical river running between earth and sky. It is so still at noon. I was never there before the river left, to hear the thousand swirling sounds it made for Rodney's Landing, but could it be that its absence is so much missed in the life of sound here that a stranger would feel it? The stillness seems absolute, as the brightness of noon seems to touch the point of saturation. Here the noon sun does make a trance; here indeed at its same zenith it looked down on life sacrificed to it and was worshipped. (*ES,* 293)

Thus, in terms familiar to traditional Gothic description, Welty describes the sun worship of the "proud and cruel . . . elegant . . . and ruthless" (*ES,* 293) Natchez Indians in enough detail to suggest her belief that some essence of that ancient nation remains to affect the visitor through the very power of its sun god. This appeal to more than living memory, to an abiding essence with its hint of supernatural force, together with her many references to the aura of place, provides the impetus for an inquiry into her understanding of gothic effect and how it is achieved.

The most basic element of Gothic fiction is the gothic space, the defi-

---

6. Elizabeth Bowen, Rejected pages for the Eudora Welty article, in Bowen Collection.

nition of which proceeds from the earliest literary appropriations of laby-rinthine enclosures, such as cathedral and castle dungeons, as well as from a general awareness of a psychological or parapsychological realm that impinges upon the everyday world of actuality. The gothic space is a complex and unpredictable setting that surrounds a center of suspense; and, paradoxically, its snares are often part of a bare-stage wasteland that heightens the exposed nature of the human being who is trapped there. It is always mysteriously charged with power. Gothic spaces, according to Judith Wilt, engender anxiety, dread, and the sense that escape is not possible. Many heroines of Gothic literature are confined in such spaces, and this fact has led to the tracing of the theme of enclosure and escape in writing by women and to the coinage of the term *female Gothic* to designate a literary subgenre. Both Ellen Moers, in *Literary Women,* and Sandra Gilbert and Susan Gubar, in *Madwoman in the Attic,* discuss the female Gothic in terms of spatial images of heroines who "characteristi-cally inhabit mysteriously intricate or uncomfortably stifling houses [and] are often seen as captured, fettered, trapped, even buried alive." Even Gothic fiction itself seemed unnaturally trapped in a restrictive form, creating what George E. Haggerty calls the "challenge to the Gothic writer . . . [of] the paradox between the subjective world of dreamlike private experience and the public objective world of the novel." Thus the convergence of the Gothic dilemma with form and the dilemma of the self, which, according to Eve Sedgwick, in such fiction is "massively blocked off from something to which it ought normally to access." [7]

The female Gothic may be variously defined, its major modes the "popular" and the "serious." Both kinds, according to Juliann E. Fleenor, are written in response to social realities; they focus on repression, seg-regation, or dichotomy rather than wholeness; they are formless except as quests; and they use traditional spatial images to represent the culture and the heroine. Serious female Gothic fiction often focuses on grotesque characters, but male and female writers usually depict them differently. Claire Kahane, for example, characterizes female grotesques as resulting from self-hatred; Irving Malin describes human (male or female) narcis-

7. Wilt, *Ghosts of the Gothic,* 10, refers to Mario Praz's Introduction to *Three Gothic Novels,* ed. Praz (Hammondsworth, 1968). According to Praz, the perfect symbol of the gothic space is the prison, whose ancestor is the gothic madhouse and whose current topos is the mad city. Ellen Moers, *Literary Women* (New York, 1976), 90–112; Sandra M. Gilbert and Susan Gubar, *Madwoman in the Attic: The Woman Writer and the Nineteenth-Century Literary Imagination* (New Haven, 1979), 83; George E. Haggerty, *Gothic Fiction/Gothic Form* (University Park, Pa., 1989), 20; Eve Kosofsky Sedgwick, *The Coherence of Gothic Convention* (New York, 1986), 12.

sistic grotesques whose self-love causes them to see distorted "truths." Welty's use of the Gothic grotesque incorporates not only the concept of the grotto as a natural feature of landscape, as well as its extension in the "grotesque" or ornate decor of gothic architecture, but also her unique concept of the grotesque in human character, a mode historically more often associated with American Gothic, and especially Southern Gothic.[8]

The classic Gothic tradition of Walpole and Lewis has undergone many transformations. Jane Austen transposed the castle-and-cloister high Gothic to the key of parlor life in England; later, Charles Brockden Brown and James Fenimore Cooper translated its settings to that of the American wilderness; and still later, Hawthorne and Faulkner extended the trope of labyrinthine wilderness to houses and families. Additional modifications were made by American writers Charlotte Perkins Gilman, Evelyn Scott, Ellen Glasgow, and Kate Chopin, who adapted American Gothic conventions to depict the realities of women's confinement by houses and customs and of their psychological distress, as had Emily and Charlotte Brontë in England. The damaging effect on the human psyche, not only of social forces but also of an individual's own choices, was exemplified by Sherwood Anderson, who defined the modern grotesque character, and by the Southern Gothic grotesques of Faulkner, McCullers, O'Connor, and Capote. But through these modulations of emphasis on character and setting, the fundamental image of the gothic space has remained a source of creative energy for modern writers, as it was for their forebears.

Eudora Welty distinguishes between what she calls the supernaturalistic fictions of Gothic writers such as Poe and her own admitted belief in "mystery and magic," which she relates to her use of mythology to suggest something timeless (*C,* 343). And one must also distinguish between Welty's use of functional gothic conventions and the much broader genre of melodrama that includes stories of "violence, mysteries, improbabilities, morbid passions, inflated and complex language of any sort."[9] Welty is correct in exempting herself from this broad category.

What counts in Eudora Welty's use of some conventions of the Gothic

8. Juliann E. Fleenor, ed., *The Female Gothic* (Montreal, 1983), 15; Claire Kahane, "The Maternal Legacy: The Grotesque Tradition in Flannery O'Connor's Female Gothic," in *The Female Gothic,* ed. Fleenor, 243; Irving Malin, *The New American Gothic,* (Carbondale, 1962), 14–49.

9. Richard Chase makes the distinction between any current usage of *Gothic* and the more general melodramatic style. Richard V. Chase. *The American Novel and Its Tradition* (Garden City, 1957), 36.

tradition is that both she and her audience are knowledgeable about its many subgenres, and thus are able to communicate—even on a subconscious level—through its codes of theme, structure, and devices of setting or character. Welty's ability to utilize a poetics that incorporates such conventions can, as Robert Scholes says of the modern writer's use of the fantastic, "serve to break down the barriers between the sacred fields of *belles lettres* and the profane marketplace of popular culture." In such a dialogical poetics, Tzvetan Todorov has said that "every word smells of the context and contexts in which it has lived its intense social life; all words and all forms are inhabited by intentions." [10] Welty herself has made a similar assertion: "We start from scratch, and words don't" (*ES,* 134). Thus, Welty's understanding of the "haunting" of places by active spirits of the past ("A place that ever was lived in is like a fire that never goes out") is here translated into a working theory of language as a locus of similar "haunting."

But Welty's link with, and difference from, the Gothic tradition is in more than words and in more than devices. Through the work of Joseph Wiesenfarth we can discover a further distinction. Wiesenfarth has traced the path from the "old Gothic" to the "new Gothic," beginning, as he puts it, when "Jane Austen sandbagged the old Gothic novel in *Northanger Abbey*" and continuing through many transmutations to John Fowles's use of the conventions of "a fiction of Gothic manners" in *A French Lieutenant's Woman.* The improbable and unmotivated actions of the old Gothic romance, Wiesenfarth asserts, were phased out in its synthesis with the nineteenth-century British novel of manners, wherein the manners themselves became the threatening "gothic" enclosures of modern characters and wherein "respectability replaces Gothic horror because it denies legitimacy to strong feeling." The new Gothic is seen, he says, in Emily Brontë's psychodrama that domesticates its horrors at Heathcliff's hearth in Thrushcross Grange, a world in which "the niceties of moral conduct and warm generosity [are] grossly irrelevant." Here, Wiesenfarth says, the "labyrinthian architecture of Gothic fiction (the dark passages, subterranean tunnels, and secret doors of castles and monasteries) give way to the labyrinthian machinations of one whose own domestic arrangements are actually very simple." But Heathcliff's machinations result from psychological motivations, however bizarre; and thus the new Gothic has developed in a direction that makes it very much

---

10. Scholes, Introduction to *The Fantastic,* by Todorov, trans. Howard, vii; Tzvetan Todorov, *Mikhail Bakhtin: The Dialogical Principle,* trans. Wlad Godzich (Minneapolis, 1984), 56–57.

related to reality. As Heilman observes, the Victorians' appropriation of gothic conventions allowed the genre to "move into the lesser known realities of human life."[11]

One of these realities, which assumes primary importance in contemporary uses of gothic conventions and especially in Welty, is the theme Wiesenfarth identifies in Dickens' *Great Expectations:* that involving varieties of love and the individual's "search to be free from society's stagnant myth of concern." Such a "myth of concern" Weisenfarth also sees in George Eliot's *Middlemarch* in terms of the internal and external laws that conflict, such that "to grow into one's best self . . . is to grow into alienation from society." Since marriage is, as Tony Tanner says, "the structure that maintains the Structure" of such a confining and concerned society, the institution of marriage is instrumental in the contemporary depiction of gothic manners. Thus, according to Sandra Gilbert and Susan Gubar, "to be a happy wife to a dead man is to be buried alive." Because Eudora Welty is a writer immersed in this tradition of British fiction, and because she is conscious of the continuous development from British Gothic thrillers to the serious American Gothic romance and thence to the modern fiction of alienation, I mention the gothic in terms of Welty's fiction in the qualified sense of the Gothic tradition's evolution, through many manifestations, to a fiction that has come to deal in psychological realism. As such, its conventions are available, not in terms of outmoded historical "trappings," but in terms of directly relevant modern narrative themes and techniques. Especially relevant is the tradition as revised by Emily Brontë, who depicted female freedom not as escape "from a dark usurper into marriage," believes Syndy Conger, but as a release like that sought by young Cathy in *Wuthering Heights:* "to be a girl again, half savage, and hardy, and free."[12]

Alice Walker once asked Eudora Welty whether she had ever been called a Gothic writer, to which Welty replied, "They better not call me that!" In terms of the genre generally understood by that term, she is correct. Yet Welty's extensive adaptations of gothic attributes and her

11. Joseph Wiesenfarth, *Gothic Manners and the Classic English Novel* (Madison, 1988), 3, 21, 197; Emily Brontë, *Wuthering Heights* (1847; rpr. New York, 1959), 57, 77; Robert B. Heilman, "Charlotte Brontë's 'New Gothic,'" in *The Brontës: A Collection,* ed. Ian Gregor (Englewood Cliffs, 1970), 99, 101.

12. Wiesenfarth, *Gothic Manners and the Classic English Novel,* 12, 100; Tony Tanner, *Adultery in the Novel: Contract and Transgression* (Baltimore, 1979), 15; Gilbert and Gubar, *Madwoman in the Attic,* 503; Syndy McMillen Conger, "The Reconstruction of the Gothic Feminine Ideal in Emily Brontë's *Wuthering Heights,*" in *The Female Gothic,* ed. Fleenor, 92; Brontë, *Wuthering Heights,* 124.

conscious manipulations of gothic conventions, including its themes, to her own purposes constitute a decided link with the Gothic tradition. She told Walker that she thinks she has been "inevitably" called Gothic because it is apparently "easy" to categorize southern writers as such; and she is again correct, because her true relation to that tradition has not been properly understood. Both Walker and Welty say they do not know what is meant by the label; for Welty, as no doubt for many, it calls to mind, as she says, "a Gustave Doré illustration for 'The Fall of the House of Usher.' Anyway," she asserts, "it sounds as if it has nothing to do with real life, and I feel that my work has something to do with real life" (*C*, 152).

Welty's fiction does indeed have to do with real life; but since a major theme relates to the gothic device of confinement (in Welty's case, the various symbolic, psychic, as well as actual, spatial, confinements of women in marriage, family, and society), the considerable number of her narrative strategies that are informed by the Gothic constitutes a significant factor in her fiction. Welty's confining spaces are related to those of the European Gothic but utilize the natural wilderness, or some other American equivalent of the classic Gothic's haunted ruins, to create the mysteriously affective settings that encourage suspension of disbelief without violating their basis in visible reality. Thus, according to one critic, her sense of place—that is, the richly detailed verisimilitude she achieves in setting—"helps to contain" her antimimetic tendency toward "elusiveness" that results from her extensive use of myth and symbol.[13]

The coincidence of artistic convention with the features of a natural wilderness that engenders instinctive human fears has an ancient heritage dating from primitive grotto murals to their extravagant modern adaptations. The landscapes of Welty's fiction that reflect the natural world or some analogy of it are complex and entangling gothic spaces, often including mazes, caves, tunnels, and dense forest undergrowths. According to Philip Thomson, the grotesque (from *grotte*, Italian for "caves") existed as an artistic mode in the early Christian period of Roman culture in an intricate stylistic interweaving of human, animal, and vegetable elements in the same painting. Murals of this kind in excavated Roman caves were first described, around A.D. 1500, as decorations representing "monstrous forms rather than . . . clear images of the familiar world. Instead of columns they paint fluted stems with oddly shaped

13. Waldemar Zacharasiewicz, "The Sense of Place in Southern Fiction by Eudora Welty and Flannery O'Connor," *Arbeiten aus Anglistik und Amerikanistik*, X (1985), 189–206.

leaves and volutes, and instead of pediments arabesques. . . . The little stems . . . support half-figures crowned by human or animal heads." [14]

Such "grotesque" landscapes in Welty's work, though they may have their basis in an actual location, are chosen for some inherent distancing factor that separates them in some way from the everyday world. In this regard, Cooper's novel *The Spy: A Tale of the Neutral Ground* is an instructive predecessor of Welty's work. For Cooper too adapts gothic conventions, though he and others intent on creating an American literature agreed that the authentic Gothic was unsuited to the new democratic country because there was "nothing to awaken fancy in that land of dull realities . . . ; it contains no objects that carry back the mind to the contemplation of early antiquity; no mouldering ruins to excite curiosity in the history of past ages . . . no traditions and legends and fables to afford materials for romance and poetry." And yet *The Spy* is set in a time and place that is significant in the actual history as well as in the romantic folk tradition of New York. Notwithstanding Cooper's reservations about its potential, the "neutral ground" of the subtitle of *The Spy* was an area that had a flourishing oral tradition of folklore and legend, including the Dutch and German ghost stories and the colonial American witch tales on which Washington Irving so felicitously capitalized. For, as Donald Ringe reminds us, Ichabod Crane scares himself with Cotton Mather's tales of ghosts and witches. [15]

Much of this folk tradition relates to the history surrounding Cooper's subject in *The Spy:* to the villainy of Benedict Arnold and his escape, including a fund of anecdotes and tales about the Cow-Boys and Skinners, the mercenary bandits who plague British Loyalists, American revolutionaries, and private citizens alike in the unprotected New York countryside. Cooper studied the details of the history, terrain, and oral tradition of the area; and his daughter Susan recalled his listening to workmen around his home in Scarsdale tell tales about spies and caves and a grove "called the Haunted Wood—ghosts had been seen there!" His transformation of these informants' accounts into the mood of terror and desolation in his novel is evidence of his success at adapting the European Gothic for American use by giving it a firm basis in reality. He made the New York woodlands into a gothic space, an American

14. Philip John Thomson, *The Grotesque* (London, 1972), 10–19. Thomson quotes Wolfgang Kayser, *The Grotesque in Art and Literature,* trans. Ulrich Weisstein (Bloomington, 1963), 20.

15. James Femimore Cooper, *The Spy: A Tale of the Neutral Ground,* ed. James H. Pickering, (1821; rpr. New Haven, 1971), 10–12; Donald A. Ringe, *American Gothic: Imagination and Reason in Nineteenth-Century Fiction* (Lexington, 1982), 92.

version of haunted ruins, which, as Charles Brockden Brown argued for his own work, was sufficient; indeed, Brown found it "far more suitable for American settings [than] would be European Gothic castles and chimeras."[16]

The actual ruins that existed in Cooper's New York were mostly battleworks from the Revolutionary War on both shores of the Hudson and on what is now known as Constitution Island, where old gun emplacements and redoubt walls still stand, as does at least one deteriorating "castle" on the hill above Garrison, New York, on the east shore. During the winter months when foliage is sparse, one can glimpse a castle-like structure from across the river at West Point, as I discovered when I visited the area in 1986. It may well have been the one Cooper referred to when, fearing the displeasure of his female audience, he wrote in his preface to *The Spy:* "If we have got no lords and castles in the book, it is because there are none in the country. We . . . traveled a hundred miles to see a renowned castle to the east but, to our surprise, found it had so many broken windows, was such an outdoor kind of place, that we should be wanting in Christian bowels to place any family in it during the cold months."[17] For such a land, bereft of "authentic" Gothic ruins, Cooper's subtitle appropriates the historical designation of the site of his revolutionary spy's activities—the "neutral ground"—to add romantic interest to the terrain itself as a border territory where anything might happen, in fiction as well as in real life. As such, it is a credible precedent for Eudora Welty's *The Robber Bridegroom.*

In *The Spy,* war and outlaw raids are superimposed on the gothic space of the neutral ground between two armies. Cooper creates the tale out of the fabric of history but ornaments it with Gothic trappings; thus he provides a basis in reality from which "to express dark and complex truths unavailable to realism," a power Richard Chase claimed for the

16. Susan Cooper is quoted by James H. Pickering, ed., in his Introduction to *The Spy,* by Cooper, 10–14. Pickering refers to the McDonald Papers, interviews made in 1944–50 with elderly New York residents, recorded in manuscript by the Huguenot Historical Association, New Rochelle, N.Y. The New York State Historical Association holds an extensive collection of recorded tales from the oral tradition in New York. From this collection, selections have been published in Harold Thompson's *Body, Boots, and Britches* (Philadelphia, 1940), and Louis C. Jones's *Things That Go Bump in the Night* (Syracuse, 1983). Charles Brockden Brown, in "To the Public," an introduction to *Edgar Huntly, or The Memoirs of a Sleepwalker* (1799; rpr. New Haven, 1973), 29, asserts that for sources of inspiration, the "moral painter" (as he called himself) no longer need resort to "puerile superstition and exploded manners, Gothic castles and chimeras . . . [, because] the incidents of Indian hostility and the perils of the Western wilderness are far more suitable."

17. Cooper, *The Spy,* 32–33.

romance in general, describing it as "a kind of 'border' fiction." For although *The Spy* is a Scott-like border romance, it addresses the serious questions that war poses: the human capacities for deception and cruelty as well as for survival and heroism, questions that Welty too addresses in her "adult fairy tale" based on legendary bandits, or as Robert M. Coates calls them, "land pirates," of the Natchez Trace wilderness.[18]

The Spy is replete with sufficient mystery and terror to reveal the New York "neutral ground" of the subtitle as a fit province for the novelist's imaginative use of the Gothic conventions of sentimental fiction: the hero-villain and the terrified heroine, ghastly apparitions and secret caves in the forest. Cooper's protagonist, Harvey Birch, represents the historical character whose dual cover was that of a Yankee peddler and a Loyalist spy, said to be George Washington's favorite. Settings in *The Spy* are made doubly ominous by Cooper's conscious manipulation of them by dream-work, unexplained appearances, and similar devices that portray the cleverness of the spy while also evoking mystery. Such appearances by the spy, combined with his prophetic warnings to those he accosts in the forest, have the effect of the actions of a ubiquitous ghost character; and Birch's dying father in a white nightshirt is taken for a real ghost by the superstitious rural folk. Cooper not only introduces ghostlike apparitions as functional parts in the plot; in a similar vein, he has the army's physician confess to acts that would conjure up tales of the horror Gothic for a readership well versed in the popular genre: Dr. Sitgreaves robs graves for specimens to dissect.[19]

Similarly, Cooper's female protagonist, Frances Wharton, though a minor character in the novel, recalls the standard terrified Gothic heroine as she makes a night journey through the forest to the cave where Harvey Birch meets General Washington. In the dark she bumps against the scaffold where her brother is to hang at dawn. Like the spunky American girls made famous later by Henry James, Frances overcomes her fright and successfully goes about her errand. She is a courageous but not complex Jamesian prototype, and she remains one of Cooper's chaste heroines, and a character not so far removed from the long-suffering heroines of the Gothic romance.

Thus Cooper's *Spy*, an important step in the what Donald Ringe calls the "domestication of literary Gothicism in America," can be seen as a conscious precedent for American authors' adaptations of Gothic literary

18. Chase, *The American Novel*, xi, 19; Robert M. Coates, *The Outlaw Years: The History of the Land Pirates of the Natchez Trace* (New York, 1930).

19. Cooper, *The Spy*, 196.

conventions; as a source of terminology conversant with Gothic tradition that is helpful in discussing works like Welty's independent adaptations, such as *The Robber Bridegroom;* and as one of Welty's links to the early American literary mainstream.[20] The devices of disguise and deceit, the prophetic dream, the ghostly apparition, and the heroine are characteristic of all early American Gothic romances, beginning with those of Charles Brockden Brown.

Crucial to the tradition appropriated by Eudora Welty, and employed throughout her canon, is Cooper's development of the gothic space as a "neutral ground," a wild and alien landscape where outlaws menace society and ordinary law is suspended. In this setting, characters are threatened or confined in various dark tangles, and mystery prevails. Further, the setting itself, in Welty as in Cooper, takes on an active, characterlike function. Joel Porte says that nature in Cooper is used not only "to reflect or influence states of human thought or feeling . . . [but also as] a paradigm for authentic utterance of any sort . . . [because it] cannot falsify; it cannot deceive." Cooper often uses nature, Porte asserts, "to suggest dark undertones of meaning . . . [and even as] a landscape of nightmare . . . , an allegory of horror, where the meaning of events is inscrutable." Through the works of Cooper, Poe, Hawthorne, Melville, and James, Porte traces America's "fictional quest for knowledge of the wilderness" and finds it "synonymous . . . with the desire and need to explore the self."[21] Welty's subtle and sophisticated depictions of the mysteries of nature and human nature owe much to this tradition of the American romance.

Welty's use of historical borderland settings derives naturally from Mississippi's forested lands near the great river, where so much significant history has transpired. An undercurrent of America's dream-nightmare relationship with the wilderness is felt throughout Welty's oeuvre, perhaps because of her references to "progress" and to the clearing of the wilderness, and because of her use of the Turner thesis in *The Robber Bridegroom.* Lisa Miller has shown that Welty was almost certainly aware of the celebrated professor's former tenure at the University of Wisconsin whose influence was still strongly felt on the campus during the time Welty was a student there. Miller argues that the foreboding atmosphere of *The Robber Bridegroom,* written in the 1930s, may have been a reaction to Turner's overly optimistic thesis of progress, which

20. Ringe, *American Gothic,* 108.

21. Joel Porte, *The Romance in America: Studies in Cooper, Poe, Hawthorne, Melville, and James* (Middleton, Conn., 1969), 30, 32, 227–28.

ignored the destructive aspects of industrialization.[22] But this undercurrent is also due to Welty's appeals to more ancient mythologies of the forest, some depicting it as a sacred grove, consonant with Cooper's most memorable use of it in the Leatherstocking Tales, others using it as a symbol of the dark and tangled psyche, as interpreted by Hawthorne in "Young Goodman Brown" and *The Scarlet Letter.*

The sense of place in Welty's early stories freely partakes of sacred-nature and threatening-nature mythologies; and the magic and mystery she imagines in terms of either tradition endow her landscapes with the conventional qualities of a gothic space: a haunted territory subject to its own laws, a place where anything could happen to, or be imagined by, her characters. In Welty's first published story, "Death of a Traveling Salesman," the danger of the natural world is only imagined by Bowman, the ailing salesman, who is inexplicably lost in the "desolate hill country" (*CS,* 119) and who loses his car to a tangle of grapevines when it falls into a ravine. The threatening power of nature is seen through his eyes in the harsh winter sun that "seemed to reach a long arm down and push against the top of his head, right through his hat" (*CS,* 119) and also in the anxiety he feels upon entering the backwoods house. The fire has gone out; it is cold and very still. To Bowman the "silence of the fields seemed to enter and move familiarly through the house. The wind used the open hall. He felt that he was in a mysterious, quiet, cool danger" (*CS,* 123). Thus, the "gothic" content of this story is in the mind of the salesman. In Vande Kieft's words, he senses "trembling, rushing, and waving of the light . . . [and even] the walls, suggesting the instability and delirium of his impressions."[23]

Ironically, Bowman is in serious trouble because of his heart condition, the fatal nature of which is foreshadowed by his crawling after Sonny through the "underworld" of the wilderness—a tunnel in the thicket—for a drink of buried whiskey. Bowman has nothing to fear from the wilderness or its inhabitants, for Sonny rescues his car, and the man and wife offer him the hospitality of their simple home; but he has misunderstood the situation. It is only his customary isolated life in the

---

22. Lisa K. Miller, "The Dark Side of Our Frontier Heritage: Eudora Welty's Use of the Turner Thesis in *The Robber Bridegroom,*" *Notes on Mississippi Writers,* XIV (1981), 18–25. Welty received her B.A. in 1929. For evidence of Turner's continuing influence at the University of Wisconsin, see David Kinnett, "Miss Kellogg's Quiet Passion," *Wisconsin Magazine of History,* LXII (1979), 267–99. Albert J. Devlin notes Turner's influence on Welty, in Devlin, *Eudora Welty's Chronicle: A Story of Mississippi Life* (Jackson, 1983), 34–35.

23. Ruth M. Vande Kieft, *Eudora Welty* (Rev. ed.; Boston, 1987), 43.

artificial world that makes the intimacy of this natural world so threatening. The "conspiracy" he senses between the couple is no Gothic plot but, ironically, only the "secret" of their coming child and "the ancient communication between two people," only that of love: "That simple thing. Anyone could have had that" (*CS*, 126, 129). But Bowman will never have it, for he dies of a heart attack, irrationally fleeing the cabin, alone, in the middle of the night.

It is Bowman's mental parody of the Gothic that energizes "Death of a Traveling Salesman," but in "A Curtain of Green" Welty evokes for the reader the terror of a gothic labyrinth in Mrs. Larkin's dense, tangled garden. This grotesquely overgrown yard is both solace and threat to Mrs. Larkin as she loses herself in frenzied cultivation of the virtual jungle to cope with her husband's accidental death from a falling tree. But her feverish activity cannot keep out the memory of the love she had been powerless to protect, nor can it hide her in its tangle; and she thinks of some revenge for such loss and such merciless exposure to the world: "She felt all at once terrified, as though her loneliness had been pointed out by some outside force whose finger parted the hedge" (*CS*, 110), the "curtain of green" of the title, which has hidden Mrs. Larkin but now parts to expose her human vulnerability. It is not her loneliness that is gothic but her terror and the fact that she feels, even in the depths of her custom-made wilderness, exposed and vulnerable to some supernatural "finger." The "callous" and "inexhaustible" natural world, combined with the presence of the innocent child Jamey, constitutes an incongruous situation that causes her a "feeling of stricture, of a responding hopelessness almost approaching ferocity." At this moment of temporary madness, with her hoe raised above the boy's head, she sees her own helplessness in Jamey's, whose "head she could strike off" (*CS*, 109–11). As in "Death of a Traveling Salesman," the terror originates, not in the external world, but in the mind of the protagonist. But in "A Curtain of Green," nature, though impersonal, is yet mysteriously healing; for with the first drops of rain, Mrs. Larkin's trance is broken, and she acquiesces to its balm.

It is not nature that is the spirit of healing in "A Worn Path," but human love and endurance, in spite of a world that might seem Gothic to those less grounded in reality than is Phoenix Jackson. Although it is justly celebrated for its humorous and inspirational depiction of Phoenix's love and of her clever adaptability in the natural world, even "A Worn Path" contains images of a gothic space and situation. The old woman with the exotic name walks through a winter wasteland from the Natchez Trace, up the hill through "dark pine shadows" and then down under live oaks, where "it was as dark as a cave" (*CS,* 142–45), to the town of Natchez. Not only gothic entrapment but also the historical reality of slavery in the South is suggested by Phoenix's own image for her weariness— "Seem like there is chains about my feet, time I get this far"—and by the thorny bush and barbed-wire fence that entangle her along the way (*CS,* 143). The "ghost" in this story is only a scarecrow; but she is menaced as well by a real black dog and by "big dead trees like black men with one arm," and a row of weathered houses appears in gothic array like "old women under a spell sitting there" (*CS,* 144). It even seemed necessary for Welty to explain the story's motivation, in "Is Phoenix Jackson's Grandson Really Dead?" (*ES,* 159–62), to readers who believed the grandson, too, was a ghost, so fully "mysterious" is this most-magic work. The fact that Phoenix is associated with magic and with conjuring is a part of the realistic depiction of black culture, in which "women have long possessed 'magical' powers."[24] Thus the story illustrates the felicity of gothic images to deal with the many mysterious but very real facets of life as it is lived.

It is that combination of the real and the imaginary that characterizes the life of Phoenix Jackson. Besides the obvious qualities of faith and love that impel such a journey in the first place, her equanimity is due to several other aspects of her complex personality. If, for example, Phoenix seems remarkably without bitterness for an elderly, poor black woman in a forbidding, cold, white world, it is at least partly because she lives imaginatively. For one thing, she lives by her wits; thus, in the white man's South she uses good humor and frank admission of need to gain assistance from a hunter, a shopper, and a nurse. In addition, she respects the world and its powers and mysteries: "Thorns," she says, "you doing your appointed work. Never want to let folks pass, no sir" (*CS,* 143). She also works her own magic, conjuring in the direction of perceived motion in the thicket: "Out of my way, all you foxes, owls, beetles, jack rabbits, coons and wild animals! . . . Keep out from under these feet, little bob-whites. . . . Keep the big wild hogs out of my path. Don't let none of those come running my direction. I got a long way" (*CS,* 142; Welty's ellipses).

Gothic images are used lightly, almost playfully, in the stories of Bowman, Mrs. Larkin, and Phoenix Jackson. In the same collection, however, both "Clytie" and "Old Mr. Marblehall" boast literal Gothic houses: as

24. Marjorie Pryse, "Zora Neale Hurston, Alice Walker, and the 'Ancient Power' of Black Women," in *Conjuring: Black Women, Fiction, and Literary Tradition,* ed. Marjorie Pryse and Hortense J. Spillars (Bloomington, 1985), 3.

dark and mazelike as a dungeon or a forest, full of exotic old furnishings that nobody comes to see. Here Welty is perhaps closest to the Southern Gothic of, for example, Faulkner's "A Rose for Emily" or, later, Capote's *Other Voices, Other Rooms.* Gothic presences are suggested in "Clytie" by personifications of objects such as the "ivory hands" holding back the red curtains and the bronze Hermes holding the gas fixture. The ivory hands suggest other "dead hands," like those "preternatural shapes" that Judith Wilt, in another context, says must seem "immense and solid . . . in the souls of the women whose inner lives these shapes seek to master and emblematize." Wilt's book *Ghosts of the Gothic* traces the modern uses of the Gothic romance by Jane Austen, George Eliot, and D. H. Lawrence, all of whose works we know that Eudora Welty admires. But Welty's image of the "ivory hands" could as well call to mind contemporary poet Adrienne Rich's "Aunt Jennifer's Tigers," in which the persona's hands, even after death, remain "terrified," as they had been in marriage while she lived.[25] Indeed, the dead hands in "Clytie" seem to have more power than do the occupants of the tomblike, "airless" house, who themselves are reified by the narrative: Octavia is "like one of the unmovable relics of the house" (*CS,* 82). Claude Edmonde Magny has noticed the same phenomenon of reversal in Faulkner, and uses Sartre's terms the *ensoi* and the *pour soi* to denote the exchange of attributes between human beings and things. Similarly, Donald Ringe describes Hawthorne's Clifford and Hepzibah Pyncheon, and also Hester Prynne and Arthur Dimmesdale, as such "living ghosts."[26] The spell of the virtual prison and its haunted occupants has taken its toll on Clytie, who has apparently been forbidden a love affair, or denied some measure of ordinary life, long ago. She is the only member of the Farr family who goes out of the house; and though she continually searches about town for a (lost lover's?) face, she sees instead a tangle of faces, some living and some dead: "the face of Octavia . . . thrust between, and at other times the apoplectic face of her father, the face of her brother Gerald and the face of her brother Henry with the bullet hole through the forehead" (*CS,* 86). Thus the family, or Clytie's perception of it, is symbolic of a mysterious force that confines her mind, if not her body. Eventually, her obsessive search of the faces that haunt her drives her to drown herself in the rain barrel, where she has finally found the face of one from whom she has been the

25. Wilt, *Ghosts of the Gothic,* 179; Adrienne Rich, "When We Dead Awaken: Writing as Re-Vision," *College English,* XXXIV (1972), 22.

26. Claude Edmonde Magny, *The Age of the American Novel: The Film Aesthetic of Fiction Between the Two Wars,* trans. Eleanor Hochman (1948; rpr. New York, 1972), 199; Ringe, *American Gothic,* 159–69.

most devastatingly separated—herself. For Clytie has been, like Virgie and Miss Eckhart of *The Golden Apples,* "wandering on the face of the earth" without meaningful human connections.

It is the protagonist's frantic doubling of his human connections in "Old Mr. Marblehall" that contributes to this grotesquely humorous tale with its subversive suggestion of gothic cruelty. Mr. Marblehall's frankly Gothic house appears as a dark tunnel with a back garden, some of which has "crumbled away, but the box maze is there on the edge like a trap, to confound the Mississippi River." Inside the house, the Marblehall family live surrounded by "domestic dark," "deathly-looking tapestry," and "brocades as tall as the wicked queens in Italian tales" (*CS,* 92). Old Mrs. Marblehall "has spent her life trying to escape from the parlor-like jaws of self-consciousness. . . . When she walks around the room she looks remote and nebulous, out on the fringe of habitation, and rather as if she must have been cruelly trained" (*CS,* 91). Although his wife has no means of escape from what is obversely suggested as the "jaws" of her parlor, Mr. Marblehall has escaped one life to live another (as Mr. Bird) in the separate community under the hill in Natchez. In this alternate life he reads *Terror Tales* and *Astonishing Stories* under a naked light bulb in "a great fourposter with carved griffins" (*CS,* 96). The stories "scare [Mrs. Bird] to death" (*CS,* 95), but to Mr. Bird they help to "kill time, and get through the clocking nights" (*CS,* 97). The Gothic is represented, in this early story, in the confining house, the grotesque furnishings, and the images of violence and terror that surround both wives and, ironically, Mr. Marblehall/Bird too, in spite of his apparent freedom to move between two worlds.

One might reasonably expect a Gothic plot in a Gothic house with a duplicitous "hero" like Mr. Marblehall, but perhaps not in the story of a child's visit to two elderly ladies. Yet, to a child, much in the adult world must seem "gothic"; so it is not surprising that, in "A Visit of Charity," Marian, a "Campfire Girl," finds the "Old Ladies' Home" a metaphoric gothic maze of cubicles. Her visit in the room of two residents is, to her, "like being caught in a robbers' cave, just before one [is] murdered" (*CS,* 113, 114). During the surrealistic experience of her visit, she sees the old ladies "from all sides, as in dreams" (*CS,* 117). Through the fourteen-year-old's imagination, we are told that the old ladies speak like robbers and witches: " 'Did you come to be our little girl for a while?' the first *robber* asked" (*CS,* 114; emphasis added). One points a witch's "horny finger," one speaks in a "menacing voice" (*CS,* 116), and the spell of the place so frightens the girl that she cannot speak coherently or remember her own name. As she flees in terror from the place, Marian's red coat and white bonnet flash in the sun, recalling Red Riding Hood's escape from the wolf-grandmother. Although *The Robber Bridegroom* is commonly assumed to be Welty's only fairy tale, "A Visit of Charity," especially because of its theme and its child protagonist, is surely another. Such stories as these provide evidence that the conventions that create fairy-tale terror parallel and overlap those of the Gothic, and evidence as well of Welty's relation to both traditions. Moreover, any adult who has lived in, or even visited, a nursing home perhaps knows the surreal, often dehumanizing, atmosphere that often seems to prevail.

These stories from *A Curtain of Green* illustrate Welty's early dependence on the Gothic tradition, as well as her growing metaphoric use of gothic convention to establish an atmosphere appropriate to the inherent mystery of the unfathomable natural world and of the human personality as well. As in "Clytie" and "Old Mr. Marblehall," Welty may assign the attributes of a gothic wilderness to a mazelike house or garden that is "on the fringe of habitation," and the qualities of a Natchez Trace robber's den to a home for senior citizens. But in "The Purple Hat," collected in *The Wide Net* and said to be Welty's only ghost story, the setting is the "neutral ground" of a New Orleans bar. In another parody of "robbers' dens" or cavelike settings, the bar is "a little hole in the wall . . . [like] a mousehole" (*CS,* 222).

The story has been identified as a parody of the Gothic that "comes close to pure Gothic supernaturalism, despite its realistic frame setting of a New Orleans bar."[27] The bartender, the proverbial neutral listener, who has a "baby-pink nose" and "sad, black eyebrows raised like hoods on baby-carriages," is discussing, with two customers, a middle-aged woman who gambles daily at the Palace of Pleasure (*CS,* 222, 224). The woman is said to be a ghost who wears a "great and ancient and bedraggled . . . monstrosity" of a purple hat embellished with a glass vial (of poison?). More than the woman herself, the purple hat mysteriously seems to seduce the same young man at the Palace "from year to year" (*CS,* 223). One of the customers, a casino guard with "small, mournful lips" and "fat little hand[s]," claims that the woman is a ghost, because during the thirty years of her patronage at the casino he has "seen her murdered twice" (*CS,* 224). The other customer strangely resembles the young man who, like the woman of the purple hat, and like a ghost, never ages; he simply comes to look "a little stale, a little tired" (*CS,* 224). The three men, even the godlike guard, who looks down on the action from a catwalk over the gambling tables and predicts the lady's third murder,

27. Vande Kieft, *Eudora Welty* (1987), 40.

take leave of each other without having solved the mystery. The dominant impression of the story is of the mouselike and infantile images of the men compared with the huge and indomitable ghostly seductress with a "large-sized head," a "face [that] spreads over . . . a wide area," and features that seem to expand surrealistically as she courts her victim (*CS*, 226). Ironically, "The Purple Hat," which Welty herself says is "no more than a playful ghost story" whose failings she realized when she saw it dramatized off-Broadway in 1971 (*C*, 68), seems only marginally magical and mysterious. This failure of atmosphere, combined with (perhaps because of) the lack of development of the male-female comparison, results in what is for some the least satisfying of Welty's stories. Yet "The Purple Hat" too creates a gothic space in codings recognizable to readers familiar with gothic conventions: a marginal zone somewhere between imagination and reality (a neutral territory), ghostly apparitions, and the hint of implicit and repeated violence that haunts a place.

A Welty character may be defined by his or her relationship to the natural world as gothic space, whether that world is perceived as threatening, as it is by Bowman in "Death of a Traveling Salesman," or whether it is the reader who is most aware of the nature of the relationship, as in "A Curtain of Green." Or a character may experience the place as a sort of vacuum or theater that is separate from the ordinary world and that has perhaps been set apart as the scene of a special vision. Two stories from *The Wide Net*, "First Love" and "A Still Moment," take advantage of historical characters associated with the Natchez Trace as the impetus for such epiphanies. In "First Love," Joel, a young deaf-mute, is witness to Aaron Burr's late-night conferences with Harmon Blennerhassett just prior to Burr's scheduled trial for treason. The story's memorable first line could stand as introduction to many of the landscapes in Welty's fiction: "Whatever happened, it happened in extraordinary times, in a season of dreams." In this bitter winter on the Natchez Trace, there is snow—strange for Mississippi; and we are told that the "Mississippi [River] shuddered and lifted from its bed, reaching like a somnambulist driven to go in new places" (*CS*, 153).

Welty recalls that she learned the word *somnambulist* while watching "in terror" *The Cabinet of Dr. Caligari* and that for her, even now, the word vividly calls up the Gothic villain in a frightening scene from that silent film (*OWB*, 36), perhaps the more vivid because of the nature of a silent film, which so forcefully engages the visual imagination. Given this context for her language, her intention to create a landscape of gothic terror in "First Love" seems clear. Images of suffering, entrapment, and death in the unusual cold and "snare-like silence" of the now "glassy tunnels" (*CS*, 153) of the Trace prepare us for Joel's precarious existence as a boot boy who must go at night among sleeping men at the inn to gather up their boots and clean them. These nightly rounds seem even more ominous to a reader who knows that Welty's imagination is informed by the Grimms' tale "The Robber Bridegroom," in which the young protagonist, escaping a band of sleeping robber-ogres in their forest hut lest she become their next meal, "had to walk over . . . [the] sleepers . . . lying on the ground in rows . . . , and she was very much afraid of waking them." [28] For Joel also "it was dangerous to walk about among sleeping men. More than once he had been seized and the life half shaken out of him by a man waking up in a sweat of suspicion or nightmare. . . . It might seem to him that the whole world was sleeping in the lightest of trances, which the least movement would surely wake. . . . Once a rattlesnake had shoved its head from a boot as he stretched out his hand; but that was not likely to happen again in a thousand years" (*CS*, 156). Welty's language, including the idea of a trance, the fairy-tale time of "a thousand years," and the unexpected violence in this scene suggest dangers similar to those that face the young girl in the story by the Brothers Grimm.

In addition to working in a sleeping world, Joel lives in a literally silent dream world because of his deafness. A long description of the gothic space Joel inhabits precedes the narrative of his witnessing, in his own room, the nightly secret meetings of Burr and Blennerhassett. It is as if the boy were seeing a mysterious vision. As he has been literally "seized . . . and shaken" by awakened men, so now he is "seized and possessed by mystery" (*CS*, 158). During the last night before he is to be tried, Burr falls asleep on a table often used to lay out men killed in duels. Joel watches him cry out, convulsed with a nightmare; and his feeling of closeness to the sleeper engenders within him a new sense of human relationship—his "first love," an emotion as mysterious as the gothic landscape around him. Although he knows no names for "the places of the heart . . . and its shadowy and tragic events," he comforts the dreaming man by holding his "burning" hand, which warms the boy as if he had entered the world of Burr's dream (*CS*, 165). But it also brands him, changes him; and he weeps for the loss of his parents (representing his former innocence) as he enters the alien outside world, following the trail of the disguised Burr, who is escaping just ahead of a posse, through the dense winter wilderness.

28. Jakob and Wilhelm Grimm, "The Robber Bridegroom," in *Grimms' Tales for Young and Old: The Complete Stories,* trans. Ralph Manheim (1819; rpr. Garden City, 1977), 148.

In "First Love," Joel's entire life is grotesquely still and silent, while "A Still Moment" is charged with noise and motion, as Welty makes the Natchez Trace the meeting place of the fantastic evangelist Lorenzo Dow, the outlaw James Murrell, and the naturalist John James Audubon. Indians and serpents threaten Dow, but his religious ecstasy makes him fearless of the dangers of this wilderness. More than most of Welty's characters, Dow is aware of the intersection of space and time, and of the wilderness/psyche analogy. "Inhabitants of Time!" he shouts. "The wilderness is your souls on earth!" He is joined on the trail by "a dark man," Murrell, who shouts, "I'm the Devil!" Murrell tells tales of his own prior evils to Dow, his "victim-to-be" (*CS,* 191–92). Together they come upon Audubon in a low marshland that Dow has seen in dreams. As the men measure each other, a white heron alights, creating the still moment of the title, and creating as well the imaginary neutral territory, in this case a moment when time and place essentially vanish for the three men. It is the equivalent of a supernatural revelation for each, and a very different experience for the reader than that provided by the recognition scene in Sarah Orne Jewett's "The White Heron," a story that, in other ways, has some distinct parallels with Welty's.[29]

As a result of the charged moment, Murrell, too, now understands the space/time connection, for he realizes that with the disappearance of the Trace, his "conspiracy . . . will be disclosed" (*CS,* 196): time will ruin him by exposing the murders the wilderness has hidden. As for Audubon, his pure vision of the heron at the moment he kills it bares to him the inevitable limit of his own effort to preserve its beauty; but he also experiences for the first time "horror in its purity and clarity" in the "bright blue eyes" of Dow (*CS,* 197), whose reaction to the ornithologist's shooting of the heron registers a self-conviction that Audubon, like Hawthorne's amoral scientists, has never considered in connection with the "victims" of his own scientific endeavors. It is Lorenzo Dow's vision after Audubon kills the heron that gives voice to one of the most abiding themes in all of Welty's fiction, a theme first identified in 1944 by Robert Penn Warren: love and separateness. The sudden impact of the irrationality of death, the separation from life because of, and especially after, the knowledge of Audubon's love for the bird, causes Dow to experience the physiological equivalent of Gothic terror as he ponders the mysterious gap between human logic and divine chronology: "The hair rose on

29. See Joseph Rosenblum, "A New England Heron on the Natchez Trace: Sarah Orne Jewett's 'A White Heron' as Possible Source for Eudora Welty's 'A Still Moment,'" *Notes on Mississippi Writers,* XXII (1990), 69–73.

his head and his hands began to shake with cold, and suddenly it seemed to him that God Himself, just now, thought of the Idea of Separateness. For surely He had never thought of it before, when the little white heron was flying down to feed. He could understand God's giving Separateness first and then giving Love to follow and heal in its wonder; but God had reversed this, and given Love first and then Separateness, as though it did not matter to Him which came first" (*CS,* 198). Dow cannot abide what must seem to him a vision of blasphemy, and he flees, shouting "Tempter!" (*CS,* 199). Thus, in "A Still Moment," from historical characters and a literal wilderness Welty has created a gothic neutral ground and a portentous moment outside of time.

Whatever function Welty gives the landscape, the space itself has as much significance as the human characters. Welty has said, in her own analysis of "No Place for You, My Love," that its atmosphere, which is based on the reality of the unclear border between the natural elements of land, water, and air in the Louisiana delta, is so nearly tangible as to constitute a "third character" in the plot. The charged atmosphere, which holds the two northern travelers as if they were in an active chemical medium, is a character, Welty says, in the sense that it plays the role of a relationship between the man from Syracuse and the woman from Toledo (*ES,* 112). The idea that the third character will play a powerful role is introduced early in the story during a meditation on the propriety of the two strangers' taking a side trip from their chance meeting in New Orleans: "Had she felt a wish for someone else to be riding with them? . . . Whatever people like to think, situations (if not scenes) were usually three-way—there was somebody else always. The one who didn't—couldn't—understand the two made *the formidable third*" (*CS,* 471; Welty's emphasis). They are slowly seduced by this "third" as they cross the ferry, drive through "a sort of dead man's land, where nobody came" (*CS,* 468), and approach each other tentatively. Their point of closest communication is at the appropriately named beer shack Baba's Place in Venice, Louisiana; for this is a never-never land as far from their ordinary lives as that of Ali Baba's adventures. Even the ferryboat has seemed in a "trance" (*CS,* 469), and on board are two boys with a chained alligator, described as "the last worldly evidence of some old heroic horror of the dragon" (*CS,* 470). The spell of Baba's Place temporarily makes the woman into a heroine, as "she accepted it that she was more beautiful or perhaps more fragile than the women they saw every day of their lives" (*CS,* 476). And the terror of gothic cruelty is not missing from the story either, though Welty's glancing narrative skims by it: as the couple dance, "she became aware that he could not help but see the bruise at her temple. . . . She felt it come out like an evil star" (*CS,* 477). It is a sign, perhaps, of a cruel relationship from which she has fled. Although they dance like "professional, Spanish dancers wearing masks" (*CS,* 478), the mysterious neutral ground of the beer shack, condensed in the bare stage of the dance floor and further condensed in the circle of their own arms, allows the masks to drop for a significant moment: "Surely even those immune from the world, for the time being, need the touch of one another, or all is lost. Their arms encircling each other, their bodies circling the odorous, just-nailed-down floor, they were, at last, imperviousness in motion. They had found it, and had almost missed it: they had had to dance. They were what their separate hearts desired that day, for themselves and each other" (*CS,* 478).

The third character evoked by the sense of place is a role appropriate to the economy of a gothic setting. It gives the two the sense of moving, "immune from the world," in an incredible dream world that is somehow threatening to their more "real" worlds: "For their different reasons, he thought, neither of them would tell this . . . : that, strangers, they had ridden down into a strange land together and were getting safely back— by a slight margin, perhaps, but margin enough" (*CS,* 480). The felicity of the story's title is its double meaning: "no place" announces its locus as a neutral zone, with all its dangers and possibilities; and "for you, my love" suggests their present acceptance of the journey's reality *for* each other, but also their future denial of it. And when they pass the town of Arabi on their way back to New Orleans and their flights home, the transition is momentous. "We're all right now," he says; and confirming the apparitional quality of the "formidable third" character that is the catalyst in the story, the omniscient narrator asserts: "Something that must have been with them all along suddenly, then, was not. In a moment, tall as panic, it rose, cried like a human, and dropped back" (*CS,* 480). The centrality of such gothic effects to Welty's sense of the *realistic* surfaces of her own fiction is summed up here. For Welty has called this story a realistic story in which

> the reality *was* mystery. The cry that rose up at the story's end was, I hope unmistakably, the cry of that doomed relationship—personal, mortal, psychic—admitted in order to be denied, a cry that the characters were first able (and prone) to listen to, and then able in part to ignore. The cry was authentic to my story: the end of a journey *can* set up a cry, the shallowest provocation to sympathy and love does hate to give up the ghost. A relationship of the most fleeting kind has the power inherent to loom like a genie—to become vocative at the last, as it has already become present and taken up room; as it has spread as a destination however unlikely; as it

has glimmered and rushed by in the dark and dust outside, showing occasional points of fire. Relationship *is* a pervading and changing mystery. (*ES,* 114; Welty's emphasis)

Here Welty's own analysis adopts the language of the literary Gothic. In the story, gothic convention has been appropriated in the description of the couple's leaving New Orleans "as though following a clue in a maze," by the terror of their helpless exposure to each other, and by the personified haunted landscape that holds them in thrall. The equivalent of a supernatural spirit is the fleeting relationship that can "loom like a genie" and "spread," suggesting the surrealistic spreading face of the ghostly seductress of "The Purple Hat." It is a force that exists beyond the human and beyond time, which enters time and stops it for a magic, uncanny moment. In "No Place," this "third character" banishes the separateness of the two strangers for a brief time in an intense moment of wholeness, which Michael Kreyling finds depicted often in Welty's fiction. Welty's valorization of such a moment in an extramarital situation adds an additional level to the no-man's land inhabited by the couple in "No Place for You, My Love," and may reflect a similar usage of the wayward dalliance in the fiction of E. M. Forster, a writer whose work Welty has long admired. Carolyn Heilbrun describes Forster's use of the device in terms of "the importance to personal salvation of the odd and momentary relationship, the flash of love between two people who are not joined according to any of the conventional unions sanctioned by society." In Welty's fiction, this functional, ghostly, "third character," which itself operates on the margins of culture and consciousness, is Welty's adaptation of a classic Gothic attribute to depict modern alienation and miraculous, fragile, and potentially dangerous human connection.[30]

In spite of the gothic attributes (now reduced to their metaphoric, lower-case manifestation) of Welty's landscapes, her adherence to the verisimilar in basic settings includes her frequent historical and biographical research for details that concretely reflect human experience.[31] She herself has commented on the attraction historical settings have for her:

Indians, Mike Fink the flatboatman, Burr and Blennerhassett, John James Audubon, the bandits of the Trace, planters, and preachers—the horse fairs, the great fires—the battles of war, the arrivals of foreign ships, and

30. Michael Kreyling, *Eudora Welty's Achievement of Order* (Baton Rouge, 1980), 11–13; Carolyn G. Heilbrun, *Toward a Recognition of Androgyny* (New York, 1973), 100.
31. See Peggy Whitman Prenshaw, "A Study of Setting in the Fiction of Eudora Welty" (Ph.D. dissertation, University of Texas, 1970), 233–34.

the comings of floods: could not all these things still move with their true stature into the mind here, and their beauty still work upon the heart? Perhaps it is the sense of place that gives us the belief that passionate things, in some essence, endure. Whatever is significant and whatever is tragic in its story live as long as the place does, though they are unseen, and the new life will be built upon these things—regardless of commerce and the way of rivers and roads, and other vagrancies. (*ES,* 299)

Every description of the Natchez country, like Cooper's of the Hudson Highlands, evokes a mysterious no-man's land that Welty, like Cooper, transforms into a gothic space to serve the ends of her fiction. Her native region is a unique part of Mississippi dominated by a ridge atop loess bluffs, where "a gate might have been shut behind you for all the difference in the world" (*ES,* 287). The ruins here are those of Indian mounds and plantation mansions. In "Some Notes on River Country," she describes the ruin of Windsor, with its twenty-two Corinthian columns, remembering its five stories and the observation tower that helped Mark Twain to sight his position when he piloted a steamboat on the Mississippi River (*ES,* 288). Windsor was the model for the ruin in Welty's story "Asphodel"; and it is situated near Rodney's Landing between the Natchez Trace and the Mississippi River, as is Clement Musgrove's house in *The Robber Bridegroom.*

The old Sunken Trace itself is today a ruin of a road, preserved in two short places adjacent to the paved two-lane Natchez Trace Parkway that links Jackson and Natchez. Now measuring from six to fifteen feet wide, it was worn deeper than a man's height first by the buffalo and then by the Indians and other desperate men who replaced the buffalo in the seventeenth century and then succeeded each other. It is overhung by Rodney cemetery, which is described, in "At the Landing," as "a dark shelf above the town" (*CS,* 243) and which in that story serves as the fictional neutral ground between Jenny's grandfather's home and the outside world. Here Jenny meets Billy Floyd when she visits her mother's grave. In the story, Welty depicts the forest along the Natchez Trace as the dark scene of temptation and initiation of Jenny, who, like her mother before her, has been kept from the harsh world in the virtual prison of the house. She is allowed out only to go to the cemetery. Ironically, it is in this place of death that she finds new life in her love for Billy Floyd; but she also finds an introduction to a new kind of death or, as Suzanne Marrs notes, "destruction."[32] Jenny looks from the cemetery across the Trace at Billy

32. Suzanne Marrs, *The Welty Collection: A Guide to The Eudora Welty Manuscripts and Documents at the Mississippi Department of Archives and History* (Jackson, 1988), 86.

Floyd standing in a meadow awash with sunlight, a world in which she imagines her freedom from the constraints of home. But even as she looks, a premonition of danger is implied in Welty's description of her as "a child who is appalled at the stillness and unsurrender of the still and unsurrendering world" (*CS,* 243).

"Go back," Jenny says, as if instinctively fearing what she desires. But it is too late; the spell is cast that "could make a strange glow fall over the field where he was, and the world go black for her, left behind. She felt terrified, as if at a pitiless thing" (*CS,* 244–45). Thus, from elements that could have composed a romantic idyll (as indeed Jenny composed for herself)—a sunny meadow and two young lovers—Welty creates an atmosphere of gothic dread for her heroine. And Jenny's premonition comes true; for at the end of the story as in the beginning, the freedom of the "pasture, the sun and the grazing horse were on his side, [while there was a closure like] the graves on hers" (*CS,* 244). Like other ambivalent "saviors" in Welty's fiction, Billy Floyd makes love to her and saves her from the river's flood; but then he leaves her to wait for him in the shantyboat along the river, where her heroine's life of habitual obedience overcomes her earlier moment's impulse toward sexual freedom. The result of her training in this culturally enforced role of obedience to patriarchal domination is her docile endurance of sexual confinement at the whim of the fishermen who "one by one . . . came in to her" (*CS,* 257). The text implies that, at the very least, she suffers multiple rape, and suggests the possibility of her continuing life as a riverfront prostitute, waiting in despair for Billy Floyd, who, in his own eager quest for life, may have simply forgotten her. As she has feared, the world has "go[ne] black for her, left behind."

Jenny's quest has been cut short; for it is subsumed in the romance plot in which she becomes a victim of romantic thralldom. However, in Jenny's story, as in traditional romance plots, "nonpossession of the hero or nonaccess to marriage" exemplifies "the negative print of marriage," the script that called for the "narrative death" of Flaubert's Madame Bovary, of Lily Bart in Edith Wharton's *The House of Mirth,* and of Edna Pontellier in Kate Chopin's *The Awakening.* Jenny Lockhart is lured into a cultural hiatus like that which has been called, in the case of those nineteenth-century heroines, a "distorted, inappropriate relation to the social 'script' or plot designed to contain her legally, economically, and sexually . . . [because of the] energies of selfhood, often represented by sexuality[, which are] expended outside the 'couvert' of marriage or valid romance."[33] Accordingly, in the economy of the romance plot, Jen-

33. DuPlessis, *Writing Beyond the Ending,* 15–17.

ny's "invalid romance," signified by her "nonpossession of the hero and nonaccess to marriage," necessitates her narrative death-in-life on the shantyboat.

"At the Landing" utilizes the Natchez landscape for the sense of place in its physical setting only; "First Love" and "A Still Moment" make use of the physical setting as well as of characters associated with its history. But in *The Robber Bridegroom,* Welty, like Cooper in *The Spy,* not only depicts a physical setting that is a no-man's land of limitless imagination but also brings together historical characters, legendary figures, and a situation of intrigue based on historical events. She says the tale is "not a *historical* historical novel"; but it takes place, nevertheless, "in the Natchez country of the late eighteenth century, in the declining days of Spanish rule" (*ES,* 300, 302) when, in fact, Indians, bandits like the historical Harpe Brothers, and murderers like the legendary Mike Fink actually menaced the area (*ES,* 299). In her essay "Fairy Tale of the Natchez Trace," Welty relates her method of combining the plot of the Grimms' fairy tale "The Fisherman and His Wife" (which, she says, "exceeds my story in horror") with history, which "tells us worse things than fairy tales do. People were scalped. Babies had their brains dashed out against tree trunks or were thrown into boiling oil when the Indians made their captures. Slavery was the order on the plantations. The Natchez Trace outlaws eviscerated their victims and rolled their bodies downhill, filled with stones, into the Mississippi River. War, bloodshed, massacre were all part of the times. In my story, I transposed these horrors . . . into . . . the fairy tale" (*ES,* 309).

Welty's use of history in *The Robber Bridegroom* can be seen in her creation of figures based on the lives of outlaws Joseph Thompson Hare, Thomas Mason and his gang, and the Harpe Brothers. By adding to folk legends specific details from actual journals and histories, and details of the actual landscape, Welty creates a sense of the magnitude of human experience in a place, both that of the past and of the yet possible. Such a strategy allows the fictional setting to exceed the literal and operate symbolically as an expression of theme, as Peggy Prenshaw has observed. It is in this regard that Welty's choice of the fairy tale for modern fiction is particularly astute. For the fairy tale can accommodate effects similar to those of the Gothic; in addition, the unrealistic nature of folk or fairy tales, like that of the Gothic, is important precisely because, according to Bruno Bettelheim, it makes obvious the fact that such tales' concern is "not the external world, but the inner processes taking place in an individual." It is, rather, the so-called realistic novel that Ronald Sukenick finds to be the actual "fairy tale" because, he says, it "whispers assurance that the world is not mysterious, that it is predictable—if not to the characters then to the author, that it is not only under control but that one can profit from this control." Welty's stories, on the other hand, bear out R. Buckminster Fuller's assertion about the "absolute mystery of the universe" (*C,* 68). In fact, in answer to a question about her work as "sort of a map of Mississippi," Eudora Welty has said that she thinks of it more as an "internal map . . . a map of minds and imagination. Of course, it has to be laid somewhere. But what guides you is what is inside of the characters" (*C,* 178).[34]

Welty is not, then, adapting gothic attributes to American settings for the sake of those settings themselves, as were early American novelists, such as Cooper, Irving, Charles Brockden Brown, and William Gilmore Simms, in their attempts to create an American literature. Welty manipulates gothic and fairy-tale conventions, physical settings, and personal situations, both consciously and intuitively, in a process that she often explains as the result of a lyrical impulse of "attentiveness and *care* for the world . . . and a wish to connect with it," an attempt to be "*attentive* to life, not closed to it but open to it" (*C,* 261; Welty's emphasis). The mystery in a Welty story is not the mystery of the classic Gothic, whose aim was to create physiological sensation in its readers. Although gothic conventions may be used to portray it, the mystery is, instead, the inherent mystery of the relationships between people and between people and places, even across time. Welty's treatment of the theme of the mystery of human relationships in a full-blown fairy tale indicates her belief in the continuing efficacy of that genre for communicating psychological truth.

In *The Robber Bridegroom,* mysterious communications are carried on through dreams and through various enigmatic presences that contribute to the human situations of the tale. A talking raven is introduced early in the story as the companion of one of the outlaws Clement Musgrove is assigned to room with on his way home from a trip down river. In all situations of imminent danger—and there are many that complicate this innocent planter's dream of pastoral harmony—the raven repeats the refrain "Turn back, my bonny, / Turn away home" (*RB,* 78). Clement's roommates at the inn—Jamie Lockhart, the bandit of the Natchez Trace, and Mike Fink, the giant flatboatman—are not the only

34. Prenshaw, "A Study of Setting," 220; Bruno Bettelheim, *The Uses of Enchantment: The Meaning and Importance of Fairy Tales* (New York, 1977), 25; Ronald Sukenick, "Twelve Digressions Toward a Study of Composition," *New Literary History,* VI (1975), 429.

outlaws in the tale. Little Harp is waiting for the chance to take over Jamie's gang and his wife. His mischief is masterminded by the talking head of his brother, executed highwayman Big Harp, whose head, coated with a layer of blue Mississippi River clay, is carried about in a trunk by the feisty bandit. The head serves as an evil counterpart to a talking locket that chides Clement's daughter Rosamond like a good conscience, "If your mother could see you now, her heart would break," when she elopes with Jamie in the forest (*RB*, 43). The tale even includes a warning "from another world," but it is not "a message from out of the past for the old ghost," as Mike Fink thinks; rather, it is the news "from out of the future" that Jamie Lockhart is soon to be the father of twins. Since Fink thinks he murdered Jamie in the inn scene of the opening action, Jamie is proclaimed throughout the story to be a "ghost." In Welty's humorous tale, of course, such "ghosts" are taken in stride; and Fink, the murderer-turned-mail-carrier, remarks mildly upon the paternity, "Ghosts are getting more powerful every day in these parts" (*RB*, 177–78).

If these mock-supernatural spirits were the only elements lifted from the Gothic, Welty's story could be seen simply as a fairy-tale parody of the genre. But in the context of the entire Welty canon, these, together with more ominous devices, combine to suggest their utilization in the American literary tradition of the serious romance. And indeed the novella treats another serious theme: that of the destruction of the wilderness, as Michael Kreyling has shown.[35] But it also treats the characteristic theme of the terror Gothic genre: betrayal and entrapment; specifically, the premeditated abduction and seduction of a young girl. Recalling Frances Wharton's night journey through the forest in Cooper's *The Spy*, and indeed all the perils of Gothic heroines who enter dark and frightening places, Welty's Rosamond, on a similar journey after her wicked stepmother has stolen her talisman locket, discovers a formerly pastoral forest turned suddenly hostile; and no wonder, for it is inhabited by many human evils. The deceit of Cooper's armies, outlaws, and spy is overmatched by that of Welty's robber bridegroom, several outlaws, and even by the lies of the heroine Rosamond herself. The violence of war in *The Spy* is echoed by that of the savage (however "elegant") Natchez Indians who have thrown Rosamond's baby brother in boiling oil, and who torture Salome, her stepmother, making her dance until she dies. And the gang rape, mutilation, and murder of the Indian maiden Jamie's bandits mistake for Rosamond matches any Gothic horror. The story's fairy-tale-gothic villainy includes not only Jamie Lockhart's plot, as "gentle-

---

35. Kreyling, *Welty's Achievement,* 36.

man," to rescue and marry Clement Musgrove's cinder-stained "silly daughter" for her father's money. It extends also to his other berry-stained, bandit self's seduction of Rosamond's other romantic-heroine self. He steals Rosamond's clothes on one occasion, rapes her on another, and then knocks her unconscious before he drags her off to bed, even after they elope.

But Rosamond, no sentimental heroine, is unfazed by the theft of her clothes and by Jamie's chivalrous offer of death instead of the traditional dishonor his rape has ostensibly caused. "Why, sir, life is sweet," she responds, "and before I would die on the point of your sword, I would go home naked any day" (*RB,* 50); and she does, a short time later consenting to elope with him to his forest hideout. Washington Irving's Rosetta, in a similar bind, is speechless; but neither Rosamond nor her voice are diminished. In the formula romance plot, which the fairy-tale script follows, survival by any means, blatant or devious, is scandalous behavior for a damaged heroine. If she chooses, heroically, to live, then she has also, ironically, chosen to be as much of an outcast as the bandits. "A female hero has no alternative community where the stain of energy (whether sexual or, in more general terms, passionate) will go unnoticed or even be welcomed," according to Rachel Blau DuPlessis. Thus, Rosamond's behavior is early evidence that Welty is not writing sentimental fiction. Jennifer Lynn Randisi exempts Welty from the sentimentalism of antebellum southern romance writers because, she says, unlike their unselfconscious transmission of a cultural mythology, Welty consciously manipulates that tradition.[36] Although the setting of *The Robber Bridegroom* is in a dreamscape of romance, Rosamond is forever being awakened before she gets her "dream dreamed out" (*RB,* 61)—an indication that Welty's forte is irony, not sentiment. And what Welty has called being open to life and trying to see it without (even rose-colored) distortion is suggested by Rosamond's washing the berry stains off the face of her robber bridegroom.

Perhaps most important, we are prevented from reading the story *only* as a fairy tale by Rosamond's poignant, and anachronistically modern, expression of her right not to be used as a heroine—that is, not to be kept without knowledge and confined, like Psyche by Eros, in a relationship of the night: "My husband was a robber and not a bridegroom. . . . He brought me his love under a mask, and kept all the truth hidden from me, and never called anything by its true name, even his

36. DuPlessis, *Writing Beyond the Ending,* 16; Jennifer Lynn Randisi, *A Tissue of Lies: Eudora Welty and the Southern Romance* (Washington, D.C., 1982), x.

name or mine, and what I would have given him he liked better to steal. And if I had no faith, he had little honor, to deprive a woman of giving her love freely" (*RB*, 146). Neither is the happily-after-after ending without its modern emendation; for the double natures of Jamie as bandit-gentleman and Rosamond as liar-lover are changed hardly at all when they are transformed into rich merchant and wife in New Orleans. Having heeded her sexual self, Rosamond is now a mother, who has much in common with her powerful and mercenary "wicked" stepmother, a development that attests to the psychological validity of the enigmatic conflict of mother-daughter as evil-good doubles. Furthermore, studies by Juliann Fleenor and Karen Stein allege that generational alter egos are often instrumental in women's ambivalence toward themselves, a theory that has been the basis for much female Gothic fiction of the past and that has now been affirmed by the psychological research reported in Nancy Chodorow's *The Reproduction of Mothering.*[37]

Arvid Schulenberger notes that Cooper discovered promise in a synthesis of elements from three genres—the sentimental novel, the Gothic novel, and Scott's historical romance. Similarly, Eudora Welty freely draws from the conventions of these "escape" literatures, as well as from those associated with other genres, including fairy tale, myth, and legend, creating her unique contribution to the American romance, a genre that, according to Stanley Bank, brings truth closer to the reader instead of moving it farther away, as in the classic Gothic or the pastoral romance. She transforms such conventions as suit her purpose into the moods of terror and wonder that depict her characters' complex feelings. Most of the characters in these works, and throughout the Welty canon, are not fully drawn; in fact, they often seem to be mere caricatures. Yet, the "complexity of feeling" that Allen Tate recognizes in the American novel since Hawthorne is routinely accomplished without complexity of character, but rather, as Richard Chase says, with a kind of "abstracted simplicity" in both character and event; and the juxtaposition of this complexity and this simplicity, Chase believes, exemplifies the "radical disunities" that contribute to the romantic character of the American novel. The complexity of feeling that Welty achieves is in large part due to her success in adapting a core of materials from the European Gothic, as it has evolved through the British novel of manners and through the American serious romance, the latter with its melding of the actual and

---

37. Fleenor, ed., *The Female Gothic,* 16; Karen Stein, "Monsters and Madwomen: Changing the Female Gothic," *ibid.,* 123–37; Nancy Chodorow, *The Reproduction of Mothering: Psychoanalysis and the Sociology of Gender* (Berkeley, 1978).

the imaginary. Her work provides a modern exemplar of the romance's ability, to use Chase's phrase again, "to express dark and complex truths unavailable to realism." It is in the tradition of romantic, psychological realism, then, that Welty's stories belong; and their truths most often emerge from a feeling for an actual place imaginatively transformed into a gothic space.[38]

38. Arvid Schulenberger, *Cooper's Theory of Fiction: His Prefaces and Their Relation to His Novels* (New York, 1972), 10; Stanley Bank, *American Romanticism: A Shape for Fiction* (New York, 1969), 11; Allen Tate, "Techniques of Fiction," in *Essays of Four Decades,* by Tate (Chicago, 1968), 130; Chase, *The American Novel,* 5, 6, 13. Chase refers to Howellsian realism, I presume, which did not dwell on the darker truths.

II

Spatiality and the Short Story
The Lyric Technique

To speak of Eudora Welty's infusion of an actual landscape with an imaginative atmosphere, creating thereby a "neutral territory," is to use the vocabulary not only of Fenimore Cooper but of Nathaniel Hawthorne, who explained his fiction as a moonlight-induced transformation of the familiar into what is a dramatic locus, and very often a gothic space: a "neutral territory, somewhere between the real world and fairy-land, where the Actual and the Imaginary may meet." The concept has remained a significant one throughout American literary history, restated by Henry James in "The Art of Fiction" in terms of the combination of the realistic and the imaginary, and by Marianne Moore in her poem entitled "Poetry," in which she advocates "imaginary gardens with real toads in them." Richard Chase employs the same vocabulary to describe the American novel in general; its setting, he asserts, is "conceived not so much as a place as a state of mind—the borderland of the human mind where the actual and imaginary intermingle."[1]

This, then, is the general principle that governs Welty's writing and identifies her with the main currents in American prose and poetry: a basic realism is energized by the free play of the imagination. But equally important is her participation in what Chase has said is the American extension of that principle: the use of setting as a "borderland of the human mind." For she transforms the raw material of experience into what Hawthorne, in "The Custom-House," called "things of intellect," by which he meant things of the imagination as opposed to things of the real world. The raw material of place becomes, then, in Welty's fiction, not so much a place as a state of mind. The mysterious events that transpire in the supercharged spaces of her stories are psychological, not supernatu-

1. Chase, *The American Novel,* 19.

ral, phenomena. Welty intellectualizes her landscapes—that is, she externalizes internal emotions in narrative patterns—in ways that recall Hawthorne's. Like him, she selects times, and especially places, that allow the reader's imagination to range freely, as in some dreamlike "legendary mist" that, like the classic Gothic, offers a potentially dramatic space. From this basis in place, imbued with the lively presence of history (timebound) and myth or legend (timeless), she creates for each story an aesthetic space like that which Hawthorne called "a proper theatre" for fiction.[2] Like Hawthorne's, Welty's artistic vision is crucially informed by her dramatic visual imagination. She conceives of her fiction in scenes as vivid and as spatially realized as the scaffold scene in *The Scarlet Letter* or the forest tableau in that novel, in which the river both physically and symbolically separates little Pearl from her parents. The memorable opening scene at the prison in *The Scarlet Letter* and the confining weight of ancestral guilt in *The House of the Seven Gables*—both spatial presentations of psychological realities—are only two examples in Hawthorne that provide credible precedents for Welty's pervasive images of confinement.

Although her essentially celebratory tone has prevented most readers from seeing her work in relation to the gloomy Hawthorne, and although she is not mentioned in Samuel Chase Coale's account of American writers who work "in Hawthorne's shadow," her own darker vision is always there under the optimism. As she says of writers in general, "It was the dark that first troubled us" (*ES,* 151). Several commentators have remarked briefly on Hawthornian traits in Welty. Michael Kreyling, for example, has realized that there exists between Welty and Hawthorne a kinship in moral vision that functions "imaginatively rather than intellectually" in devices such as Hawthorne's veil symbolism, manifested in the veil of Welty's evil beeman in the manuscript of "The Delta Cousins." He also notes that the relation manifests itself thematically in the futile dreams of order and harmony of, for example, Clement Musgrove in Welty's *The Robber Bridegroom* and Miles Coverdale in Hawthorne's *The Blithedale Romance.*[3] And indeed it is through such aesthetic patterns of

2. *Ibid.;* Hawthorne, *The Scarlet Letter,* 31. See also Hawthorne's preface to *The House of the Seven Gables,* ed. Richard Harter Fogle (1851; rpr. New York, 1962), which he calls "a Tale [that] comes under the Romantic definition, . . . a Legend, prolonging itself from an epoch now gray in the distance, down to our own broad daylight, and bringing along with it some of its legendary mist" (15); and see his "Alice Doane's Appeal," in *The Complete Short Stories of Nathaniel Hawthorne* (New York, 1959), 561, and his *Blithedale Romance* (1852; rpr. New York, 1986), 1.

3. Kreyling, *Welty's Achievement,* 58. See also Vande Kieft, *Eudora Welty* (1987), 163; Randisi, *A Tissue of Lies,* vii; Marie-Antoinette Manz-Kunz, *Eudora Welty: Aspects of Fan-*

her fiction that we may perceive many of Welty's themes, especially that of the conflict between what confines the human spirit and what impels it to break free of constraints.

With Hawthorne, American Gothic romances became so intense a quest into the depth of the human mind and heart, into the human personality's doubleness, separateness, and essential mystery, that writers who have followed his lead create the lineage of what might be called the serious romance in America: a way of knowing reality that is a very different product from the early Gothic entertainments of Europe. My reading of Hawthorne is in line with Michael Davitt Bell's assessment of him as a "romancer," a term of Hawthorne's own making, in a culture hostile to the idea of granting validity to the imaginative faculty. Such a reading marks Hawthorne as what Bell calls a "deviant" in the literary profession of his age, regardless of the fact that he was uncomfortable with this position, and no matter how conservative he may have been in other areas of his life. I do not see Hawthorne in the more conservative (neutral) tradition of the Gothic romance writer of escape fiction, a position that is assigned him by Richard Chase, Perry Miller, and Joel Porte, as Bell points out.[4]

Welty's place in the Hawthornian tradition of the serious romance is commonly overlooked. But if she does not share Hawthorne's extreme pessimism, still she shares with him the fascination with the romantic idea of the primitive and fragmented self: of doubleness and loneliness; of love versus freedom, and enclosure versus escape; of strong women and ambivalent, vulnerable, or passive men; and of the formal shaping of fictional space to establish those themes.

Welty's relation is not to the tradition of the classic Gothic romance per se, but primarily to the nineteenth-century "new" Gothic tradition that merges with that of the developing American short story. For Welty creates the kind of functionally active atmospheres and symbolic spatial structures that have been identified as marks of the American lyric short story since Poe, its primary theorist, and Hawthorne, its most influential practitioner. And like those early short-story writers, Welty is a conscious

tasy in Her Short Fiction (Bern, 1971), 25; Gary Carson, "The Romantic Tradition in Eudora Welty's *A Curtain of Green*," *Notes on Mississippi Writers,* IX (1976), 97–99; Jan Nordby Gretlund, "Out of Life into Fiction: Eudora Welty and the City," *Notes on Mississippi Writers,* XIV (1982), 46.

4. Michael Davitt Bell, "Arts of Deception: Hawthorne, 'Romance,' and *The Scarlet Letter,*" in *New Essays on "The Scarlet Letter,"* ed. Michael Colacurcio (Cambridge, Eng., 1985), 29–56.

narrative theorist whose literary critical language often recalls theirs. Mary Rohrberger cites Hawthorne, not Washington Irving, as the first American short-story writer; and she defines the "lyric" short story, after Poe's dicta, as "characterized by symbolic substructures . . . [that are part of] a steady rhythmic process toward a particular ending necessitated by the pattern involved." In line with the "single effect" theory codified by Poe in his reading of Hawthorne's tales, but also with James Joyce's concept of the literary "portrait of the artist" as "not an identificative paper but rather the curve of an emotion," is Welty's telling comment that she "think[s] in terms of a single impulse, and . . . of a short story as being a lyric impulse, something that begins and carries through and ends all in the same curve" (*C*, 345). Related to his unity-of-effect concept is Poe's theory of the short story as analogous to a painting, as he said in a review of Dickens' tale "The Pawnbroker's Shop." As Robert Jacobs observes, such a pictorial concept is "spatial: a design extended in space, not a movement in time."[5]

It becomes apparent that Poe and Hawthorne should be recognized as influences that complement Welty's modernist literary forebears when one recognizes her similar transformations of actual landscapes into imaginary gothic spaces. While the ghostly presences and passions of actual history haunt Hawthorne's stories with a heavy sense of the sins of his own ancestors in early Salem, Welty's best-known setting is the Natchez Trace wilderness of Mississippi, which was a literal "neutral ground" in the late eighteenth century when it was the Spanish frontier. Indeed, it has been such a seminal component of the writing of Welty and others that an annual literary conference is now devoted to the literature and history of the Trace.[6] It is a place possessed of lively historical spirits that live on in some sense, Welty believes, creating the *locus ge-*

5. Heilman, "Charlotte Brontë's 'New Gothic'"; Mary Rohrberger, "Between Shadow and Act: Where Do We Go From Here?," in *Short Story Theory at a Crossroads*, ed. Susan Lohafer and Jo Ellyn Clarey (Baton Rouge, 1989), 40; Rohrberger, *Hawthorne and the Modern Short Story: A Study in Genre* (The Hague, 1966), 58, 141; Edgar Allan Poe, *The Complete Works of Edgar Allan Poe*, ed. James A. Harrison (1902; rpr. New York, 1965), IX, 48; Robert D. Jacobs, *Poe: Journalist and Critic* (Baton Rouge, 1969), 164; James Joyce, "A Portrait of the Artist," *Yale Review* (1960), rpr. in Joyce's *A Portrait of the Artist as a Young Man*, ed. Chester G. Anderson (New York, 1977), 258. Joyce's analogy of the artist's portrait to the shaping "curve" of a story is remarkably like Welty's comment that "it is through the shaping of the work in the hands of the artist that you most nearly come to know what can be known, on the page, of his mind and heart" (*ES*, 144).

6. The first Natchez Trace Literary Celebration was held June 7–9, 1990, in Natchez, Mississippi. For published selections from this conference, see the Natchez Literary Celebration Special Issue of *Southern Quarterly*, XXIX (Summer, 1991).

nius that now thickens the atmosphere of the actual place and pervades the ominous silences of many of Welty's fictional spaces, thus creating the proper aesthetic "theatre," to use Hawthorne's term. As Welty explains it, since "passionate things, in some essence, endure . . . [,those which are] significant and . . . tragic . . . live as long as the place does, though they are unseen" (*ES,* 299). Hawthorne appropriates the figure of Cotton Mather to lend authenticity to Boston's Gallows Hill in "Alice Doane's Appeal"; similarly, Welty casts, for her fictional "theatre," legendary outlaws such as Mike Fink in *The Robber Bridegroom* and other historical figures such as Aaron Burr and Harmon Blennerhassett in "First Love" and John James Audubon in "A Still Moment."

George E. Haggerty has recently connected many strands of the literary history and criticism of the Gothic in a way that is useful for illuminating the narrative techniques in Welty's short stories in terms of the affective aesthetic forms both she and Hawthorne employ. Haggerty's work relies extensively on that of contemporary theorist Charles E. May, who has expanded on Russian formalist short-story theory, and also on Northrop Frye's work on the revolutionary nature of the romance, which he describes as "introverted and personal . . . , deal[ing] with characters in a more subjective way . . . [in terms of] treatment, not subject matter." May suggests that the Gothic, a romantic and highly *affective* (esthetically subjective instead of realistically objective) medium, is more amenable to the form of short fiction than to the novel. In a passage that seems to echo Hawthorne, May argues that the short story "breaks up the familiar life-world of the everyday, defamiliarizes our assumption that reality is simply the conceptual construct we take it to be, and throws into doubt that our propositional and categorical mode of perceiving can be applied to human beings as well as to objects, . . . [leading to] intense focusing for the totality of the narrative experience." Such defamiliarization is also a known component of the Russian short-story tradition, to which Welty claims kinship through Chekhov (*C,* 83); but Welty's use of the technique has not been well recognized in terms of its connection with the American tradition. Actually, Welty enjoys a dual heritage in terms of short-story technique: (1) the tradition of the mythic and aesthetic (metaphoric) reality of the primal story patterns derived from myth and folk tale, a reality that always has mystery as its center, and (2) this same tradition of mythic "storyness" as transformed by Irving, Hawthorne, Poe, and Melville, who, as May notes, "subjected those conventions to the demands of *vraisemblance,* or realistic motivation . . . by presenting them as basic psychic processes" through the (metonymic) press of event and realistic detail. The two modes alternate in primacy among the stories of Eudora Welty; that is, sometimes an outward realism is haunted by an aesthetic infrastructure of primal mystery, and sometimes a stylized or dreamlike lyrical surface dominates, or competes for dominance, with a realistic structure of chronological event.[7]

A primary component of the technique Welty has developed from these sources is the gothic convention of the labyrinth, which she adapts in various image patterns that give focus to the sense of alienation and loneliness of characters who are bewildered by a world that often seems unreal, and who move through frightening mazes of feeling. The same convention was used by Hawthorne in "My Kinsman, Major Molineux" to shape the curve of Robin's emotion as he wanders *amazed* in a pre-Joycean phantasmagoria of labyrinthine streets. Welty creates similar gothic spaces, which she fashions from actual places: from the tangled grapevines of a literal wilderness in the early "Death of a Traveling Salesman" to New Orleans streets thronged with grotesquely costumed, "blundering" Mardi Gras revelers in *The Optimist's Daughter* (*OD,* 55).

Confining houses and their tangled gardens in Welty's works are descendants of houses that reflect the troubled minds of protagonists in American Gothic romances: Henry James's *The Turn of the Screw;* Poe's *The Fall of the House of Usher;* and, of course, Hawthorne's *The House of the Seven Gables,* as well as "Rappaccini's Garden" with its deadly greenhouse. Gothic houses are part of functional settings that are central to these works, and most bear some resemblance to crypts slowly being encrusted with moss and shrouded by mists and gloomy foliage. Such settings blur the border between the inert and the living, as does Welty's graveyard in "At the Landing," in which "the moss seems made of stone, and the stone of moss" (*CS,* 243). The charged atmospheres that result from settings on the margins between the living and the dead, between the "Actual and the Imaginary," and imbued with the lively presence of history, myth, and legend, contribute to what is perhaps Welty's most obvious link with the Gothic romance: the fact that her stories court mystery and the metaphysical. They are, as she has said of Katherine Mansfield's "Miss Brill," "bathed in something of [their] own . . . [and are] wrapped in an atmosphere" (*ES,* 88), an atmosphere that, like Hawthorne's "moonlight, in a familiar room," transforms figures into "things of intellect," or imaginative constructs in the service of the story.

7. Haggerty, *Gothic Fiction/Gothic Form,* 86; Northrop Frye, *The Anatomy of Criticism* (New York, 1970), 308; Charles E. May, "The Nature of Knowledge in Short Fiction," *Studies in Short Fiction,* XXI (1984), 333–35; May, "Metaphoric Motivation in Short Fiction: 'In the Beginning Was the Story,'" in *Short Story Theory at a Crossroads,* ed. Lohafer and Clarey, 65.

But in addition, and contributing to Brooks and Warren's still-valid concept of "the logic of the whole," Welty's appropriation of gothic convention is seen not only in the static symbols of the maze but also in the dynamic patterns of enclosure and escape that permeate the fiction and constitute the essentially gothic *shape* of a plot: that is, the order of points in a story at which the writer causes the major emphases to fall.[8] In Welty's words, it is "this *ordering* of his story that is closest to the writer behind the writing, and . . . it's our perception of this ordering that gives us our nearest understanding of him" (*ES,* 105, Welty's emphasis). Such words echo the classic definition of the lyric as the subjective poetic expression of the writer, and they illustrate what is meant by the short story as an *affective* medium: even its formal structure is designed to *affect* the reader in such an intimate way that something of the subjective state of the writer's own mind is revealed. The frankly romantic attitude of Welty's words here coincides with the similar attitude that contributes to the concept of the lyric technique of the short story.

Twenty-five years ago, in tracing the derivation of the modern short story from the romantic tradition, Mary Rohrberger noticed structural affinities in the stories of Welty and Hawthorne. And since the relation of Welty's short stories to this American tradition has never been adequately explored, Rohrberger's comments are worth quoting at length:

> The short story derives from the romantic tradition. The metaphysical view that there is more to the world than that which can be apprehended through the senses provides the rationale for the structure of the short story which is a vehicle for the author's probing of the nature of the real. As in the metaphysical view, reality lies beyond the ordinary world of appearances, so in the short story, meaning lies beneath the surface of the narrative. The framework of the narrative embodies symbols which function to question the world of appearances and to point to a reality beyond the facts of the extensional world.[9]

Especially Hawthornian, then, is Welty's interest in perception, in the question of what is real, and in the dramatic presentation of human limitation. Welty consistently presents these themes through patterns developed from selected conventions of the European and American Gothic romance, which she combines with modernist techniques of the literary and visual arts, to portray the individual's frequent losing battles with self or world, but also his or her epiphanic moments of what may seem un-

---

8. Cleanth Brooks and Robert Penn Warren, *Understanding Fiction* (New York, 1943), x.

9. Rohrberger, *Hawthorne and the Modern Short Story,* 141.

reasonable optimism. Her aims are not those of the classic (old) Gothic of Horace Walpole or Anne Radcliffe, which elicit the vicarious thrill, the gratuitous physiological *frisson.* The "gothicism" implied by romantic conventions and settings in Welty's fiction is not a matter of using outmoded literary forms. Rather, it is suited to the present in the way that Joyce Carol Oates means when she speaks of gothicism as "a fairly realistic assessment of modern life." For the Gothic continues to be adaptable to modern cultural formations, making possible the twentieth century's repossession of a literary and cultural past "made plastic again," Richard Brodhead believes, because there is "something *to*" Hawthorne's work that speaks to contemporary culture. That "something" is, I believe, what Peter Brooks points to as a textual function that corresponds to a psychic function, a technique known since Vladimir Propp and the Russian formalists first discussed the difference between the *sjuzet* or *récit* (plot, or the order of events as presented) and the *fabula* (story, or the order of events referred to by the plot).[10] And because Cleanth Brooks and Robert Penn Warren's *Understanding Fiction* reasserted "literary study's role in mental training," in part by the example of such textual functions in Hawthorne's "The Birth-Mark," at a time when Eudora Welty was coming to maturity as a writer, it is perhaps not beside the point that Welty often includes "The Birth-Mark" along with her own work at public readings.[11] Brooks and Warren's comment that Aylmer's "possession of the questing spirit which will not resign itself to the limitations and imperfections of nature" would be grounds enough for showing Hawthorne's influence on Welty's treatments of human, especially artistic, rebellions against limitations.[12] It is apparent in stories like "A Still Moment," for example, in which Audubon must kill the beautiful heron to "perfect" his own art, or like "June Recital," in which Miss Eckhart's passion erupts in a violent piano performance, startling her young students. But beyond that, the plot structure of "The Birth-Mark," in which the metonymic figure of contiguity shows Aylmer's growth toward intellectual freedom and discovery as opposed to his wife's concomitant move toward psychic imprisonment and death, provides a model of structural dynamics to which Welty's stories exhibit a clear relation.

Indeed, Welty's stories are more significantly "plotted" than has been recognized. As her modern protagonists struggle to free themselves from

10. "Joyce Carol Oates: Writing as a Natural Reaction," *Time,* October 10, 1969, p. 108; Richard H. Brodhead, *The School of Hawthorne* (New York, 1986), 210 (his emphasis); Brooks, *Reading for the Plot,* 23, 90–91.

11. Brodhead, *The School of Hawthorne,* 210–11.

12. Brooks and Warren, *Understanding Fiction,* 104.

enclosures that often are as alien and menacing as the past that haunts Hawthorne's characters, Welty moves them not only in space but in significant sequence, not only in metaphoric but also in syntagmatic relationships that trace patterns of desire: the narrative desire of writers and readers to "rescue meaning from temporal flux." Such desire corresponds to what Susan Lohafer cites as our need for "'storyness' [, which is] pre-effable, centered not in language but in a cognitive strategy, . . . [as in folktales, which] have their roots in the unspoken and unspeakable." As in Hawthorne, so in Welty, characters are often enclosed by the force of another's, or what Michel Foucault has called society's, "carceral" desire, or they are crushed under the weight of memory and tradition. In such stories characters are propelled in space and time by increasingly suffocating loves or by inducements to conformity that unnaturally confine him or her—in Welty, most often *her*. And the sequences of their movements constitute plots that are "enchained toward a construction of significance," to use Peter Brooks's words.[13]

Many of Welty's stories depend less upon the literal complexities of natural landscape, which lend themselves to presentation as gothic qualities, than on an analogous sense of threatening enclosure that she creates by manipulating the *sense* of space and motion in her narratives. Stories such as "Lily Daw and the Three Ladies," "The Burning," and "Going to Naples" may therefore be said to extend the concept of a landscape to that of a mindscape with a structural pattern like that which reproduces "the shape of [an] emotion," as Eileen Baldeshwiler has described in Turgenev and Chekhov, Mansfield and Woolf, Porter and Welty, tracing the development of the "lyric" short story, which "concentrates on internal changes, moods, and feelings," as opposed to stories that develop by means of conventional plots of external action. Thus they recall Hawthorne's emphasis on setting over action, which in his case is more an intellectualization of his morals than an actual concern with setting per se in *The House of the Seven Gables*. Richard Harter Fogle's analysis of the intellectualization of setting reveals metaphoric "patterns of symbol" and symbolic characters that "all make up a design." Jerome Klinkowitz, however, believes that Hawthorne compromises spatial form by asking the Pyncheon house to perform as a character; but if this "house character" results in less than a "pure spatial setting," it even more closely resembles Welty's technique, in which atmosphere often functions as

13. Brooks, *Reading for the Plot,* 90–94; Susan Lohafer, "Preclosure and Story Processing," in *Short Story Theory at a Crossroads,* ed. Lohafer and Clarey, 275; Michel Foucault, *Discipline and Punish: The Birth of the Prison,* trans. Alan Sheridan (New York, 1977), 307–308.

what she calls a "third character" (*C,* 111).[14] The most basic pattern of such mindscapes in Welty's fiction is that of a chaotic human tangle that whirls purposefully in toward a still center but that, because neither the force nor the center can hold or because of some powerful counterimpulse, reverses itself in a centrifugal motion that spins outward toward an open ending. In her most complex works, both total formal structure and individual image patterns of these shaped spaces organically embody her pervasive theme of human limitations versus possibilities, central to which is the theme of the enclosure and escape of women.

Welty's fictional mindscapes, then, result from the externalizing of inner realities; and they often do so in ways that make the question of reality itself an issue, as it was with Hawthorne, who made a pre-Freudian contribution to a new and deeper sense of reality in American fiction with literary texts that are opened to the reader by authorial questions— "Had Goodman Brown fallen asleep in the forest and only dreamed a wild dream of a witch-meeting?"—and by such multiple symbolic references as that which Matthiessen long ago noticed in the significance of Hester's scarlet *A.* Thus the dubious "reality" of Hawthorne's narratives themselves comment not upon their romantic nature so much as upon the extent to which we may know reality in general. Eudora Welty's fiction abounds in the same productive uncertainties. For example, did King Mac-Lain in "Sir Rabbit" make love to Mattie Will in the forest, or was it an adventure of Mattie's own imagining? In spite of the illusion of realism Welty's regional settings lend, one critic has said that no one quite believes a Welty story; another has said, of *Delta Wedding,* that in what looks like a "chatty, domestic novel . . . [Welty] is not to be trusted"; yet another that Welty's "radically unstable" texts leave us "in a state so divided that anything like conventional closure is out of the question." Perceptive critics, therefore, have understood that the surfaces of Welty's stories, which may resemble bright patchwork quilts, are often held together by dark infrastructural threads that can be attributed to what Margaret Walker Alexander has recently called Welty's "gothic imagination." [15]

14. Eileen Baldeshwiler, "The Lyric Short Story: The Sketch of a History," in *Short Story Theories,* ed. Charles E. May (Athens, Ohio, 1976), 202–206; Hawthorne, *The House of the Seven Gables,* ed. Fogle, 8–9; Jerome Klinkowitz, "The Novel as Artifact: Spatial Form in Contemporary Fiction," in *Spatial Form in Narrative,* ed. Jeffrey R. Smitten and Ann Daghistany (Ithaca, N.Y., 1981), 42.

15. F. O. Matthiessen, *American Renaissance: Art and Expression in the Age of Emerson and Whitman* (London, 1941), 276; Patricia S. Yaeger, "'Because a Fire Was in My Head': Eudora Welty and the Dialogic Imagination," *Mississippi Quarterly,* XXXIX (1986), 569; Carol S. Manning, *With Ears Opening Like Morning Glories: Eudora Welty and the*

Welty's own delight in mysterious unknowns, as well as her habitual reliance on the vocabulary of the Gothic in discussing her craft, suggests her cognizance of gothic conventions as viable components of image systems amenable to non-Gothic literary aims. For example, in "Place in Fiction" Welty describes the writer's responsibility to "disentangle the significant," to hack "his way through a forest . . . [that] is a new and different labyrinth every time" (*ES,* 120–21). This same figure is used to describe the coherence of form and content in traditional Gothic fiction, both old and new, works that are noted for their "labyrinthine narrative structures wherein are inscribed gothic ambiguities."[16] One cannot but be aware of the suggestive nature of such language. Beyond Welty's images of writing as an activity in a tangled (potentially gothic) space is her extraordinary attention to the structural dimensions of fiction itself, which she commonly describes in spatial terms. And it is the spatial structure that is the crucial link between her gothic landscapes and her various treatments of the theme of human limitation. For the essence of her characters' confining situations is conveyed through scenes constructed from the shapes and patterns of enclosure. Welty is concerned with "seeing that [fiction's] inner and out *surfaces* . . . lie . . . close together" and with giving fiction "a *surface* that is continuous and unbroken, never too thin to trust, always in touch with the senses." Her goal is a story that is "steadily visible from its outside, presenting a continuous, shapely, pleasing and finished surface to the eye" (*ES,* 120, emphasis added). The surface appearance of a Welty story may be more accurately described as a collection of pieces in a spatially relative puzzle than a backdrop for a narrative of causal continuity. Always aware of the spatial properties of literary art, she admires Flaubert's statement that "poetry is as precise as

---

Love of Storytelling (Westport, Conn., 1985), 100–103; John F. Fleishauer, "The Focus of Mystery," *Southern Literary Journal,* V (1973), 68; Joyce Carol Oates, "Eudora's Web," in *Contemporary Women Novelists: A Collection of Critical Essays,* ed. Patricia Meyer Spacks (Englewood Cliffs, 1977), 171; Ruth M. Vande Kieft, "'Where Is the Voice Coming From?': Teaching Eudora Welty," in *Eudora Welty: The Eye of the Storyteller,* ed. Dawn Trouard (Kent, Ohio, 1989), 197; Margaret Alexander, Paper given at Natchez Literary Festival, June 9, 1990, in Natchez Literary Celebration Special Issue of *Southern Quarterly;* See also Danièle Pitavy-Souques, "'Shower of Gold,' ou les ambiguités de la narration," *Delta,* V (1977), 77. Pitavy examines the role of Kate Rainey as unreliable narrator/creator of characters. Regarding the depiction of King MacLain, for example, Mme Pitavy notes that, ironically, "au lieu de servir le but avoué de Kate Rainey (démasquer publiquement l'imposteur) le glorifie, sinon aux yeux du narrataire, du moins à ceux de la narratrice."

16. Claire Kahane, "The Gothic Mirror," in *The (M)other Tongue: Essays in Feminist Psychoanalytic Interpretation,* ed. Shirley Nelson Garner, Claire Kahane, and Madelon Sprengnether (Ithaca, N.Y., 1985), 334.

geometry," and notes that place, "to the writer at work, is seen in a *frame."* She asserts that "when the good novel is finished, its cooled out-side *shape"* has the illusion of reality (*ES,* 124–25, emphasis added).

Thus, Welty's expression of her own literary theory in these spatial terms invites a reading of her work in terms of its spatial form. She takes her point of departure from the real world, including its artistic conventions and its cultural mythologies, then consciously reinterprets these inherited forms, avoiding representational reality in favor of distillations, artistic distortions, and impressions at least as significant for their formal shapes and sensual evocations as for their story lines. The result of this approach is writing that challenges the reader intellectually and imaginatively to "disentangle the significant" from Weltian "labyrinths," to meet the author in realizing the embedded potential of the fiction—that is, to recognize the literary transformation of experience into "things of intellect." In her early story "A Memory," Welty's young protagonist makes this artistic transformation, using a literal frame as a special controlling device by which she tries both to distance herself from and to impose order on the dangerous, as she thinks, disorder of the outer landscape that is dominated by the grotesque family on the beach.

Like the beach in "A Memory," which has its origin in the Jackson park Welty enjoyed as a child, all of Welty's regional landscapes are related to literal historical ones, as are Fenimore Cooper's in *The Spy,* as well as to metaphoric spatial settings of the imagination in the manner of Hawthorne. But they are also related to abstract tableaux with the spatial components of painting, theater, and dance, making her fiction not only intertextual but multimedial. In fact, when her collection *The Wide Net* was published, it was criticized for being "a book of ballets, not stories." [17] It is, in fact, a collection of "at hand" images, the relation of which to her known world the artist sacrifices to the felicitous freedom of creating a new reality: a poetics of surprise, perhaps for author and reader alike, at the creation that is coming into being on the page and that results in what has been called, in another context, "a particular rapport with reality sufficiently permanent that we may for a time share it." [18] Such settings are foundations for the construction of the freestanding artifact Henry James called a house of fiction, and they have the potential of virtual gothic spaces with or without the "furniture" of a house or a

17. Diana Trilling, "Fiction in Review" (Review of Eudora Welty's *The Wide Net*), *Nation,* October 2, 1943, p. 286; H. D. Vursell, Review of *The Best American Short Stories,* ed. Martha Foley, in *Tomorrow,* III (November, 1943), 53.
18. Sukenick, "Twelve Digressions Toward a Study of Composition," 429.

forest. For example, the gothic theme of confinement can be effectively communicated by the painterly disposition of figures in an essentially "bare stage" narrative, which Welty is especially adept at creating, by image patterns that keep foremost in the reader's mind the figures' positions and movements in space. A reviewer of *The Golden Apples* recognized, in 1949, that Welty had such an "extraordinary sense . . . of human beings and other objects in space" that a reader has the sense of "standing before a canvas by one of the great . . . masters of space, color, and light, before a masterpiece of Pissarro, Seurat, or Villon."[19] Welty herself has said that she thinks of landscape as a stage—in the case of the bleak hill-country setting of *Losing Battles,* as a "clear stage" to depict "rock bottom" poverty of people during the years of the Great Depression (*C,* 54).

That the illusion of the spatial dimension in the ostensibly temporal medium of literary narrative has special relevance to Eudora Welty's fiction is apparent not only from examination of spatial form in her stories but also from her own and other writers' extensive critical commentary about Welty's version of the craft of fiction. Four specific areas of Welty's aesthetic can be profitably approached by means of reading for spatial form. The most obvious of these is Welty's concentration on place in fiction, which provides the basic illusion of reality and often contributes to the motivating force by means of gothic conventions: certain actions can be expected to happen in certain types of spaces. Proceeding from the connection of narrative to environment, and the relatively subtle sensations elicited by place, is a second extensive use Welty makes of spatial form: in stylistic techniques that borrow from the plastic and performing arts. Through the medium of such techniques, mental space and time are externalized on the printed page less in terms of semantic meaning than of suggestive sensual imagery, especially visual imagery. Geometric lines of relationship and perspective as well as centripetal and centrifugal motions around a point of suspense subvert the progress of the narration in time as they enrich and advance the theme. Alun R. Jones has described Welty's thematic structures as "centripetal, . . . with an intuited center and everything subdued to the demands of this central insight," but he does not identify the centripetal and centrifugal counter motions in her narrative patterns.[20]

19. Francis Steegmuller, "Small Town Life," *New York Times Book Review,* August 21, 1949, p. 5.

20. Alun R. Jones, "The World of Love: The Fiction of Eudora Welty," in *The Creative Present: Notes on Contemporary American Fiction,* ed. Nona Balakian and Charles Simmons (Garden City, 1963), 182.

Cinematic techniques like freeze-framing and jump-cutting direct attention more to individual scenes than to development of causal action. Welty, an admitted "constant moviegoer" who has said she would like to write an original screenplay, displays a special affinity for the arts of stage and screen. She especially admires the "lyric [and] mood films" of French *nouvelle vague* filmmaker Jean Renoir, and explains that he was "trained in a world of art . . . in a painter's household." She sees a close relation between the lyric film and the short story in their "fluid forms . . . [that] can move . . . back and forth in time . . . , can elide . . . , compound, [and] exaggerate" (*C,* 165, 187–89). Repeated spatial patterns and leitmotifs constitute a continuum throughout Welty's work, like the process that Joseph Frank, in his analysis of Proust's method, has called "reflexive reference," denoting the reference of one part of a work to another, a method that provides unity through simultaneity. "Proust's purpose," says Frank, "is achieved only when these units of meaning are referred to each other reflexively in a moment of time." Such spatial reflexive references enhance Welty's more conventional unifiers such as temporal flow of action or narrative point of view. The spatial illusion also extends to the painterly or sculptural attributes of, as well as perspectives on and by, what E. M. Forster called "flat" characters, who do not develop through time.[21]

A third aspect of Welty's aesthetic is related to that which Peter Brooks has recently analyzed in terms of the various definitions of *plot* that he finds in the *American Heritage Dictionary:* as a "measured area of land," a "ground plan . . . [or] diagram," the "series of events . . . of a narrative or drama," and "a secret plan to accomplish a hostile or illegal purpose; scheme." Essentially, what Brooks describes are several strategies for both writing and reading in terms of spatial and temporal organization of fiction, and even in terms of subtle or embedded meanings and "subterranean logic connecting these heterogeneous meanings" in the dictionary. To the foregrounding of space and what Ronald Sukenick calls the "spatialization of time" and point of view must be added a fourth aspect of Welty's spatial form: that of the writer-reader nexus. For Welty's "mindscape" stories impose a more difficult burden on the reader than does the conventional novel of causality. The spatial form that temporarily suppresses and upstages causal narrative is composed of very subtle patterns, many of which are themselves unobtrusive. To experi-

21. Joseph Frank, *The Widening Gyre: Crisis and Mastery in Modern Literature* (New Brunswick, 1963), 25; E. M. Forster, *Aspects of the Novel* (1927; rpr. New York, 1954), 103–108.

ence more fully the potential of a work, the reader must join with the writer in the technique of romantic irony, which involves deliberately destroying the illusion of "reality" and accepting the fiction as an artifact, a created product that exists in space as an entity that can be apprehended entire, a technique that I will shortly discuss in connection with "Lily Daw and the Three Ladies." Romantic irony occurs when the reader is led to view units of meaning in a work of art *only through* relation to the whole, thereby deflating the work's claim to be a self-contained "imitation of reality." The technique is traced by Ann Daghistany and J. J. Johnson to its philosophical basis: the phenomenon of human inadequacy before the vastness of the universe. Reading for spatial form reveals the poetic effect of the cumulative whole of Welty's fictions, and thus her themes; but it requires the shared imaginations of writer and reader that Welty hopes for (*C,* 168).[22]

The effective spatial depiction of human limitation and enclosure in Eudora Welty's early work makes a unique contribution to the grotesque mode that had its beginning in Gothic fiction. Asked about the "grotesque and grim" in her first stories, Welty replied that in the collections *A Curtain of Green* (1941) and *The Wide Net* (1943) she needed the device of the grotesque "to differentiate characters by their physical qualities as a way of showing what they were like inside—it seemed to me then the most direct way to do it. . . . It's instinctive for a writer to show acute feelings or intense states of emotion by translating it into something visible. . . . But it's not necessary. I believe I'm writing about the same inward things now without resorting to such obvious devices" (*C,* 93–94). But even early literary grotesques, such as the protagonists of "Petrified Man," "Lily Daw and the Three Ladies," and "Clytie," are not simply vehicles of social or psychological commentary, though they are inescapably that. Welty has dismissed these grotesque characters as elements in a somewhat elementary technique, yet they are nonetheless evidence of a poetic phenomenology that is interested more in creation than re-creation, and in essential states of being more than representational reality. Welty's ability to speak to ontological essence with gravity and infinite suggestibility through this "elementary" technique is an attribute she shares with American writers of the Southern Gothic, but which also has roots in the grotesques of Kafka and Chekhov. Welty her-

22. Brooks, *Reading for the Plot,* 11–12; Ronald Sukenick, *In Form: Digressions on the Art of Fiction* (Carbondale, 1985), 9; Ann Daghistany and J. J. Johnson, "Romantic Irony, Spatial Form, and Joyce's *Ulysses,*" in *Spatial Form in Narrative,* ed. Smitten and Daghistany, 54. See also Oskar Franz Walzel, *German Romanticism,* trans. Alma Elise Lussky (1932; rpr. New York, 1965), 43.

self, of course, has recognized an affinity with Chekhov, especially, as she told Linda Kuehl, because of his love of "the singularity in people, the individuality" (*C,* 83)—in other words, in the very attributes that often give rise to the grotesque in Southern fiction, according to Carson Mc-Cullers in *The Mortgaged Heart.* The affinity was corroborated by scholars from the Gorky Institute, in Moscow, who attended a Soviet-American Symposium on Eudora Welty, in Jackson, Mississippi, in June, 1991. Both Welty and Chekhov, the Russian scholars agree, combine a gentle comedy with serious philosophical truth; and both emphasize the common people and a love for the land.[23]

The apparently simplistic surface of these stories belies their complex use of shaped fictional space. Her best work spatializes the narrative line such that it achieves the effect that one spatial critic has called, in another context, "a whole whose unity lies not in temporal relationships but in a closed system of spatial relationships. Dread of space has been replaced by dread of time." Dread, the quintessential emotion of Gothic fiction, exists in a new guise in Welty's fiction, where attenuation of time leads to a more complex experience of space.[24]

Welty's eclectic appreciation of many art forms is perhaps responsible for what may seem strange bedfellows in her fiction. In their oblique reflection of gothic conventions, for example, the "singularity" of Welty's characters and the "clear stage" (*C,* 54), stylized setting of many stories contribute to the correspondence of her fiction with the tradition of folk arts, which exhibits a personal instead of historically received style and which conceives of a work of art as a made thing as much as a culture expressed or a tale told. Her work also resembles the fine art of post-impressionist painters, who, unlike their Impressionist predecessors, abstracted reality, desiring to create form rather than imitate nature. The post-impressionists expressed an inner vision by manipulating color, line, and composition of space—the formal components of painting. This late-nineteenth-century interest in the expressive rather than the imitative is represented in American art by visionary painters of "inner states," such as Benjamin West, Georgia O'Keeffe, and Andrew Wyeth; and the movement coincided with the symbolist poets' emphasis on inner vision. Similarly, the inner world created by American visionary painters resembles

23. The round-table discussion at the symposium has been transcribed and reproduced, along with four essays by Russian scholars who attended, in a special issue of *Southern Quarterly* devoted to Eudora Welty. See especially "Eudora Welty and Southern Literature in World Perspective," *Southern Quarterly,* XXXII (1993), 31–39.

24. Daghistany and Johnson, "Romantic Irony, Spatial Form," in *Spatial Form in Narrative,* ed. Smitten and Daghistany, 50.

the earlier *literary* visionary tradition of Poe and Hawthorne, which Welty follows in her own way by creating stories that approach the status of abstract visual artifacts. Indeed, the great mystery of Welty's art may reside in the paradox of her wide and sympathetic knowledge of human history and culture and her equal capacity to "forget knowing" in order to make each work a new beginning—a new creation, like Elstir's roses, which were, as Proust's Mme Verdurin remarks, "a new variety with which this painter, like a skillful gardener, has enriched the family of the Roses." [25]

Not only is each story an artifact, but the entire Welty canon is decorated with folk arts, from the "hemstitched pillowcases" in "Lily Daw and the Three Ladies" to the breadboard in *The Optimist's Daughter* in which Laurel sees the "whole solid past" (*OD,* 206). A specific comparison of Welty's fiction to folk art—and one that validates my emphasis on American rather than European art—is Vande Kieft's comment that *Losing Battles* is "more like a big brown country bucket than a Grecian urn, suited to visual display as a 'period piece' of American Literature." In the 1962 version of *Eudora Welty,* Vande Kieft compares Welty's crowded scenes to Breughel canvases and to the pictorial writing style of Elizabeth Bowen, who, like Welty, "began with a youthful intention to be a painter." In her revision of this text (1987), Vande Kieft suggests the comparison of Welty's fiction to folk art and specifically to American, rather than European, art. Welty's interest in American primitivists is suggested by her composition of a humorous lyric about Grandma Moses as part of a song entitled "Fifty-seventh Street Rag-Ballet." The song, which satirizes arty trends, was included in *What Year Is This?,* which Welty wrote in collaboration with Hildegard Dolson during a summer in New York, but the musical was never staged in full. Welty knew the work of contemporary Mississippi primitivists Ethel Mohammed and Theora Hamblett, who, along with Welty and Pecolia Warner, were interviewed by Bill Ferris on videotape. [26]

Like folk artists and crafters, Welty has the ability to practice what has been called, in Henry James, the "sacrifice of relation" to the outer world the better to reflect its vital inner forces; and although her practice more

25. For a discussion of these painters, see Abraham A. Davidson, *The Story of American Painting* (New York, 1974), 79–81; 99–100. Marcel Proust, *Remembrance of Things Past,* trans. C. K. Scott Moncrief (New York, 1934), II, 244.

26. Vande Kieft, *Eudora Welty* (1962), 71, 182; *ibid.* (1987), 164; Bill Ferris (dir.), *Four Women Artists* (Memphis, 1977). See also Elizabeth Evans, *Eudora Welty* (New York, 1981), 14–15; Jane Reid-Petty, "The Town and the Writer: An Interview with Eudora Welty," *Jackson Magazine,* I (September, 1977), 34.

often follows Hawthorne's, in stylized stories like "Lily Daw" she seems to "cut the cable" between imagination and any realistic sense of place. There is little more setting in "Lily Daw" than in a play of Samuel Beckett's; yet it is also marked by traits of mimetic realism. Folklorist Bill Ferris sees one of these traits as common to "both folk and literary artists": an extraordinary eye for the telling detail, to be able to recognize, for example, if a "dog's been a long way off and is headed home by the way it walks" (*C,* 181).

Welty has often commented on her visual imagination, which is certainly related to her early study of painting and to her habit of taking pictures on her job as a WPA roving reporter. Her likeness to American primitive painters includes their common unwillingness to be simply illusionists. In spite of her unerring ability to reproduce the colloquial southern idiom and manner, Welty uses that ability simply as part of her materials "at hand," as the colonial artisan would use local pigments to make paint for a three-foot-high chicken to serve as a pilot-house figure, never mind that no known chicken was such a shade of gold or such a size. In spite of the strong presence of nature and human life in such work, then, there is no attempt to create the illusion of fully detailed, representational reality.

Early American folk artists, as well as the nineteenth- and twentieth-century artists who followed their lead, evinced a paradoxical mixture of self-conscious deliberateness and unselfconscious aesthetic awareness about their craft. Folk artifacts were made, not to be enshrined as *objets d'art,* but to be practical and decorative. The sculpted weather vanes, duck decoys, and tobacconist's Indians are examples, as is the quilt that is both warm and colorful and perhaps itself "tells" the story of a region or a family. Folk artists—including the painters of intricate and beautiful Pennsylvania Dutch hex symbols, which contain no trace of narrative significance—resemble the storyteller of the oral tradition and its modern practitioners such as Eudora Welty. It is in no way reductive to suggest that her work, like theirs, fits Constance Rourke's definition of "applied art." [27] Welty's stories naturally differ from static visual art in their temporal component and from all "applied art" in that they do not illustrate a "recipe" that can be reproduced. Yet they can be seen as applied art in the sense that they not only entertain but also *serve* as skilled transmitters of a unique part of America's cultural heritage. Her stories

27. Suzette Lane and Paul d'Ambrosio, *A Shifting Wind: Views of American Folk Art* (Cooperstown, N.Y., 1986), n.p.; Constance Rourke, *The Roots of American Culture and Other Essays,* ed. Van Wyck Brooks (1942; rpr. Westport, Conn., 1980), 12.

not only are items of "piece work" but are also veritable encyclopedias of cultural history. Paradoxically, they are also adaptations of the modernist idea of art for art's sake. Although Welty, like Faulkner, says she simply wants to tell a good story the best way she can, her stories are finely crafted verbal artifacts; she has consciously made the storytelling art a part of her own sophisticated vision, as critical works such as Carol Manning's *With Ears Opening Like Morning Glories* have shown.

A recognition of aesthetic similarities between Welty's fiction and the visual arts is not an attempt to draw lines of direct influence but rather to say that hers is a poetics as much of space and motion, of shape and color, as of language. Nevertheless, the bold lines of folk art, a medium that perennially has energized fine art, are reflected in the stylized characters of Welty's fiction. Her grotesques make primarily visual, not psychological or social, statements. Thus the tonglike legs of Clytie drowning in the rain barrel, the pyramid that distributes the characters around Little Leroy in "Keela, the Outcast Indian Maiden," and the cone of light Virgie Rainey perceives connecting her to the moon in "The Wanderers" are as abstractly geometric designs as those in the fiction of other line- and color-conscious writers. The spatial images that Welty herself has admired come to mind: the "funnel-shaped tracks in the heavy sand" that point toward and away from the climactic action in the last scene of Stephen Crane's "The Bride Comes to Yellow Sky" (quoted in *ES,* 87), and the fusion of Coronado's ancient sword with the contemporary plow against the prairie sun in Willa Cather's *My Antonia* (*ES,* 43). Such decorative shapes, which upstage the linear narrative and yet perfectly signify—let us "see"—the artist's intent, as Cather's image dramatically and economically juxtaposes two historical eras, are typical of Welty's visual imagination; and in her fiction such shapes combine with equally decorative characters, moving and speaking in a significant economy of stylized patterns.

In some of Welty's stories, two-dimensional figures embody a concept of abstract art that is as integral a part of her total vision as are the masses of light and shade in the art of Whistler, whose painting of his mother is, significantly, entitled *Arrangement in Grey and Black No. 1: The Artist's Mother* (1871). The best of Welty's "flat" characters achieve the same complex effect as that of the flat surface of Grant Wood's double portrait *American Gothic,* which suggests by its title and confirms by its intricate design and by the haunting gazes of its ostensibly simple, wholesome subjects, the underlying negativity of American rural life, perhaps the dark underside of the American dream. And it is at least as much Wood's complexity of feeling and sophistication of technique as it is Thomas Hart Benton's "simple" celebrations of homespun ruggedness in paintings whose surfaces often belie the sophisticated techniques of their creators, and thus whose work Welty's resembles.[28] For although Welty herself prefers criticism that simply celebrates art rather than analyzes it, and although much critical comment has justifiably emphasized *Welty's* celebration of human life and human mystery, there is much in the fiction itself that is not celebratory. Constantly countering the felicitous triumph of her artistic creation is the grotesque reality of human finitude that provides vital tension to her work. Danger lurks behind the "curtain of green" in Welty as does potential violence behind the Grant Wood pitchfork.

The art with which Welty's painterly methods have most in common is perhaps Andrew Wyeth, whose work is informed by the nonobjective artists and whose "Magic Realist" style, which has elements of an almost photographic realism, is nevertheless imbued, usually by unique perspective, with an element of fantasy or of the bizarre or grotesque. And certainly Welty's version of the grotesque in the early stories bears at least as much relation to spatially realized inner states, such as those depicted in the compositions of Wyeth, as to the psychologically deformed characters of Flannery O'Connor and Carson McCullers.

Welty creates stories that seem virtual collages of the visual arts and the gestures of the drama and of dance. To establish her important theme of cultural confinement of women, she employs structures like those that contribute to what Joseph Frank identified as spatial form in literature, in which the primary temporal component of fiction is supplemented, and often subverted, by what has been called a "spatial secondary illusion." [29]

Through the guidance of Welty's visual imagination, we "see" the limited and distorted perspectives and prospects of her characters in a manner analogous to that by which we view those in Wyeth's paintings. His best-known work is no doubt *Christina's World* (1948), in which a crippled girl in a faded pink dress drags herself up a hill of waving yellow grass toward a small paintless frame cabin set starkly alone. The model for this painting, and for some of Wyeth's other most acclaimed works, was Christina Olson, whom the painter knew in Cushing, Maine. Although severely restricted by a childhood attack of polio, Christina is described as having "a force of character that would make any condescension to her paralysis an insult." Wyeth has said that his inspiration for the painting was the sight of Christina, crawling across a field, a com-

---

28. Thomas Hart Benton, *An American in Art: A Professional and Technical Autobiography* (Kansas City, Kans., 1969), 137; Benton, *Thomas Hart Benton: A Personal Commemorative* (Joplin, 1973), 25–26.

29. Joseph A. Kestner, *The Spatiality of the Novel* (Detroit, 1978), 13–32.

ment similar to Eudora Welty's description of the inception of "A Worn Path."[30] Of the inspiration for Phoenix Jackson in that story, Welty says that she witnessed a "small, distant figure come out of the woods and move across the whole breadth of my vision and disappear into the woods" (*C,* 186).

One of Welty's most stylized stories, "Lily Daw and the Three Ladies," utilizes painterly techniques similar to those in *Christina's World.* Through the disposition of the three figures around Lily, we are drawn into the scene, to Lily, as by the line of perspective in a painting. And the description of Lily as small, as compared with the larger figures that loom threateningly over her, contributes to our heightened sense throughout the story of her oblique perspective below the level of and from the midst of the circling ladies. By the central functioning of angle of perception in this story, Welty suggests not only Lily's limited field of view but that as well of the ladies who focus all of their attention upon her. The spatial form of the story is seen here not only in the circling patterns but in the use of the technique of romantic irony, described by Ann Daghistany and J. J. Johnson as a "humorous reduction of finitude . . . which enforces . . . aesthetic distance." The result is the enhancement not only of pattern perception but of humor. The humorous effect of romantic irony was illustrated by Coleridge in a lecture on Rabelais, Swift, and Sterne that was reported in the *Tatler* of May 24, 1831. The journalist quotes Coleridge's description of humor as it is "displayed in the comparison of finite things with those which our imagination cannot bound; such as make our great appear little and our little great; or rather, which reduces to a common littleness both the great and the little, when compared to infinity." But more than that, romantic irony is a practice that deflates the idea of systems in general. In a recent study of Schlegel, Marike Finlay asserts that even nature is rendered by romantic irony as "*apriori* chaotic and a-systematic," and thus revolutionary. Welty's use of it in "Lily Daw and the Three Ladies" is consonant with her general valorization of the chaotic over the rigidly systematic. In "Lily Daw," the humorous deflation of both the great (ladies) and the small (Lily), which a properly distanced reader apprehends, implies the characters' equality in human finitude before the infinite universe, which itself is symbolized by the chaotic railroad station crowd that dwarfs them all at the end of the story.[31]

30. Brian O'Doherty, "A Visit to Wyeth Country," in *The Art of Andrew Wyeth,* ed. Wanda M. Corn (Boston, 1973), 32–34, 39.

31. Daghistany and Johnson, "Romantic Irony, Spatial Form," in *Spatial Form and Narrative,* ed. Smitten and Daghistany, 52–53; Samuel Taylor Coleridge, *Miscellaneous Criti-*

Welty's intertexual presentation in "Lily Daw" consists of choric movements and poetic repetition, and it results in a collage of shifting limits, like a cubist superimposition of planes, and which achieves the effect of symphonic variations on the theme of limitation. The narrative surface of the story is that of idiosyncratic regional speech, carefully selected and arranged by an omniscient authorial controller who is more precisely a choreographer of speaking statues. Yet these flat characters, by the subtle shadings of their idiolects alone, convincingly masquerade as traditional characters in mimetic fiction.

The three ladies speak and move in the manner of a chorus. There is minimal physical or psychological description of character, for these figures are more abstract items in arrangements than personalities. It is as if Welty had first imagined these characters as shadow and motion on a bare stage, in silhouette, behind a gauze curtain, as was the case in the opening scene from *Sister and Miss Lexie,* a collage of Welty's fiction originally produced in 1981. When a new adaptation by David Kaplan and Brenda Currin was performed by Currin at the Second Stage Theatre, off-Broadway, in the summer of 1985, the performance I viewed opened with "Sister," seen through a transparent curtain, at her ironing board in the "P.O."

Certainly Welty's many references to the influence of Chekhov seem justified not only by her interest in unique characters but also by her dramatically objective presentation of her characters' actions (*C,* 20, 83, 216, 252, 312). Perhaps it was Welty's fascination with the New York theater while she was a graduate student at Columbia University that led her to use the methods of almost classical dramatic movement, but her use of it in "Lily Daw and the Three Ladies" is ironic; for in this story she deflates her own stylistic suggestion of enlightened culture by the story's insistent comparison of people with poultry. Thus the "Greek chorus" of ladies amounts to parody, since they resemble nothing so much as chickens pecking as purposefully at Lily as at a juicy tidbit on the ground at their feet.[32]

The "chorus" meets at the center of communal life, the post office, where the news has arrived that Lily has been accepted at the Ellisville

---

cism, ed. Thomas Middleton Raysor (Cambridge, Mass., 1936), 113; Marike Finlay, *The Romantic Irony of Semiotics: Frederich Schlegel and the Crisis of Representation* (Berlin, 1988), 263.

32. Manning, *With Ears Opening Like Morning Glories,* 59, comments that the ladies are only amusing themselves; Vande Kieft, *Eudora Welty* (1962), 58, notes the "Greek chorus" of ladies in "Asphodel," who tell their story, "now one speaking, now another, and then all together." The pattern is analogous to that which I have identified in "Lily Daw."

Institute for the Feeble-Minded of Mississippi: "What will Lily say," beamed Mrs. Carson. . . . "She'll be tickled to death," said Mrs. Watts. . . . "Don't you all dare go off and tell Lily without me!" called Aimee Slocum (*CS*, 3).

The ladies confront Lily Daw in her home, a structure reminiscent of the house in *Christina's World* and one that reflects the incongruity and illogic of the characters' actions and speeches: "[Lily Daw's] paintless frame house with all the weather vanes was three stories high in places and had yellow and violet stained-glass windows in front and gingerbread around the porch. It leaned steeply to one side, toward the railroad, and the front steps were gone" (*CS*, 5). Inside, Lily sits in her petticoat on the floor by an old trunk lined with a paper whose circular patterns repeat the circular motions of the three ladies and also provide a graphic symbol of limitation. The three, alternately or in unison, stand and sit, converging upon Lily. First, from their rocking chairs, they question her about her recent decision to marry a traveling musician whom she describes only as "a man last night" (*CS*, 7). The trio then begins an incantation aimed at protecting Lily's virtue by committing her to the asylum: "'Why don't you go to Ellisville!' [said Mrs. Carson]. 'Won't that be lovely?' said Mrs. Watts. . . . 'It's a lovely place,' said Aimee Slocum" (*CS*, 6).

When this does not convince Lily, they add choral movements to their performance; and the narrative commentary at this point resembles stage directions. First they move in unison: "All the ladies *leaned down* toward her in impressive astonishment"; and they gasp in unison. Then they move in sequence: "Mrs. Watts *stood up* and balanced herself. . . . 'What?' demanded Aimee Slocum, *rising up* and tottering before her scream. 'What?' . . . 'Don't ask her what,' said Mrs. Carson, *coming up* behind" (*CS*, 6–7, emphasis added). The three-beat kinetic rhythm is reinforced by the triple repetition of *what*, as Welty manipulates the colloquial speech patterns in a manner that impresses the reader as it is meant to impress Lily. It confirms Welty's adjective *impressive*, used instead of the expected "*impressed* astonishment": their look of surprise is for Lily's benefit; for the ladies' exhortations, as well as their gyrations around Lily, constitute a performance intended to exert control over the weak-minded girl:

> "I'll give you a pair of hemstitched pillowcases," said Mrs. Carson.
> "I'll give you a big caramel cake," said Mrs. Watts.
> "I'll give you a souvenir from Jackson—a little toy bank," said Aimee Slocum. "Now will you go?"
> "No," said Lily. (*CS*, 8)

The up-down movement continues, first in unison: "They sat sunken in despair." Then, as Lily weakens: "Silently they rose once more to their feet" (*CS*, 8). And as she finally agrees, they nod, smile, and back away together. The rhythmic aural and visual elements create what Edwin Muir calls a "widening present," due to the time delay that results from the text's calling attention to its own spatial patterning. Thus, in spite of the "cliffhanger" plot with its last-minute "escape," in this story space is more important than time, the narrative's traditional medium.[33]

The circle is one of Welty's favorite images of the power to contain, to include or exclude; and it functions in "Lily Daw" as part of a larger symbolic network of images of mental and physical limitation, of the mindless human wilderness of small-town society that opposes the ironi-cally contrasting clarity of Lily's *tabula rasa* conscience at the center of the story's design. A spatially designed story built around an unchanging core, which may be a nondeveloping (Forster's "flat") character, such as Lily Daw, is described by David Mickelsen through the metaphor of an orange, consisting of numerous segments, all tending toward the core. Jeffrey Smitten sees it in terms of Joseph Frank's theory of closed spatial form, a system of interlocking reflexive references, "all bearing on a single theme or core," as opposed to Roland Barthes' concept of "open spatial form [in which] relations extend infinitely outward from a point." In the plot structure of "Lily Daw," Welty combines these systems to produce a pattern that first converges on a still center, then reverses to open out in what emerges as a centripetal-centrifugal design.[34]

Counterpointing the syncopated movements of the three ladies as they converge on the slow-witted girl, and reversing the centripetal to centrifugal motion, is the frenzied comic activity that erupts at the train station as Lily Daw is put on board for Ellisville. The town has turned out and the band arrives, without orders and with false signals to play. A crate of baby chicks breaks open, Aimee screams, bells ring, the brass horn sounds, and the train steams. The commotion is like the crowded murals of Thomas Hart Benton or the bright splashes of color in the stitchery art of Mississippi primitivist Ethel Mohammed, which Welty knows well. Welty's story is a collage not only of motion but of colors throughout: from the pink hands of Mrs. Watts to the orange Ne-Hi that Estelle drinks; and it shifts from the muted earth tones of the earlier choric scene, in

---

33. Edwin Muir, *The Structure of the Novel* (London, 1928), 24; Émil Borel, *Space and Time* (1926; rpr. New York, 1960), 163–64; Kestner, *The Spatiality of the Novel*, 17.

34. David Mickelsen, "Types of Spatial Structure in Narrative," in *Spatial Form in Nar-rative*, ed. Smitten and Daghistany, 72; Jeffrey R. Smitten, Introduction to *ibid.*, 23–24.

which the ladies look "mutely" at each other, with brown, green, and Lily's "milky-yellow hair" (*CS*, 6), to the brash reds, blacks, and whites in the explosive depot scene. Lily's stranger himself, the catalyst for the comic madness, has red hair, a red coat, and a red notebook. With this live prospect at hand, the ladies quickly pull Lily off the train, and now they circle around a new target: the xylophone player. "Here's your little Lily," [said Mrs. Watts]. . . . "My husband happens to be the Baptist preacher . . . ," said Mrs. Carson. . . . "Oh, I feel just like crying . . . ," said Aimee Slocum (*CS*, 11).

Earlier, when the ladies first attempt to arrange Lily's future, Lily gazes directly at Aimee and remarks, "You've got bumps on your face" (*CS*, 6). Welty gets dual service from the line: for the reader, noting the over-achieving ladies' attempts to remove Lily from temptation, it has the ironic force of the biblical injunction to remove the mote from one's own eye; but it is also evidence that Lily is literal minded. Like the "daw" that her name suggests, she lives entirely in the present. She gives so freely of herself without thought of consequences that the three ladies see fit to confine her for her own good, as Ibsen's Henrik tried to contain his "little bird" in *A Doll's House.* And lest we mistake Welty's views on that kind of paternalism, we need only remember her dislike of "stultifying" security, which she once illustrated by quoting the witch's line from *Macbeth:* "security / Is mortals' chiefest enemy" (3.5.31–32, quoted in *ES*, 130), an axiom she has dramatized in story after story. In the process of providing such confining security for Lily Daw, the ladies themselves are shown as limited and confined in many ways. Their obsession with restraint and "big sister" watchfulness perhaps betrays an ulterior wish to see that others are likewise restrained, as Jinny Love Stark in "The Wanderers" wants to "drive everybody . . . into the state of marriage along with her" (*CS*, 445). The ladies often leave sentences unfinished, censoring their own verbalization about what they fear is Lily's scandalous predicament: "'Last night at the tent show—' said another, and then popped her hand over her mouth" (*CS*, 3).

Mrs. Carson carries a tape measure on her bosom. Mrs. Watts knows "how to pin people down and make them deny what they'd already said" (*CS*, 6). Aimee Slocum makes her living stamping and bundling mail; and she even observes the ten-word limit in her telegram to Ellisville. Mrs. Watts, who is ready to accompany Lily as far as Jackson, is confined in a tight corset from which she plans to free herself as soon as the train pulls out, all the while attempting to restrict even Lily's view from the train: "'Look,' Lily said, laughing softly through her fingers," to which Mrs. Carson replies, "Don't look at anything till you get to Ellisville" (*CS*,

10). Lily's stranger is limited, too, and confesses that he doesn't hear well. And in the crowd of symbolically limited folk in the final depot scene are those described as small, as one-eyed, and finally as cheering without knowing why.

More serious implications of limitation result from the grotesque comparisons of humans with animals and inanimate objects. Aimee wonders which is more terrible, "the man [or] the hissing train"; and the narrator implies a connection as the "bell began to ring hollowly, and the man was talking." The ladies cluck their tongues and make noises "sad as the soft noises in the hen house at twilight"; people and chicks run wild on the station platform; and Lily, named for a jackdaw and sucking on a zinnia between her teeth, makes a sound "exactly like a jay bird." (Her name is ironic, for the symbolic purity of "Lily" is at once deflated by the dual meanings of "daw": a black, crowlike bird as well as a simpleton.) Pictures of redbirds on a school tablet adorn wires *inside* the store, while Estelle perches *outside* on a rail fence. The story reads like the script for an absurdist comedy in which the silent and controlled pantomime of modern dance alternates with the apparent randomness of a theatrical "happening." And, of course, Lily's beau is a stylized "performer" who has already taught Lily part of his stock repartee: "Hello, Toots. What's up—tricks?" (*CS,* 5–11).

"Lily Daw" is a modern slice-of-life story, a subgenre that is the perfect medium for spatial form.[35] Yet it exhibits the rhetorical patterning of a folk or fairy tale, in which things often happen in threes. To this modernist form and this ancient fairy-tale pattern, Welty adds the mnemonic qualities of the oral folk tradition as well as the rhythms and shapes of the drama and of the plastic and painterly folk and fine arts. The story depicts the individual's lyric impulse toward freedom in Lily's carefree bestowal of favor and unconventional behavior. And it portrays the culture's myth of concern: its conditioned tendency to limit such freedom because of its threat to "safe" conventions and its attempt to hide, behind institutional walls, the other than "normal"—that which cannot be neatly "stamped and bundled," like the mail put up by Aimee Slocum. Not least, it reveals the ironic situation of women, who, blessed and limited by fertility, must therefore, polite society dictates, be controlled when they are "mature for their age." In this story, Welty manipulates the traditional American wilderness image by portraying its miniature in a well-meaning

---

35. Robert Scholes and Robert Kellogg, *The Nature of Narrative* (New York, 1969), 13; Mickelsen, "Types of Spatial Structure in Narrative," in *Spatial Form in Narrative,* ed. Smitten and Daghistany, 76.

but self-castrating community tangle of women who close in around a little innocent "wild" life to see her safely entrusted to one institution or another—to the asylum or to marriage. Thus, the controlling metaphor of "Lily Daw" anticipates the development of the motif of family and cultural wilderness in *Delta Wedding, The Golden Apples,* and stories from *The Bride of the Innisfallen* such as "Going to Naples."

The "flat," unrealistic characters in "Lily Daw" are somehow hauntingly real, as King MacLain is "flat . . . , undeveloping, mythical, existing outside the complex moral world" and yet is "absurdly human," as Vande Kieft notes; yet their very abstraction suggests them as metaphors for the flat, unreal lives that are often forced by men on women in the South of Welty's fiction. But in "Lily Daw," as in other Welty stories, a young woman's role as ward of society is enforced by other women, who have become so rigid in their own assigned roles that they do not realize they are performing too. In their own way, like Fay in *The Optimist's Daughter,* they are "making a scene." But their about-face decision to get Lily married after all is evidence that the ladies are like the "hypocrite women" in Denise Levertov's poem of that name, who "with . . . psychopomp / . . . play and plead—and say / nothing of this later," and thus, according to Rachel Blau DuPlessis, perpetuate the romance script of culture, "hid[ing] the intensity of the conflict from themselves . . . , rejecting their capacity for growth, and denying their inmost selves." Such women's self-censorship hides the fact that they, like women throughout both actual and literary history, "assume the mask their culture has long made available . . . [,] repress[ing] whatever they feel—even their own self-doubt—to preserve a generous, unruffled surface."[36] Thus the ladies identify with Lily more than they would admit, as they deny her, as well as their own, potential for growth.

The triumph of the American spirit of the individual is seen here less in Welty's characters than in the boldly conceived, modernist style of the author. In the characters of the ladies the bold spirit is perverted by a will to power that is manipulative, and it is never developed in Lily Daw. While such human concerns are important in the story, the piece itself is less a social treatise than an abstract design that evokes a sense of grotesque human limitation. Its treatment in spatial, more than temporal, terms underscores its metaphoric confining lines and spaces. Even the language, reflecting as it does the society's limited concept of maturity, itself functions as a metaphor for limitation. For, as Welty has said, "We

36. Vande Kieft, *Eudora Welty* (1962), 114–16; Denise Levertov, *O Taste and See* (New York, 1964), 70; DuPlessis, *Writing Beyond the Ending,* 124.

start from scratch, and words don't" (*ES,* 134), her own critical vocabulary suggesting a linguistic dimension of the concept of limitation. Language is not only loaded with accumulated meanings, but it is also a grotesquely limited and delimiting automatism that Welty extends by the illusion of spatiality. "Lily Daw and the Three Ladies" is Welty's earliest portrait of the virtual confinement of women in society by this inscription in its linguistic and cultural codes. Lily herself symbolizes the victim of such limitation as well as the hope of escape; and the circling, threatening, talking ladies reveal woman's own complicity in what Michel Foucault has called a "carceral society." For such a society not only supervises criminal incarceration, it also incorporates a series of enclosing devices, a network of forces, including "walls, space, institutions, rules, discourse," all intended to normalize human beings in accord with the prevailing cultural mythos.[37] The few props in the setting for "Lily Daw" contribute to the sense of a "bare stage" on which Lily is cruelly exposed to the "carceral" elements in her world that threaten her freedom as surely as those in any gothic space; but it is a setting that, together with the oblique perspective, invests her slight figure, however deflated, with dramatic monumentality.

"Lily Daw" anticipates some major patterns that Welty has developed throughout her career, at all stages of which her fiction shows, under the apparently simple surface of the colloquial style, the complexity of the American experience, but also of the universal female experience. By employing the abstract qualities of American folk and fine art, Welty has energized her story with something that haunts the reader as from the distance of legend, with all the "primitive severity of myth" that has been said to characterize some of Katherine Anne Porter's stories.[38]

At the end of the story, Lily understandably hangs her head, for her hope chest is gone on the train to Ellisville, while she herself is as trapped as the hat thrown into the telephone wires overhead. Denied the freedom to marry as a result of her natural instinct, Lily now merely submits unhappily to the same match at the ladies' direction. She is not able to articulate what is clear to the reader: the ironic double reversal from her naïve hope of free choice, to her "escape" to Ellisville, to her enclosure in the redefined "asylum" of marriage. But Lily's pout is not to be our final impression. Rather, Welty leaves us with the more complex and ambiguous image that results from a distanced perspective: one as

37. Foucault, *Discipline and Punish,* 307–308.
38. M. E. Bradford, "The Passion of Craft," in *The History of Southern Literature,* ed. Rubin *et al.,* 376.

graphic and functional as that of the fused sword and plow that she admires in Cather's *My Antonia.* In the final scene, those telephone lines, like the lines of perspective in a painting, now draw our attention past the diminished figure of Lily to the focal point that represents her: the hat itself, an object caught. Yet lest we misread the scene as pure pessimism, we do well to remember Welty's insistence upon both the mystery and the duality of life. After all, wasn't the hat thrown up randomly, in celebration?

Spatial patterning to suggest society's encircling bonds and the individual's countermotions is also central to *The Bride of the Innisfallen and Other Stories* (1955), especially in Welty's creation of the aesthetic shapes of implosion and explosion. In "The Burning," for example, Miss Theo and Miss Myra stand frozen in genteel disbelief before the Union soldiers who converge on them to rape them and destroy their home. The ritual nature of the burning is emphasized by "the screams that soon took over the outdoors and circled that house they were going to finish for sure now" (*CS,* 485). The still center of this turbulence is even more profound after the burning; for the center, scarcely holding, is made up of the stunned trio: the two ladies and their black servant, Delilah. They walk aimlessly through the devastated area, "holding hands all three, like the *timeless time* it snowed, and white and black went to play together in hushed woods" (*CS,* 487, emphasis added). Here Welty has banished time from the text, employing an explicitly and exclusively spatial image to denote the utter unreality of such a scene in the South. The reversal of the centripetal force of convergence to that of centrifugal dispersion is seen in the departure of the soldiers, in the kitten who "ran ahead to the woods, where she was never seen again" (*CS,* 485), and in the chickens, who "had gone to roost in a strange uneasy tree against the cloud where the guns still boomed" (*CS,* 492). It is also seen in Delilah's scattering of ashes to collect the bones of the baby Phinny, killed in the fire, and in the minds—first closed, then scattered—of Theo and Myra. After helping the spinsters hang themselves under a tree (a bow to the conventional death for dishonored sentimental heroines), Delilah herself undergoes a miniature convergence-dispersion experience when she loses herself in dazed contemplation in the mirror she finds in the ruins of the burned house. In another Weltian timeless moment, a spatial perception of temporal simultaneity framed in the mirror, she sees images that are "quivering, leaping to life, fighting, aping old things Delilah had seen done in this world already, sometimes what men had done to Miss Theo and Miss Myra and the peacocks and to slaves, and sometimes what a slave had done and what anybody now could do to anybody. Under the flicker of the sun's licks, then under its whole blow and blare, like an unheard scream, like an act of mercy gone, as the wall-less light and July blaze struck through from the opened sky, the mirror felled her flat" (*CS*, 493). Following this inward focusing through the mirror of memory, which opens toward the past and which includes gothic images of cruel, "wall-less" exposure and of silent screaming analogous to those in "Music from Spain," is the outward motion of a new mental chaos when she looks up from it to perceive, even in the mundane buzzing insects and changing leaves of an autumn day, the equally appalling images of a barely credible Civil War present:

> She put her arms over her head and waited, for they would all be coming again, gathering under her and above her, bees saddled like horses out of the air, butterflies harnessed to one another, bats with masks on, birds together, all with their weapons bared. She listened for the blows, and *dreaded* that whole army of wings—of flies, birds, serpents, their glowing enemy faces and bright kings' dresses, that banner of colors forked out, all this world that was flying, striking, stricken, falling, gilded or blackened, mortally splitting and falling apart, proud turbans unwinding, turning like the spotted dying leaves of fall, spiraling down to bottomless ash; she *dreaded* the fury of all the butterflies and dragonflies in the world riding, blades unconcealed and at point—descending, and rising again." (*CS*, 493, emphasis added)

Here Welty combines a basic element of classic Gothic fiction—the female dread of powerful and grotesque male forces—with the modernistic attenuation of time to depict the very realistic horror and confusion that epitomized the Civil War. The circles and spirals not only serve as metaphors for Delilah's confusion; they also function metonymically as links in the chain of significance, a chain that allows us to perceive the young slave's move out into wider and more frightening circles of freedom as a result of the terrors that have set her mind spinning in a new way, out from the still center of shocked disbelief. Thus the relatively straightforward spatial patterning that Welty employed in "Lily Daw and the Three Ladies" has developed, in *The Bride of the Innisfallen,* into a sophisticated postmodernist psychodynamics of alienation, conveyed by a surprisingly congruent melange of images from the Gothic and from physical geometry.

In the conclusion of "The Burning," Delilah, fleeing the ruin alone, wades into the Big Black River, "submerged to the waist, to the breast, stretching her throat like a sunflower stalk above the river's opaque skin" (*CS*, 494). The scene recalls a similar one toward the end of Welty's "The Wanderers," in which Virgie Rainey, after her mother's funeral, remembers wading naked, breast deep, into the same river. In that story too, images combine: a geometric shape with the suggestion of a silenced cry that could as well come from a Gothic heroine, here collapsed into the single image of "a long silent horn"; and the combination makes visible to readers the mysterious sensation Virgie feels as the focal point between two realities: two times, which are represented by two points in space and the geometric figure that connects them. She imagines that "from the eyes to the moon would be a cone, a long silent horn, of white light. It was a connection visible as the hair is in air, between the self and the moon, to make the self feel the child, a daughter far, far back" (*CS*, 454). The fact that Delilah can be appropriately compared with Virgie, because of their visions and their analogous positions in the narrative shapes of their stories, is evidence that Delilah is the true protagonist of "The Burning." Miss Theo and Miss Myra are only parodies of what has been called "the refined, sheltered, helpless Southern lady" of the plantation literature of the Old South. Delilah, whose limitations are real, but whose possibilities will also be real with the abolition of slavery, is the character who keeps this story from being a standard reproduction of either the romantic literature of nostalgia for the Old South or that of the Southern Gothic, with its grotesque characters and situations and its depiction of the "kind of musty Gothic interior" that characterizes Faulkner's "A Rose for Emily."[39]

The lone individual in Welty's stories is often depicted as a finite point in space between dual expansions outward from, as well as deep into, the self. This image is realized in "The Wanderers" by the cone of light, an alternate manifestation of the spiral shape, that links Virgie to the moon, on the one hand, and to her child-self, on the other. Here Welty uses the image of life's vital continuities in a way that seems a virtual illustration of what Michel Butor calls a "cone of memory," in his discussion of novelistic techniques and of the spatial metaphor Henri Bergson used to "make us aware of certain continuous aspects of our experience."[40] In "The Burning," this continuity is presented by the corresponding extensions Delilah sees, first into the mirror—backward into memory, then, in her imagination, into some far-flung, chaotic future. In both stories the symbolic shape of the light cone projects infinitely outward but implies its inverse in the receding "shape" of memory, in a realistic appropriation of the physics of shapes in motion, which in turn replicate the cognitive patterns Peter Brooks has identified as a "double

39. Appel, *A Season of Dreams*, 83; 131.
40. Michel Butor, *Inventory*, trans. Richard Howard (New York, 1968), 22.

operation on time." For it is Virgie's and Delilah's recognition of a same-but-different dynamic of memories and possibilities that gives these passages their literary power.

Circular images and alternating centripetal and centrifugal motions also dominate the little-known story "Going to Naples," in which they assume an even more complex role in the narrative design. Welty's familiar circular images, which often grow into convergence-dispersion motifs, as in "Lily Daw," and to double spiral patterns, as in Delilah's mirror in "The Burning," in "Going to Naples" achieve the additional resonances possible to the longer story. Here Welty realizes the advantage Poe claimed for "the dropping of the water on the rock"; for the mere duration enables the preliminary images of Gabriella's physical and social confinement, and small ruptures of her confines, to anticipate similar images of her subsequent psychological enclosure, its reversal, and the buildup of momentum for her escape. The story takes place on board the *Pomona*, bound from New York to Palermo and Naples. Gabriella Serto is the raucous but lonely eighteen-year-old whose position in the center of a group of chaperoning mothers and other passengers is in many ways like that of Lily Daw among the ladies. Gabriella's complaints that she "was happy in Buffalo" and sees no reason for the trip is answered only by Mama Serto's "Enough for you it is *l'Anno Santo*" (*CS,* 567). The several Italian mothers' unabashed matchmaking between the six young women and six young men on the ship, especially that of Mrs. Serto on behalf of her daughter and Aldo Scampo, is described in terms analogous to the subtly ominous circling of the ladies around Lily Daw. Spatiality is first suggested by the sculptural rotundity depicted in the narrator's introduction of the "largest mother [of the] largest daughter" on board. In the same paragraph, spatial form is closely tied to the theme of enclosure and escape, and, in turn, the theme focused on Gabriella, by the (otherwise apparently random) detail that "a hole broke through her stocking and her flesh came through like a pear" (*CS,* 567). The sensuous image of the pear in the torn stocking is a strand in a pervasive thematic web of Welty's in which vibrant life continually breaks through to upset orderly but confining situations. As Richard Gray has noted, a movement from order to confusion is characteristic of Welty's fiction: after the exposition of a particular order "life will somehow break in to destroy it."[41] In her typically paradoxical adherence both to order and openness, Welty connects place with the vocabulary of spatial pat-

---

41. Richard Gray, *The Literature of Memory: Modern Writers of the American South* (Baltimore, 1977), 176.

terning as she describes place as a "*locus* . . . where the particular story [a writer] writes can be pinned down, the circle it can spin through and keep the state of grace, so that for the story's duration the rest of the world suspends its claim upon it and lies low as the story in peaceful extension, the *locus* fading off into the blue" (*ES,* 129).

Thus, Welty articulates the connection between freedom and control in terms that relate to a major structural pattern in her fiction: the fixed center and the impassioned, circular "spin" outward from it that constitutes the creative urge not only in life and art but also in the physical reality of the universe. This aesthetic pattern, this "shaping of the work," is the truest link between Welty's intellect and her story. It is, as she says, what allows us to "come to know what can be known, on the page, of [the writer's] mind and heart" (*ES,* 144). Both the overall narrative pattern of "Going to Naples" and the particular dynamic of its protagonist, Gabriella, embody the author's theory of what Welty calls the *locus* of the story and the "circle it can spin through" (*ES,* 129). In this story, as in Welty's fiction in general, the locus is a foreboding, shifting "neutral ground," an expanded narrative time that must be experienced in a spatial borderland where linear time is held in abeyance, as the world's time or, in Welty's words, the world's "claim upon it," is suspended for the passengers on the *Pomona.*

The vaguely threatening atmosphere aboard the otherwise (but perhaps superficially) festive ship is not only a function of its isolation in time and space, on the ocean between continents, but also of bizarre elements of setting. Gabriella's constant rushing and screaming is echoed by the diving, calling island birds (*i gabbiani*), which have flown too far to return to land and thus are easy prey for the sailors who use them for target practice, and for which Gabriella seems aptly named, in all respects. Also ominous are the strangely silent crew, "wild in their half-undress" (*CS,* 568), and the equally silent two black passengers, whose "four feet formed a big black M, for getting married, set out for young girls to fall over" (*CS,* 569)—the latter hardly an optimistic image of marriage. And, throughout the story, startling, onomatopoeic interruptions suggest warnings: the repeated "*Attenzione!*" of the ship's loudspeaker; the "Tweeeeet!" of old Papa's tin whistle; the "*Ecco!*" of Mr. Ugone and Mrs. Serto; and, not least, "the crack of [Mama's] wedding ring [on Aldo's head that] went out all over the Mediterranean night" (*CS,* 569, 571, 583, 584, 589, 591).

The close quarters of the ship contribute both to the spatial form of the narrative and to the theme of enclosure: "There was nowhere to go but in a circle" (*CS,* 568). Mrs. Scampo's choice for her daughter is represented by the typical Weltian male protagonist as free-spirited sun god: Aldo stands "as though the breezes had just set him down . . . [; his] forehead was all bright copper, and so were his nose and chin, his chest, his folded arms" (*CS*, 569). He appears "almost luminous" (*CS*, 571), while Gabriella is described as a trapped, and even physiologically limited, wild creature, who is silently screaming when not actually screaming "as though some *captive*, that had never had news of the world, land or sea, would sometimes stand there and look out from that pure arch—but *never to speak; that could not even be thought to hear*" (*CS*, 571, emphasis added).

In addition to the mother's unsubtle pushing of the courtship of a daughter she intends for a romantic heroine, Gabriella's own advances toward Aldo are loud, brash, and awkward. In fact, her behavior suggests a lower-class version of the young Emma, whom Rachel Blau DuPlessis calls a "babbling girl hero" before Jane Austen finally molds her into a proper heroine.[42] In Welty's story, Gabriella pulls Aldo out of a deck chair to the floor, and they confront each other on hands and knees "ringed around with the well-filled benches," the "circle of feet," and the legs as "dense and still as a ring of trees" (*CS*, 573). A ritualistic mating dance takes place between the two young people in this arena: "She set her teeth into his sleeve . . . , and he moved like a spring and struck at her with his playful weapon. . . . In return she butted his chest, driving her head against the hard, hot rayon, while . . . he pecked with his little beak that place on the back of the neck where women no longer feel" (*CS*, 573). During this ritual, the surrounding "circle was still"; and when, at the climax of the circling couple's exertions, Aldo buries his face in Gabriella's blouse, there is a mysterious still moment for them as well as for their audience of elders, who "felt something of an old, pure loneliness come back to them—like a bird sent out over the waters long ago, when they were young" (*CS*, 573–74). Here the memory projects backward from the circle, as the mating ritual in its center implies the future.

Soon after, there is an even greater still moment for Gabriella, as she and Aldo walk in "the deepest part" of the ship, where "the engines pounding just within that open door made a human being seem to go in momentary danger of being shaken asunder." At the still center of this noise she imagines that "she and Aldo [are] walking side by side in some still, lonely, even high place never seen before now, with mountains above, valleys below, and sky" (*CS*, 576). It is a place of power and sensual energy like that which Judith Wilt has remarked in Doris Lessing's

42. DuPlessis, *Writing Beyond the Ending*, 8.

Four-Gated City when Martha Quest discovers a separateness apart from love and apart even from the physical act of sex: a "high vibrating place" that is visited only by "her brain, cool and alert, watching and marking," a "dark place" from which she sees visions like scenes. The passage in Lessing resembles many such descriptions in women's writing, and it provides a context in which a pervasive pattern of images in Welty's fiction comes into focus: of train trestles and marriages, of mysterious "neutral grounds" and high places of (mostly female) assertion of essential human separateness in the midst of confluence, and of questing wanderers. One of the most familiar images in this system is the one of "confluence of the waters" Laurel sees in the rivers on the high trestle south of Cairo, as she and Phil travel to Mount Salus for their wedding in the final chapter of *The Optimist's Daughter* (*OD,* 186). The pattern can be seen in miniature at the wedding dance in *Delta Wedding,* as both Shelley and George experience "vision[s] of choice"; as "Shelley's desire fled . . . to an open place, . . . to an opening wood, with weather—with change, beauty" (*DW,* 220); and, in seeming confirmation of her own heart's confluence with theirs, as Ellen, who was already experiencing "a kind of vertigo . . . , saw [George's] mind—as if it too were inversely lighted up by the failing paper lanterns" (*DW,* 221). The passage in which Martha Quest's "body was in a fine high vibration like a wire at very high tension" also suggests the final scene in "Lily Daw and the Three Ladies" in which a straw hat is caught in the high-tension telephone wires, an image that implies that Lily's mind may be on some plane far above the milling crowd, although she hangs her head in the midst of her own wedding plans (*CS,* 11). Gabriella's vision of herself and Aldo "as if [they] were] walking side by side in some still, lonely, even high place" (*CS,* 576), so like Martha Quest's vision of "a man and a woman, walking in a high place under a blue sky," confirms Gabriella as one of these visionary questers. And the confluence of these images at critical moments, moments that lead out of linear time into a narrative time that is meaningful in terms of a character's sense of self and self-story, is a key element in Welty's narrative strategies.[43]

For the young couple in "Going to Naples" Welty now multiplies the no-man's-land attributes of their setting both in time and space: they are on the verge of adulthood; they are physically located in a place neither on nor under the ocean; and they inhabit a place between dream and reality, between the actual and the imaginary. Moreover, in all of these

43. Wilt, *Ghosts of the Gothic,* 295; Doris Lessing, *The Four-Gated City* (New York, 1976), 59.

realms, the line between safety and danger is fragile. From their descent into this many-faceted underworld of the ship, with the all the implications of that narrative archetype from classical literary history, Aldo and Gabriella emerge upon "an altogether new deck, where the air was bright and stiff as an open eye. It was white and narrowing, set about with mysterious shapes of iron wound with chains. No passenger was in sight. . . . All was still . . . [except for] the *Pomona* . . . parting the water" (*CS*, 576–77). In another kind of story these "mysterious shapes of iron wound with chains" would serve very well as Gothic props; Welty's use of them here heightens the sense of the danger and mystery of life in the "unsurrendering world" that she wishes to suggest here for Gabriella, as she does for Jenny in "At the Landing." The image of parting water is significant also, for it is at this moment that Aldo takes from Gabriella a picture of herself as a baby; and her response—to blind him momentarily with the hem of her skirt—causes him to allow the snapshot to fall into the sea. The moment is marked by his expression of "solemnity" and his holding of his breath as well as by his throwing her down on the deck, where they lie "a little apart, like the victims of a passing wind." Then, on a ship named for the apple, an ancient symbol of initiation into the mysteries of life, time gradually begins anew for them when, after this symbolic death of childhood, their resurrection into the tentative and ambiguous state of young adulthood is suggested by the beat of a hesitant rhythm: "Presently Aldo, moving one finger at a time, began to thump on the calf of Gabriella's leg—1,2,3,4—while she lay as before, with her back to him. Intermittently, the 1,2,3,4 kept up, then it slowed and fell away. Gradually the sounds of the dividing sea came back to Gabriella's ear, as though a seashell were once more held lifted" (*CS*, 577). Aldo falls asleep, and Gabriella remains "caught in an element as languorous as it was strange, like a mermaid who has been netted into a fisherman's boat, only to find that the fisherman is dreaming. Where no eye oversaw them, the sea lifted and dropped them both, mindless as a cradle, up and down" (*CS*, 578). The still moment passes; and the lonely girl, in spite of the mating dance and all its attendant rituals during the journey, is alone on Gala Night, because Aldo, one of Welty's typically vulnerable male heroes, is seasick. As the passengers dance on the last night be fore making port in Palermo, they realize as a group that what Gabriella has experienced alone they have somehow shared; for the illusory experience has been "in front of their eyes": "Once more, slipping the way it liked to do through one of life's weak moments, illusion had got in, and they were glad to see it. How many days had they been on the water!" (*CS*, 586).

The boisterous actions that have led to Gabriella's still moment are now reversed by the beginning of the end of the journey, when the pilgrims will all be dispersed in the world. The chaos of her desperation is apparent on the last night of dancing, when it seems

> to the general eye that she might be turning around faster inside than out. For an unmarried girl, it was danger. Some radiant pin through the body had set her spinning like that tonight, and given her the power—not the same thing as permission, but what was like a memory of how to do it—to be happy all by herself. . . . The *Pomona* rose and fell, like a sigh on the breast, but Gabriella held her place—not falling: smiling, intact, a Leaning Tower. A shout of joy went up—even from those that the spectacle of an ungrasped, spinning girl was bound to have made feel worse. (*CS,* 587)

Gabriella and Aldo have shared, and then lost, a brief connection, similar to that experienced by the couple in the dream world south of New Orleans in "No Place for You, My Love," and to that of Jenny and Billy Floyd in "At the Landing," in which one could say that Jenny, like Gabriella, is "like a mermaid . . . netted, . . . only to find that the fisherman is dreaming" (*CS,* 578). Gabriella is temporarily overcome by such a sense of alienation that, as the young Italian-Americans leave Palermo for embarkation in Naples, even "the moon and star . . . looked as though they had never been close together in their lives"; and she wonders whether now is "the time to look forward to the doom of parting, and stop looking back at the doom of meeting." Thus Gabriella recognizes the mirror-image reversal of events that have taken place; and that recognition enables the psychic growth that is implied by the story's conclusion. As they say good-bye, she ponders whether "the time would be flying by" (*CS,* 590). And indeed it will be, as the "widened present" of narrative time—achieved by Welty's spatializing of time and point of view on the ship—dissipates at the story's chaotic ending in a way reminiscent of the frenzy at the depot in "Lily Daw and the Three Ladies." Fellow travelers no longer recognize each other in the melee on the dock at Naples, where the landing is announced by boys with balls, barking dogs, "horn-blowing taxis, streetcars and cars," and, "loudest of all, a crowd of little girls . . . singing like a flock of birds" (*CS,* 594). In spite of the commotion around her, however, it is Aldo's step behind her that Gabriella feels to "shake the whole scene again, as if they were treading the spokes of a wheel" (*CS,* 594); but Aldo's attention is no longer on Gabriella.

Her own despair is mirrored in her thoughts about the fiancée of Poldy, another young passenger, who is so caught up in the action on the dock that he seems in no hurry to find the bride-to-be that he has never met. Michael Kreyling identifies the kinship Gabriella feels for Poldy's bride as an example of the "sisterhood of women," from whom men walk away.[44]

Like the many writer- and artist-characters Welty invents, Gabriella imagines a narrative for Poldy and his bride; and in the writerly task of framing a story for them she sees two views simultaneously, as Welty asserts that the writer always sees double: "two pictures at once in his frame" (*ES*, 125). It is not the male and female views that Gabriella sketches out, however, but two possibilities for the bride. Watching the bridegroom, she has mixed feelings that both acknowledge and refuse identity with the bride, whose romance plot is about to be consummated in marriage. Gabriella

> could hardly take another step down for anger at that girl, and outrage for her, as if she were her dearest friend. . . . Even now, the girl probably languished in tears because the little country train she was coming on, from her unknown town, was late. Perhaps, even more foolishly, she had come early, and was languishing just beyond that gate, not knowing if she were allowed inside the wall or not—how would she know? No matter— they would meet. . . . Poor girl, whose name Poldy had not even bothered to tell them, her future was about to begin. (*CS*, 594)

Now, at Gabriella's last greeting, Aldo looks startled, "as if to see someone he had never expected to see again" (599). Gabriella's fingers touch his cello in parting, but he is already looking less familiar as he walks away. She senses that he is already fading into unfamiliarity in what Kreyling has called the "rhythmical aspect of touching and parting, of present and future."[45]

Welty concludes the story with precisely such a bittersweet, but hopeful, image of Gabriella imagining that "the golden moment of touch, just given, just taken, [somehow remains with her] . . . bright and effortless of making, in the end, as a bubble [that] seemed to go ahead of them as they walked" up the hill into Naples (*CS*, 600). Here Welty creates the kind of image that she discusses in terms of Faulkner's "The Bear," a story in which, she says, "like the skin of a balloon, time and space are stretched to hold more and more" (*ES*, 104). Thus the writer's creation of any text, as Welty describes it, corresponds to the text Gabriella creates for her own life. For Gabriella's shining balloon symbolizes life itself, which she runs toward, which she hopes will "hold more and more," and yet which she has, in one sense, always carried with her in memory, in her family's

44. Kreyling, *Welty's Achievement,* 133–34.
45. *Ibid.*

continuity with the past. Indeed, Welty, speaking of that continuity, which the artist perceives, refers to Willa Cather's use of a similar metaphor for life. She quotes from Thea's Panther Cañon meditation, in *Song of the Lark,* on art as "an effort . . . to imprison for a moment the shining, elusive element which is life itself—life hurrying past us and running away, too strong to stop, too sweet to lose" (*ES,* 46). By symbolizing the girl's shimmering hopes in a bright bubble, then, Welty has, in spatial terms, created a range of possibilities for Gabriella; and at the same time she has created what seems a dramatization of Cather's meditation on life, art, and continuity.

Gabriella's bubble not only suggests the life ahead; as the narrator tells us, it also "seems" to remain with her, as memory, representing both past and future. The bubble shape is one of contained space, like the confining circles of cultural guardians surrounding Gabriella on board ship. Yet a bubble is also a fragile shell, as ephemeral as the illusion of human connection that for a time encouraged the passengers in "Going to Naples"; and it is a shell that might be easily broken by the energetic girl, as is the "shell" of Shellmound by several characters in *Delta Wedding.* Perhaps more importantly, it provides a visible symbol of the idea that Gabriella has the power to explode the shape of memory, as she has had the power to imagine alternate narratives for Poldy's bride. She can decide for herself whether memory will confine or nourish her "shining hopes." Like any creator of stories, she is "seeing double." As Richard Gray has noted, such a process "forces author, narrator, and ourselves to remain poised between choices"; and in this story Gabriella is so poised. In spite of her admitted limitations, she, who was not seasick even when spinning, also has "the power . . . to be happy all by herself . . . not falling . . . [but] intact, a Leaning Tower." In a world characterized by physical and psychological chaos, a world where "matches" are made *for* passive women, Gabriella assumes an attitude of poise that constitutes a "tower," virtual female phallus, an image that looks forward to Welty's later uses of female aggression and penetration. Her self-text will not be the construct of prescribed and "ideologically delimited . . . vulnerability" that Nancy Miller has described as "the heroine's text"; that is, "in the first instance nothing more than the inscription of a female destiny, the fictionalization of what is taken to be the feminine at a specific cultural moment (of the rise of the modern novel)."[46]

At that cultural moment, Miller argues, a woman's self was always dependent upon, and in danger of, the "*faux pas* . . . [which,] in the politics

46. Gray, *The Literature of Memory,* 176; Nancy Miller, *The Heroine's Text: Readings in the French and English Novel, 1722–1782* (New York, 1980), x.

of seduction, . . . generally proves to be enough" to forever remove her from the good graces of society. Miller discusses two major female plots that marked the eighteenth-century beginnings of the modern novel: "euphoric" and "dysphoric" texts. The former end with "the heroine's integration into society" and the latter "with [her] death in the flower of her youth—except for Mme de Merteuil, the 'negative' heroine of *Les Liaisons dangereuses,* who is banished to a living death—and the move is from 'all' in this world to 'nothing.'"[47] Miller asserts that the "heroine's text" is alive and well in the twentieth century: that "literary femininity in the traditional novel remains faithful to commonplaces of a familiar inscription: and female *Bildung* tends to get stuck in the bedroom. . . . Because the novel, more than any other form of art, is forced by the contract of the genre to negotiate with social realities in order to remain legible, its plots are largely overdetermined by the commonplaces of culture. Until the culture invents new plots for women, we will continue to read the heroine's text. Or we could stop reading novels."[48]

Yet the whirling activity around Gabriella in "Going to Naples" represents a significant moment of inner turmoil, when she is "turning faster inside than out," the "still" center of a potential storm. The structural patterning here, as in "The Burning," presents a "metaphysical reality beyond the facts of the extensional world," and is thus consistent with the techniques of the romantic tradition of the American short story.[49] The setting thus functions as a metaphoric extension of character: a shipboard "landscape" that is truly a "thing of intellect," a mindscape. The dynamic of this externalized emotion is expressed in repeated spatial patterns describing a centripetal force that closes in on Gabriella, then reverses itself in a true denouement, an unknotting of the tenuous relationships formed on board ship, when, "through one of life's weak moments, illusion had got in." The illusion has been one of fragile and temporary order over chaos, but one that is dispelled by the inevitable disintegration of the temporary cultural enclosure, symbolized by the disbanding of the ship's microcosm of community. For, as in the aftermath of Virgie Rainey's still moment in the river in "The Wanderers" and Delilah's epiphany in "The Burning," the final movement of the story is one of dissolution.

When the chaos of reality breaks in, however, sometimes life itself breaks through, like the living flesh through Gabriella's stocking. Neither Gabriella nor Aldo is coerced by the old order; rather, each seems almost

47. Miller, *The Heroine's Text,* ix–xi.
48. *Ibid.,* 157–58.
49. Rohrberger, *Hawthorne and the Modern Short Story,* 41.

perversely impelled toward freedom, however uncertain, instead of toward the "safe" betrothal Mrs. Serto has promoted. Since, as Patricia Meyer Spacks comments, she is more Chekhovian observer than Hawthornian moralist, Welty takes leave of her protagonists as they are poised before various possibilities, in a posture that is more likely to be evinced by the female characters of the mature writer Welty has become in 1955.[50] Welty recognizes that a changing world makes individual freedoms increasingly possible; yet throughout her fiction she also recognizes the outcast status of those who insist upon such freedom in the face of the culture's myth of concern. They run the risk of being like Miss Eckhart and Virgie Rainey in "June Recital": "human beings terribly at large, roaming on the face of the earth" (*CS*, 330). What has been said about another story could apply as well to "Going to Naples": that it demonstrates an "'objective correlative' for a certain kind of shock experienced by those with courage to face life unprotected by the buffers of habit and custom."[51] Essentially, then, Welty suggests that Gabriella has such courage and that she has the potential to revise the heroine's text her mother is following: to write for herself a female hero's text.

The spatial attributes of Welty's fiction, and especially the patterns of enforced order perennially dissolving into chaos, illustrating only one type of the relationships *between* images that are central to Welty's poetics, establish a powerful sense of unity throughout the entire body of Welty's work, perhaps a twentieth-century canonwide version of a Hawthornian unity "of intellect."[52] To try to interpret every element of such an intricate system of image patterns is usually a mistake, as Welty's own critical writing makes clear (*C*, 10, 66, 273). But to fully appreciate the subtlety of Welty's vision one must recognize the complex and systematic significance of spatiality in her art, or to adapt Laurence Stapleton's formulation, the press of structure on plot.[53] More specifically, to recognize Welty's management of the theme of order and disorder in terms of an individual's interaction with culture is to notice her modernist appropriation of the Southern dream-nightmare of a closely ordered society irrevocably opened to change, whether by the Civil War's brutal refocusing of priorities or by modern technology's equally radical influence on the traditions of the human community. And by extension, one sees her

50. Patricia Meyer Spacks, Review of Eudora Welty's *The Optimist's Daughter*, in *Hudson Review*, XXV (1972), 509.

51. Jones, "The World of Love," 191.

52. Mortimer, "Image and Myth in Eudora Welty's *The Optimist's Daughter*," 618.

53. Laurence Stapleton, *The Elected Circle: Studies in the Art of Prose* (Princeton, 1973), 5.

version of modern openings in cultural and literary narratives of romance, in revisions that reflect more latitude in expectations about gender roles. The relative merits of the confinement inherent in order, as opposed to the chaos inherent in individual freedom, is a theme that permeates Welty's fiction. By her treatment of this theme with modernist spatial techniques that achieve surprisingly gothic patterns of enclosure, exposure, and escape, Welty extends into the twentieth century Hawthorne's concern with cultural ghosts, whether such ghosts manifest themselves in recognizable gothic shapes or in the equally evocative designs supplied by contemporary physics. But if Welty writes in Hawthorne's shadow, it is the selective shadow of the experimental nineteenth-century American "romancer" who transformed conventions of the Gothic into lyric techniques, especially by his contributions to the development of the short story. Gothic conventions, which, I believe, are among the devices that allowed Hawthorne to reconcile imagination and reality, also energize the fiction of Eudora Welty with a sense of mystery and metaphysics that contributes to Welty's themes about human beings on the margins, including the marginal dead space at the center of culture; about their confrontations with *themselves* as Other; and about the possibilities they see, often as artists, in the dangerous unknown spaces beyond the conventional.

The Gothic "remains to this day a major organizing grid for female consciousness . . . [, including] the masochistic powerlessness of the generic female confronted with the no-frills cruel-but-tender male," and we are "still seduced by these fictions," as is the writer character in Margaret Atwood's *Lady Oracle*.[54] Thus the contemporaneity of Welty's plots, whose patterns make visible these themes of powerlessness and of narrative desire. The plot, which is the "shape of the emotion," to recall Eileen Baldeshwiler's apt phrase, seduces reader to join writer in the search for a way out of the "grid" of the cultural text. Perhaps it is this search that Welty suggests when, in mysterious language that somehow suggests a reaction to the dilemma of both writer and Gothic heroine, she writes of following "the contours of some continuous relationship between what can be told and what cannot be told," in stories whose words are meant "to be in the silence of reading the lightest of the hammers that tap their way along this side of chaos" (*ES,* 143).

---

54. DuPlessis, *Writing Beyond the Ending,* 44–45; Margaret Atwood, *Lady Oracle* (New York, 1976).

III

Texts and Contexts of the Self
Patterns of Enclosure, Exposure, and Escape

The topic of human restraint versus human freedom is as old as lexical representations like Plato's allegory of the cave in *The Republic* and topographical depictions of actual confinements such as those of Socrates in the *Phaedo,* Boethius in *The Consolation of Philosophy,* and Augustine in the *Confessions.* It is likewise as contemporary as the "tendency in modern literature to favor representations of enclosure and, more generally, spatiality over temporality," which became especially notable in the writing of existentialists burdened with the knowledge of massive incarcerations during World War II.[1] Both the cell and the cloister have been effectively compared to the prison-world or the prison-body— human bondages that must somehow be circumvented to liberate the mind (or soul, in Platonic terms). Whether incarceration is actual or metaphysical, however, both ancient and modern texts, and both erudite and everyday language, provide means to articulate the closed-in quality of life and the constant attempt to find openings. Perhaps this primal human sense of claustrophobia contributed to the popular fascination with the Gothic novel in Europe, which was often based on the barbaric imprisonments and tortures of the Inquisition. In American literature, colonial captivity narratives and gothic adaptations of the dungeon to the forest cave precede more general representations of space-induced emotions that are not exclusive to prisons: for example, the often contradictory feelings of confinement, release, and exclusion experienced in natural and cultural wildernesses of the New World, especially when pro-

1. See Mary Ann Frese Witt, *Existential Prisons: Captivity in Mid-Twentieth-Century French Literature* (Durham, N.C., 1985), 3–13, for a discussion of the symbolic value of prisons and other enclosures as literary figures. Witt takes the concept of the "closed in" life and the search for "openings" from Georges Matore's *L'Éspace humain* (Paris, 1962), 181.

gressively closing frontiers have caused backward-looking minds to turn in upon themselves.[2]

Eudora Welty's emotionally charged fictional wildernesses directly follow those which elicited similar ambivalent feelings in the works of Cooper, Hawthorne, and Faulkner. In the most intimate terms of family and small community, she depicts a culture like that which Michel Foucault, in describing modern culture's supervision of sociopolitical correction and coercion, calls a "carceral society." Unlike the system based on a sovereign (for example, the king whose personal honor was said to be affronted by criminal acts in *l'ancien régime* of France), the carceral society is no longer dependent upon a simple power base. Instead, it relies upon a network of forces including "walls, space, institutions, rules, discourse," all intended to normalize human beings in accord with the prevailing cultural mythos. Ironically, however, because of the increasing subtlety by which the power of the state is abetted, and at the same time "humanized," by acculturating traditions, the system provides, Foucault believes, a model of cultural coercion that essentially makes those royal Gothic barbarisms metaphoric equivalents of "civilized" human behavior.[3] Welty's modern images of enclosure reflect the limitations imposed from without by cultural traditions—that is, by civilization's web of restraints—as well as those inner exigencies willed by the self or inflicted by memory. Her family-centered stories abound with characters whose daily lives are lived within this web of society, some who are like the mutually supportive but equally limited cellmates in Plato's cave, but others who, alone, unattached, and vulnerable, fling themselves out of familiar protective custody into the dazzling glare of the mysterious world.

Eighteenth-century innovations in Gothic form were attempts to add "the great resources of fancy" to the modern romantic novel, in which, according to Horace Walpole, such imaginative resources had been "dammed up, by a strict adherence to common life." George Haggerty describes these innovations in terms of a conflict between the formal structures necessary to evoke the desired emotional reader response,

---

2. See Harold P. Simonson, *The Closed Frontier: Studies in American Literary Tragedy* (New York, 1970), 38, on the once-open American frontier blocked by the "solid wall" at the end of westward expansion; Lewis P. Simpson, "What Survivors Do," in *The Brazen Face of History: Studies in the Literary Consciousness of America,* by Simpson (Baton Rouge, 1980), 238, 241, on the southern mind that turned in upon itself when severed from tradition; and Albert J. Devlin, *Eudora Welty's Chronicle: A Story of Mississippi Life* (Jackson, 1983), 20, 210–12, who draws upon Simonson and Simpson in discussing Welty's fictional escapes from the bonds of southern literary "piety."

3. Foucault, *Discipline and Punish,* 39, 74, 198, 307–308.

and the "common life" rational responses that were expected in the conventional novel; thus, the greatest problem for the Gothic writer was how to present the dual, paradoxical realities of "the subjective world of dreamlike private experience and the public objective world of the novel." The primary images of a Gothic novel are those of "dammed up" characters. And although the Gothic novel aims at iconoclastic form, when successful it operates as a conservative, controlling function whose narrative shapes and patterns (frames, mazes) presents "the self massively blocked off from something," according to Eve Sedgwick; thus its form is particularly amenable to a fiction that concerns itself with tensions between such conservative (carceral) forces and the extravagant passions that pull against them. Indeed, the Gothic exemplifies the politics of the romance plot, which, like all literature, is "a human institution . . . organized by many ideological scripts," asserts Rachel Blau DuPlessis. "No convention is neutral, purely mimetic, or purely aesthetic," she says; rather, "narrative structures and subjects are like working apparatuses of ideology, factories for the 'natural' and 'fantastic' meanings by which we live."[4]

The American Gothic, a literary tradition that has effectively employed terror-inducing spaces to reveal to us some of those meanings, has been recognized as an obvious precedent for some of Welty's stories. Marie-Antoinette Manz-Kunz notes that in "Clytie," for example, characters are allotted progressively diminished space, like those in Poe's "The Pit and the Pendulum," and that most characters in "At the Landing" live in a state of torpor, as though they were entombed, simply waiting for the Mississippi River to flood. John Alexander Allen observes that evil in Welty's fiction is always associated with imprisonment of some kind. In fact, the entire Welty oeuvre reveals her extensive dependence upon images of confinement.[5]

Unlike Plato's cave analogue for the world-prison, most modern-day carceral reformatories—*literal* prisons—are not "inert . . . dark, abandoned region[s] but instead active forces . . . in coding [and] sometimes in recoding existences," as Foucault recognizes. A major theme in Welty's fiction is that of cultural codings or manipulations—remarkably similar to those used in actual prisons—by which human society at every

4. Horace Walpole, *The Castle of Otranto: A Gothic Story,* ed. W. S. Lewis and Joseph Reed, Jr. (1764; rpr. New York, 1982), 7; Haggerty, *Gothic Fiction/Gothic Form,* 20; Sedgwick, *The Coherence of Gothic Convention,* 12; DuPlessis, *Writing Beyond the Ending,* 2–3.

5. Manz-Kunz, *Eudora Welty: Aspects of Fantasy,* 50, 60; John Alexander Allen, "The Other Way to Live: Demigods in Eudora Welty's Fiction," in *Eudora Welty: Critical Essays,* ed. Peggy Whitman Prenshaw (Jackson, 1983), 30.

level attempts to be *formatory* and, should that effort fail, *re*formatory. A cultural community, then, wishes to mold character; but it also strives to order its world into less frightening dimensions. In illustrating the latter phenomenon, Louis Rubin has noted that Welty's fictional town of Morgana, Mississippi, "ward[s] off and mask[s], through ritual and social complexity, an awareness of the finally unanswerable and inexplicable nature of existence in time and eternity"; and, further, that "anyone who cannot enter into such a compact, cannot play the game by the agreed-upon rules, is a threat to the security and place of all the others."[6]

Welty's families, like her communities in general, close against exposure to forces operating outside their private rationales, trapping family members in the double bind of enclosure and exposure: exposed to the watchful guardians *within* the enclosure, as in a "panoptic" penal system such as that designed by Jeremy Bentham for incarcerating convicts in individual cells that are constantly monitored from a central position. It resembles a system of partitioning cities used in sixteenth-century Europe to prevent the spread of plague, the concept of which, according to Foucault, is easily extended to measures for producing "pure" communities and disciplined societies.[7] Such serious attempts at maintaining order result from that ostensibly benign social phenomenon that Joseph Wiesenfarth calls the "myth of social concern," which was dramatized as early as the Brontëan novel of manners that Robert B. Heilman calls "the new Gothic novel." Unlike the classic Gothic, it depicts not external but internal terror: "the discovery and release of new patterns of feeling." Such feelings may develop because, paradoxically, human beings are often as lost in the cultures they create to civilize the bestial energies of the world as they would be in an enclosed Gothic labyrinth like that in Jane Austen's *Northanger Abbey,* or in an exposed Gothic wasteland like the icy terrain in which Mary Shelley's creature is cruelly exposed in *Frankenstein.* Thus it is that gothic images of confinement, including those of confinement to exposed spaces, are as useful in Welty's ostensibly innocuous American novels of manners as in Brontë's "new Gothic" or Austen's novels of coercive families and confining society. Welty's admiring essay on Jane Austen should not only alert us to the difference between the two writers but should also lead us to reevaluate their similarities. In "The Radiance of Jane Austen," Welty asserts that Austen "wrote from a perfectly solid and firm foundation and [that] her world is *wholly affirmative. . . .* Jane Austen's ardent belief . . . [was] that the unit

---

6. Foucault, *Discipline and Punish,* 235; Louis D. Rubin, Jr., "Art and Artistry in Morgana, Mississippi," in *A Gallery of Southerners,* by Rubin (Baton Rouge, 1982), 62.

7. Foucault, *Discipline and Punish,* 195–228.

of everything worth knowing in life is in the family" (*ES,* 6–7, emphasis added). Certainly the family is as central in Welty as in Austen, as is the mixture of the comic and the ironic; but Welty's literary affirmations of life are hedged by pervasive acknowledgments of the pathos of human contingency—not only in society but in the face of universal forces, while Austen's own vision is influenced by the more specific contingency of women before the economic and legal systems of nineteenth-century England. Commentators mostly emphasize Welty's affirmation, noting only mildly ironic undertones, as does Jane Hinton; but some, like Margaret Bolsterli, have noticed the strong undercurrents implied by, for example, "bound" characters that result from society's myth of concern.[8]

In Welty's *The Golden Apples* some characters are, like Eugene Mac-Lain, "twined . . . in" (*CS,* 413), while others, like Miss Eckhart and Virgie Rainey, are "terribly at large, roaming on the face of the earth . . . , human beings, roaming, like lost beasts" (*CS,* 330). The contrast between those within and those without communal bonds—suggesting the threat that the individual and the society pose to *each other*—forms a close link between *Delta Wedding* and *The Golden Apples.* The alien and unpredictable presence of extreme and unseemly passion, violence, or despair in any individual conscience seems to imply something ominous beyond itself; and it must be subsumed in the family or community that attempts to isolate itself from a larger threat: from what Louis Rubin calls "the vast, ungovernable forces of human existence in the world [such as] consciousness of time and mortality."[9]

Welty makes no attempt to soften the harsh realities that engender the concern for cultural solidarity. On the contrary, she makes them visible in depictions of uncontrollable natural forces like the brooding, bandit-concealing Natchez wilderness and the flooding Mississippi River, and in images of similar phenomena in human terms: in details as small as the flesh bursting through a torn stocking in "Going to Naples," or the bulging breasts that horrify the young protagonist of "A Memory" by arousing primary body fears about sex and sudden eruptions; or in incidents as immensely grotesque as the horse ridden into the living room by the

---

8. Wiesenfarth, *Gothic Manners and the Classic English Novel,* 11; Heilman, "Charlotte Brontë's 'New Gothic,'" 99; Jane L. Hinton, "The Role of Family in *Delta Wedding, Losing Battles,* and *The Optimist's Daughter,*" in *Eudora Welty: Critical Essays,* ed. Prenshaw, 120–31; Margaret Bolsterli, "'Bound' Characters in Porter, Welty, McCullers: The Prerevolutionary Status of Women in American Fiction," *Bucknell Review,* XXIV (1978), 95–105.

9. Louis D. Rubin, Jr., *The Faraway Country: Writers of the Modern South* (Seattle, 1963), 136.

rapacious soldiers in "The Burning." William Faulkner's wildernesses continued the American Gothic tradition of symbolic landscapes, functioning both literally, as did Cooper's, and metaphorically, as did Hawthorne's, to depict the ambivalence and entangling restriction of family or culture, even as each protects its own. Welty gives new life to that impulse in terms of the family wilderness in *Delta Wedding* and in terms of the larger carceral society in *The Golden Apples.*

One of Eudora Welty's most profound thematic connections with the work of William Faulkner is her extended analogies of family and wilderness. Faulkner's method is exemplified in *Go Down, Moses,* in which the all-engulfing tangle of the Yoknapatawpha wilderness reflects the confusions of caste and blood in families such as the McCaslins, that he locates in and near it; but it also suggests the haunting, mysteriously binding legacy of the slave society of the Old South. In "The Old People," personification of the wilderness implies its empathetic relationship with humankind: "[Isaac McCaslin] stopped breathing then . . . and in the following silence the wilderness ceased to breathe also, leaning, stooping overhead with its breath held, tremendous and impartial and waiting." In "The Bear," the margin of the tangled forest seems "impenetrable"; yet just as Welty's close-knit families assimilate intruders, the forest "close[s] behind his entrance as it had opened momentarily to accept him." The frightening aspect of the deep woods is forced on any novice in this enchanted place: Isaac is "a child, alien and lost in the . . . markless wilderness." In a gesture that is a realistic representation of adolescence but is also symbolic of an entire culture's refusal to admit change in a way of life, Isaac leaves the logging camp that represents the destructive outside world and looks to the "wall of wilderness ahead within which he would be able to hide himself from it *once more anyway.*" Initiated into wilderness ways, Isaac is "not alone but solitary." In this, also, he anticipates Welty characters, not only those "lost" in family but also those who psychologically transcend a family's confining tangle while physically surrounded by it.[10]

In choosing the wilderness as a central image for their fiction, Faulkner and Welty have not only made use of the materials at hand in a land that not very long ago *was* a wilderness, they have also tapped a source vital to our Western heritage from ancient to modern times. From legends of sacred groves in Europe, of Celtic Druid oak-worship, and of Native

10. William Faulkner, *Go Down, Moses* (1942; rpr. New York, 1973), 182, 195, 208, 318, 323 (emphasis added).

American tree spirit veneration has come our inherited folklore of the forest, which was modified and intensified by the clearing of the wilderness. Both authors' work reflects the archetypal forms furnished by the old beliefs and the peculiarly American mythology involving, in Welty's case, the lore of the fertile Delta country between the Yazoo and Mississippi rivers, and the clearing, through dense and dangerous woods, of the historic Natchez Trace.

In American life and literature the relationship between humankind and the natural universe has perhaps most often meant a relationship to the wilderness. Reflecting both the American dream of an Edenic wilderness and the subsequent nightmares of its metamorphosis into something alien to humans, American works have about them a double sense of the romantic and the modern.[11] The wilderness-clearing trope is an apt metaphor for the double natures of the individual and of the human family; and human duality is part of the concept of mystery that pervades Welty's fiction, a mystery involving the idea of knowledge as well as the sanctity of the unknowable. Such emphases remind us of American writers' modifications of the gothic themes and conventions that were common in the earliest attempts at producing an American literature; but they also point to some basic dualities of the classic Gothic, such as the "real" versus the "unreal" and the comforting versus the inhibiting nature of the communal enclosure—dualities that remain viable interests for modern writers. Part of the difference Frederick J. Hoffman sees in what does not seem "realistic" to reviewers of contemporary novels is the depiction of "the world of the not-quite-real, the unexpected, in which human relations are described in something other than (higher than? weirder than?) situational terms . . . employed to secure a more than ordinary impression or effect. The difference between saying 'the August day was very hot' and describing it as follows [in the opening lines of Welty's *Delta Wedding*] is considerable: '[The land] seemed strummed, as though it were an instrument and something had touched it.' We have moved up one level by means of the imagination."[12]

In both human and natural worlds are the mysterious and eternal cycles of birth, growth, and death. Within both there exist the dualities of the individual versus the whole and of the whole versus the Other, or outside world. If we are aliens in the natural world, it is because we no

---

11. R. W. B. Lewis, *The American Adam: Innocence, Tragedy, and Tradition in the Nineteenth Century* (Chicago, 1955), 113–14.

12. Frederick J. Hoffman, *The Art of Southern Fiction: A Study of Some Modern Novelists* (Carbondale, 1967), 115–16.

longer recognize ourselves as functional parts of it. We must either explain it away, take it away, or ignore it. Instead of the primeval forests that once sheltered, later menaced, us, we moderns contend with bewildering complexities of our own making that are ironically analogous to the natural wilderness.

The complex system that is the human family is the subject of almost all of Welty's fiction. It is, perhaps, a subject that is particularly compelling in southern fiction because of the complex family structures in the South, which, in the antebellum period, were partly due to the subcaste system among the Negro contingent of a plantation. According to Raimondo Luraghi, the system contributed to an overall black-white extended family constellation that had more in common with old world seigniorial or tribal "families" than with cellular families of today. Although Welty's fiction does not focus on this kind of racial complexity, as does Faulkner's, she shares with him a concern for the complexities that cannot be revealed by "linear" narratives of individuals. Instead, they favor what Carol Kolmerten and Stephen Ross call the "backings and fillings . . . , multiple perspectives . . . , as well as the more tangled stream-of-consciousness threads of memory and perception" that characterize the novel of family and "reflect the complexity inherent in the family structure."[13] In fact, Welty has said that she found the most basic theme of her work—"the structure of the family"—in the relationships between the members of a family of circus performers in a very early story, "Acrobats in a Park" (*OWB*, 86).

Welty's comparison of family to wilderness is explicit without the oversimplification of exact analogy, her premise being that symbolic meaning must only suggest and not analogize (*TP*, 20). Thus Welty utilizes intricate matrices of narrative patternings, which subtly but dramatically point to meaning. As in "Lily Daw and the Three Ladies" and "Going to Naples," images of circles reverberate throughout *Delta Wedding*, reinforcing the idea of omnipresent encircling dangers that surround the characters in the novel. From the very first pages, where the lamp over Laura's head on the train is decorated with "a circle of flowers" and where "swallows are circling" over the country house at Shellmound, the circle is a major factor in the web of image clusters—including mazes, cages, and cycles—that extend and complicate the wilderness motif (*DW*, 3, 7). Thus Welty's domesticated metaphor of the wilderness

13. Raimondo Luraghi, *The Rise and Fall of the Plantation South* (New York, 1978), 53–54; Carol A. Kolmerten and Stephen Ross, "The Empty Locus of Desire: Woman as Familial Center in Modern American Fiction," *Denver Quarterly*, XVII (1985), 110.

is central to the narrative shape of *Delta Wedding*, in which Laura completes a circular, ritual initiatory journey through the dangers of the Fairchild wilderness.

In this novel, preservers of the family tree, the metaphoric extension of the sacred live oak in the forest, are Aunt Primrose and Aunt Jim Allen, who can remember when "this was a wilderness" and whose own house, the Grove, is "eternally cool in summer . . . like the air of a dense little velvet-green wood" (*DW*, 40). Aunt Jim Allen wants "all the ghosts kept straight" as well as "their kinfolks and their tragedies" (45). The extended metaphor of complicated family as tangled wilderness is established by forest imagery involving the house, the family, individual characters, and even their words and hopes. The description of Mary Lamar Mackey's background music, as she practices for the wedding, includes the framework for all those comparisons: the music is "isolated from them, yet near, and sweet like the guessed existence of mystery. It made the house like a nameless forest, wherein many little lives lived privately, each to its lyric pursuit and its shy protection" (*DW*, 156).

Emphasizing the analogy is the following meditation of Ellen's, which places the wilderness metaphor on a deeper, psychic level within the family and at the same time suggests enclosure by the existential world-cave, in its avatar as a gothic space: "how deep were the complexities of the everyday, of the family, what caves were in the mountains, what blocked chambers, and what crystal rivers that had not yet seen light" (*DW*, 157).[14] These complementary passages suggest the dual nature of the family wilderness: like its counterpart, the real forest, it is diverse and yet a single entity; it both isolates and protects, gives privacy and hides the light. Its tangled undergrowths are frightening but, as both the fron-

---

14. Since Welty's emphasis is always on the individual's search in the midst of both lexical and topographical enclosures, the existentialist search for the self would seem to be a ready-made topic for commentators on her fiction; and indeed brief moves were made in that direction in the early 1960s. Kurt Opitz' "The Order of a Captive Soul," *Critique*, VII (1964–65), 80–82, for example, analyzes Welty characters' "attempt[s] to escape from their situation[s] *into* the tumult of the world or, upon encountering failure in this move, through the discovery of the true nature of their predicament." Opitz calls this discovery a "leap of faith"; and he asserts that Welty's perspective is one of "philosophical engagement" that is "shaped by existential problems," however ultimately positive but nonpolemical (and therefore opposite to the perspective of many European existentialists) is her vision. Vande Kieft's early critical assessment in *Eudora Welty* (1962), 102, pointed up Welty's attempt to "answer . . . problems about how to exist in the face of potential . . . catastrophe, vulnerable to the whims of fate; how to act freely and without fear," concluding that "it is the *existential act* which makes life significant, beautiful, even heroic" (emphasis added); but in her extensive revision of that book in 1987, "the existential act" is changed to "the free act of giving" (79).

tiersman and the incarcerated prisoner know well, the opposite is also dangerous; for, as Foucault remarks, "visibility is a trap." [15]

The family circle is like the perimeter of the forest, sometimes welcoming, sometimes intimidating an intruder, and always trapping its own in its over-close embrace. It is now the magic healing circle, now the excluding barrier. Playing games on the lawn with the Fairchild children, Laura learns that "sometimes you wanted to be in a circle and then you wanted out of it in a rush. Sometimes the circle was for you, sometimes against you, if you were It. . . . It was never a good circle unless you were in it, catching hands, and knowing the song. A circle was ugly without you" (*DW,* 73).

The family is insensitive to Laura's wish to be alone, and yet her participation in the family's life is at their various whims. Her repeated attempts to penetrate the family circle leave her "a humiliated little girl whose grief people never seemed to remember" (*DW,* 54). The passage in which Maureen pushes the woodpile down on Laura emphasizes that the psychological threat of the family is more menacing than any natural physical danger symbolized by the logs. In the midst of her physical hurt, the superficial sound of the family's nearby laughter oppresses her as would the overpowering gloom of the dense forest, when a "feeling of their unawareness of her came over Laura and crushed her more heavily than the harm of Maureen and the logs of wood" (74–75).

It is, moreover, a purposeful "unawareness." In fact, as Richard Gray has noted, the plantation's name, Shellmound, is symbolic of a shield, as self-generating and subjective as those existential prisons that Mary Ann Frese Witt describes, which have been "secreted from the body"; and it operates as effectively for a group as for an individual. [16] The family's crustacean-like indifference to the outside world is well established by the fact that they simply do not notice visitors who knock at the front door and often do not answer the telephone (*DW,* 8). The family's perception that Troy Flavin's entrance with wedding presents is unceremonious may indicate his outsider status; but the Fairchilds never answer the door anyway, even when someone is expected. Thus the minister, arriving for the wedding rehearsal, "not being able to make himself heard at the door, rapped on the windowpane, causing the bridesmaids to scream at that black sight through the wavery glass" (*DW,* 183–84). It is as if an intruder has startled some little forest creatures. Welty's families cannot conceive of any intrusions from outside as being worthy of their notice.

15. Foucault, *Discipline and Punish,* 200.
16. Gray, *The Literature of Memory,* 283; Witt, *Existential Prisons,* 114.

There are, however, several shell-penetrating, circle-breaking life forces in *Delta Wedding:* Maureen, the mentally retarded child of the dead Denis Fairchild; Troy Flavin, the overseer marrying into the Fairchild planter aristocracy; Robbie Reed, the wife of George, the favorite Fairchild; and Laura McRaven, the recently orphaned city cousin. Whatever their means of access, all intruders are ultimately encompassed within the family wilderness in a coalescing action, a fluid and almost imperceptible motion, like that of the eternally mutable wilderness that surrounds it, a wilderness that, in a similar phenomenon, welcomes Faulkner's Ike McCaslin. In *Delta Wedding* the fluid shifting and continual re-forming of the family, the physical fluctuation in the lives of individuals that does not seem to disturb the essence of the family's unity, is made possible in part by the several houses on the Fairchild estate, although Dorothy Griffin argues persuasively that the degree of felicity in each house may be different. The wedding ceremony itself is described in one line: "Mr. Rondo married Dabney and Troy" (*DW,* 214), subsumed and almost lost in the undergrowth of continuous family conversation. As so often occurs in Welty's fiction, according to Albert Devlin, "human contingencies are subsumed into nature's vast articulation." [17]

The family atmosphere is superficially, even intentionally, congenial and affectionate, yet the effect on individuals is almost always negative. Thus, the very ease with which the family envelops her circle-breaking fiancé causes Dabney some uneasiness. Her marriage is an obvious rebellion against the cultural expectations of her class and family hierarchy. She not only "marries down," as John Edward Hardy has noted, but she also precedes her older sister, mildly upsetting her family on both counts. It is, in fact, the mildness of the family's protest that concerns Dabney: whether it is enough to prove their love for her. Thomas Landess has argued that she knows their permissiveness "is not the result of love but of indifference." Before her wedding Dabney uncritically sees the sky as "an unbroken circle, all around the wheel of the level world" (*DW,* 30) as she rides into a "round meadow" (32) that will be her lifelong boundary. It is a landscape remarkably like that which Louise Westling has described in Flannery O'Connor's "Greenleaf" as "the ancient circular meadow of rape in Greek religion, always the province of feminine powers," and therefore threatening, a space that in "Greenleaf" is vio-

17. Dorothy Griffin, "The House as Container: Architecture and Myth in Eudora Welty's *Delta Wedding,*" *Mississippi Quarterly,* XXXIX (1986), 529; Devlin, *Eudora Welty's Chronicle,* 16.

lated by the bull's symbolic rape of Mrs. May. Dabney's new happiness is, like George and Robbie's, "almost—somehow—threatening" to that ideally pastoral, provincial world (*DW,* 25) because, although she may not get out, she allows an alien in. Yet, as if in denial of the penetration, the Fairchild wilderness closes around the new bridegroom. His entry is accomplished with no more effort than that of a vagrant breeze that briefly ripples the leaves of the trees at the edge of a wood and disturbs not at all the indifferent undergrowth. Welty refuses to predict which will prevail, yet the preponderance of circle-breakers in the novel suggests the eventual breaking open of Shellmound.[18]

Like the wilderness and the family, the maze of a house is often a place of bewildering complexity, especially to newcomers. Richard Gray sees "a touch of the House of Usher about Shellmound . . . [, which is both] a mansion and a labyrinth, a dwelling and a kind of maze."[19] Laura thinks about the "upstairs hall where it was twilight all the time from the green shadow of an awning, and where . . . they could play an endless game of hide-and-seek in so many rooms and up and down the halls that intersected and turned into dead-end porches and rooms full of wax begonias and elephant's-ears, or rooms full of trunks" (*DW,* 8–9). Here, in a house that ostensibly protects its inhabitants from the dangerous wilderness, Welty juxtaposes artificial architectural mazes and human family tangles, including the natural labyrinth of memory, thereby problematizing the simpler (Hawthornian) analogy of forest/psyche as locus of decision to seek or shun awareness of the world. Such natural, wild tangles are believed to symbolize the unconscious, the repressed, the forgotten, or the past, while a garden, on the other hand, "where Nature is subdued, ordered, selected and enclosed . . . is a symbol of consciousness," as Barbara Harrell Carson has discovered in her research on the garden-psyche tangle.[20]

Welty's "A Memory" illustrates the contrast in human terms through the bathers who cavort in uninhibited, grotesque abandon, belying what

18. John Edward Hardy, "Marrying Down in Eudora Welty's Novels," in *Eudora Welty: Critical Essays,* ed. Prenshaw, 93–119; Thomas Landess, "The Function of Taste in the Fiction of Eudora Welty," *Mississippi Quarterly,* XXVI (1973), 557; Westling, *Sacred Groves and Ravaged Gardens,* 165.

19. Gray, *The Literature of Memory,* 183.

20. J. E. Cirlot, *A Dictionary of Symbols,* trans. Jack Sage (New York, 1962), 93, 110. Barbara Harrell Carson's earlier research, "Eudora Welty's Tangled Bank," *South Atlantic Review,* XXXXVIII (1983), 1–18, to which I am indebted for its reference to Cirlot, is now incorporated in her *Eudora Welty: Two Pictures at Once in Her Frame* (Troy, N.Y., 1992), 29–50.

the young narrator's parents believe she sees: only things that have been "strictly coaxed into place" (*CS,* 75). Similarly, in *Delta Wedding* young Laura's role is that of the ingenue who is continually astonished as she is initiated into the many-faceted world of the Delta Fairchilds, a world that often seems exotic, or even grotesque, as the "wax begonias and elephant's-ears" might have seemed to a child in the greenly lit upstairs hall "where it was twilight all the time" (*DW,* 8). Clearly dependent upon Gothic conventions is the episode in which Laura and her cousin Roy visit the decaying mansion Marmion, named for a Gothic novel by Sir Walter Scott, and "haunted" by bees and by Aunt Studney, a mysterious black conjure-woman. To get to this "silent, . . . green rank world" (*DW,* 177), a world that seems alien to Laura, the children must cross, and fall into, the "dark water" of the Yazoo (178), whose name means "river of death."

Welty's characters, like Hawthorne's Young Goodman Brown, must either come to terms with or avoid larger worlds—of family, community, universe—that will otherwise overwhelm them. In Welty's fiction, these worlds are all characterized by a mysterious duality of inner and outer reality that Vande Kieft speaks of in terms of belonging versus alienation; it is basic to "the enigma of man's being—his relation to the universe; what is secret, concealed, inviolable in any human being, resulting in distance or separation from human beings; the puzzles and difficulties we have about our own feelings, our meaning and our identity." The experience of a Welty character who enters a new world is commonly indicated by images of convolution, sometimes in terms of architectural structures, sometimes in terms of the natural world. Carl Jung, comparing the "meandering pattern" of dream images to that in a seventh-century manuscript illustration, asserts that this tangled pattern represents "the process of psychic growth." The illustration he supplies is that of an abstract design of intricately entwined floral and bestial (thus grotesque) images, which are remarkably like the verbal images Welty employs that mix human and animal, or human and vegetable, characteristics: the many bird-human comparisons in "Lily Daw and the Three Ladies," for example; or the boy with "shrimp-colored arms," the "alligator, waddling like a child to school," and the "catfish the size of a baby," the latter three of which appear in the evolution-evoking world of "No Place for You, My Love" (*CS,* 470–71, 472).[21]

John Edward Hardy suggests the combined danger and excitement that might accompany such psychic growth when he notes that Laura

21. Vande Kieft, *Eudora Welty* (1962), 17; Carl G. Jung, *Man and His Symbols,* ed. Carl G. Jung and M.-L. von Franz (New York, 1964), 160.

comes to visit the Fairchilds of *Delta Wedding* like an "adventurer [entering] an enchanted forest." At the beginning of the novel, Laura is presented on the margins of existence in several respects: she has been living in New Orleans, a city large enough to afford anonymity, and thus a virtual no-man's land in the eyes of the Shellmound Fairchilds; since her mother's death, she and her father have constituted a marginal family; and she is now on the verge of adolescence, a time when she will begin to see something of the person she is to become. In fact, Laura's self-conscious *being* and *seeing* provide an important focal point in the novel. With her observation that the novel contrasts "how to be" with "how to see," Vande Kieft suggests a concomitant to the wilderness-clearing duality. The virgin forest and those characters who relate well to it represent the American Adam's version of how to *be* in harmony with the universe, in contrast to the frontiersmen who cleared the wilderness, literally taking apart the new Eden to *see* by way of roads and clearings.[22]

Welty's complex treatment of the impact of family life on an individual's struggle with identity, surrounded but solitary, is rendered chiefly through the metaphor of the natural wilderness. Countering the ambiguous good/evil of the conserving/annihilating family in her fiction are those characters who seem at home in nature, who walk in the woods, who dream, who have something of the deep, wild, and inexplicable in them. These are often the protagonists of Welty's fiction. They represent something ambiguous, indifferent, powerful, and endowed with secret knowledge. They battle against the family's unwittingly sinister tendency to promote homogeneity as an abstract ideal of order at the expense of each individual life, and thus to see each person as *only* part of the whole. Even the title of *Delta Wedding* suggests that the civilizing agency of family will be extended, through a human rite of union, to incorporate the naturally fertile (but still primitive) Delta region.

Most members of the novel's introverted family are concerned with simply *being* Fairchilds. The exception is George (and to some extent his sister-in-law Ellen), for whom life means more than simply existing within family ties. George sees not only the forest but every tiny life therein, not only the world but his integration with it. George is a frontiersman of the spirit, a romantic anachronism, it might seem, in a changing modern South. Not only is he described as a sun-god but also, through Ellen's viewpoint, as Dionysus, "with his shirt torn back and his shoulders

22. John Edward Hardy, "*Delta Wedding* as Region and Symbol," *Sewanee Review,* LX (1952), 401; Ruth M. Vande Kieft, "The Vision of Eudora Welty," *Mississippi Quarterly,* XXVI (1973), 529.

as bare (she thought in a cliché of her girlhood) as a Greek god's, his hair on his forehead as if he were intoxicated, unconscious of the leaf caught there, looking joyous" (*DW,* 166).

Another of Welty's border figures, George is the link in *Delta Wedding* between the human and natural wildernesses. A passage that shows his unique position as somehow between and also a part of both worlds is Dabney's realization of something [George] knew all along . . . —that when you felt, touched, heard, looked at things in the world, and found their fragrances, they themselves made a sort of house within you, which filled with life to hold them, filled with knowledge all by itself" (*DW,* 34). George's special qualities make it impossible for the Fairchilds to possess him or to understand the love he has for the world, "not [for] them! Not them in particular" (*DW,* 37). In spite of Welty's pantheon of "demigods," George is her only male protagonist who achieves some measure of balance between self and family, not because of community sanction but because he manages an affectionate indifference to the confining love that "made them set little traps to catch one another" (16).

Laura, with a nine-year-old orphan's insecurity, yet with an instinctual aversion to the over-intimate but insensitive crush of relatives, recognizes a quality in George that is absent from the family as a whole: "She thought of herself as growing up beside Uncle George, the way some little flowers and vines have picked their tree, and so she felt herself sure of being near him. She knew quite objectively that he would not disown her and uproot her, that he loved any little green vine leaf, and now she felt inner warnings that this was a miracle of safety, strange in any house" (75).

"Demigods" like George resemble such paragons in Faulkner, but their purpose is not to save the forest (as indeed Faulkner's cannot) but often to "save" the female protagonist. Ironically, Welty's preternatural saviors often do as much harm as good. The Boy Scout Loch Morrison, for example, conducts a brutal resuscitation of Easter in "Moon Lake" in a resurrection ritual that is a symbolic rape; and the river god Billy Floyd saves Jenny from the flood in "At the Landing," at the same time so dazzling her with the newfound world of love—as Welty's heroes always dazzle their conquests—that she makes easy prey for the men who frequent the shantyboat where she waits for him. George Fairchild saves his retarded niece Maureen, risking his life performing as Fairchild family hero, but endangering his own marriage in the process, in this central and much-repeated tale of their narrow escape from the speeding "Yellow-Dog" train. The inexplicable (to Robbie) vaunting gesture of this characteristically aloof hero lends to the rescue the aura of an existentialist *acte gratuit,* for his only explanation for his action is, "I'm damned if I wasn't going to stand on that track if I wanted to! Or will again" (*DW,* 187).

George's posturing seems the more singular because bravado, or energetic action of any kind, is inconsistent with the view that the women of the Delta world have of this southern gentleman; he even seems strangely lackadaisical about saving his marriage when Robbie leaves him because of his family-pleasing deed. Instead of seeking reconciliation with his unhappy wife, George simply retires to Shellmound to bask in the family's adoration until Robbie is drawn back to him, exposing to the world her bare need for love in a self-abasing sacrifice that no Fairchild can understand. What can only be read as George's assumption of his own "divine" right has elicited the "death" of Robbie's pride as she descends into the inferno of a Mississippi summer, reduced to walking the long dusty way back to Shellmound after wrecking George's car, intent on her purpose of reclaiming her husband from the midst of his family. To the Fairchilds, who retain "only the romantic and the absurd" in their telling of the tale, Robbie's hurt seems only petty jealousy. But Robbie identifies so closely with George that not only he but she herself is threatened by his role as heroic incarnation of the family mythology.

The Yellow Dog episode represents "the epitome of the false position the Fairchilds put him in," for George is not as free as he seems. It is not only from the danger of the train but from the entrapment of the family mythology that Robbie has wished with "wifely ferocity" to protect him (*DW,* 188), as Gloria wishes to save Jack from the Renfro-Beecham family in *Losing Battles:* "I was going to save him!" Gloria tells the reunion, "From everybody I see this minute!" (*LB,* 198). Indeed, George Fairchild's "intolerant" sounding voice makes him "seem trapped" (*DW,* 169). Yet his refusal either to see his danger or to admit, and thus share, the danger with Robbie, or even to console her own fears—because "he wasn't used to saying anything more to women" (*DW,* 148)—further exasperates his distraught wife. Both Robbie and Gloria, at some intuitive level, sense the danger in the mythmaking power of the culture, which maintains its tenuous security only through its hold on individuals who are being "carefully fabricated" by the kind of carceral formatory processes that Foucault has described in general terms; and the Fairchild family is busily attempting to "fabricate" George in the mold of the "figural hero" that Michael Kreyling has identified as emblematic in southern culture, and thus in the world of *Delta Wedding.*[23]

23. Foucault, *Discipline and Punish,* 217; Michael Kreyling, *Figures of the Hero in Southern Narrative* (Baton Rouge, 1987), 185.

But even the panoptic attention of a society that coerces ordinary humans cannot fully control Welty's demigods. Preternatural spirits in Faulkner are for the most part treated straightforwardly as interacting with humans to remind them of some ancient good or grandeur lost from the earth. They also serve as another reflection of the mingling of past and present that is part of the tangle of all life, including the irrational yet unquenchable sense of the mystery of life and death. In Welty, however, the treatment of such spirit-characters is always ironic. As is the case with all her heroes, any good they do is offset or made ambivalent by some attendant evil. Indeed, the notion that Uncle George is a "miracle of safety" is only Laura's naïve view; for "gods" are no more islands of safety in Welty's fiction than they are in classic mythology.

In addition to George, whose "forehead, nose, and cheeks . . . fiery from the sun" (*DW,* 114) clearly help to mark him as one of Welty's preternatural demigods, there are two other spirit-characters in the novel, one dead and one alive. The spirit of Denis Fairchild, the poet-idol of the family who died young and for whom George is the designated replacement, is thought to haunt the woods he loved; and it is characteristic of the family's attitude toward nature and mystery that they must think of his ghost as "fixed—tied to a tree" (*DW,* 117). Like Eugene Mac-Lain in "Music from Spain," both Denis and George remain "twined . . . in" to the symbolic family tree. It is as though the Fairchilds refuse to acknowledge another level of being than that of the superficial relationships experienced within the family; they must keep even the souls of their dead in a recognized place where they can be readily identified, pinpointed, and thereby stripped of mystery and transposed into what J. E. Cirlot calls "symbol[s] of consciousness." Such a carceral attitude on the part of the family is analogous to that in "A Memory," which reveals a fear of things not "strictly coaxed into place" (*CS,* 75). These phenomena are valorizations of the conscious, rational mind over the mysterious unconscious. Thus Tempe "looked pleased, Dabney thought, as if she were mollified that Denis was dead if his spirit haunted just where she knew" (*DW,* 117). Welty seems to suggest that, in the *Delta Wedding* world of transition from a plantation economy to one of modern industrialism, people take pleasure in denying ancient myths and mysteries (having invented new ones, reflecting the fast-developing myth of southern aristocracy, for example); that their unease in the presence of universal mystery is tragic; and that by such pleasure, occasioned by such unease, they have alienated themselves from a true part of their own nature. Or if they should find ease, it is through a sophisticated act of will, the price of which is the loss of their organic relationship with the physical universe. This lack of sensitivity to the human relation with the natural world, which is countered by the "demigod" characters who force recognition of natural powers, has been noticed by John Alexander Allen.[24]

The lovely girl of hazel eyes, "soiled cheek [and] leafy hair" whom Ellen meets in the woods is also a forest spirit. Ellen, assuming a control that was habitual for the matron of a large plantation family, commands the spirit-girl hiding behind a tree, "Come out here in the light" and "Stand still." The beautiful waif is alive, but she is perceived as ghostly, "shadowy." In meeting her, Ellen feels a mysterious "cool breath as if a rabbit had run over her grave, or if someone had seen her naked. She felt sometimes like a mother to the world, all that was on her! Yet she had never felt a mother to a child this lovely" (*DW*, 70–71). In Ellen's thoughts as she cautions the lost girl not to "bring mistakes on [her]self" by wandering alone in the woods, we sense Ellen's own vague fear for (and of?) the lovely "ambiguous" girl "when she touched at their life, ran through their woods" (71, 80).

In addition, the complex scene of Ellen's warning to the girl may, by her recourse to the language of female solidarity and maternal wisdom, be viewed as a prophetic narrative rupture of the mythic archetype of seduction. The mother-child dyad is, according to Rachel Blau DuPlessis, "a major strategy for breaking the [Oedipal] sequence of the romance plot in twentieth-century fiction," and the significance of this female-female configuration seems the more emphatic because of its echo in the name of Partheny, the old black family retainer who banishes the Fairchild women as "Nothin'" and herself presides over the bridal dressing of Dabney (*DW*, 210). Parthenogenetic motherhood (reproduction without male participation) is an idea often used in nineteenth-century literature of female utopias, such as Charlotte Perkins Gilman's *Herland*. The image, which, as DuPlessis notes, suggests the absence of males as the "center of emotional and political life," accurately characterizes the Fairchild family in *Delta Wedding*.[25]

Although Peggy Prenshaw has pointed out that the identification of Welty's women with the life cycle contributes to the positive theme of renewal, she also correctly notes the sacrificial nature of women's place in this process. It is no doubt Ellen's current pregnancy, indicative of both her inevitable centrality and vulnerability to the process, that leads

---

24. Cirlot, *A Dictionary of Symbols*, 110; Allen, "The Other Way to Live," in *Eudora Welty: Critical Essays*, ed. Prenshaw, 27, 29.

25. DuPlessis, *Writing Beyond the Ending*, 83, 180.

her to hint at the source of danger to the lost girl, and perhaps to all women, when she explains why the girl should not be in the forest alone: "I was speaking about men—men, our lives" (*DW*, 71). Although Ellen means to warn her of the danger of male sexuality, what is unspoken perhaps is Ellen's recognition of uncontrolled *female* sexuality that the girl represents: the penetration of Shellmound's borders, which is an inversion of the physics of patriarchal power that may be somehow more unsettling to Ellen than what J. A. Bryant, Jr., has pointed out as the historically more conventional *fait accompli* of Troy, the hill-country "Trojan" who has captured his Helen. The mysterious girl's "power" is short-lived, but Ellen's moment with her in the forest is so charged that Welty has to remind us that time is passing: "The faint wind from the bayou blew in the girl's hair she had shaken out, marking somehow the time going by in the woods" (*DW*, 70). We realize that we have experienced time standing still for Ellen in an epiphany such as Virginia Woolf described in *The Waves:* one that "happens in one second and lasts forever." Such an act of female penetration, which counters and challenges that of traditional male penetration of the matriarchy and which happens in a timeless moment, constitutes a narrative pattern based on space instead of time, a pattern of violated space to which Welty will return in subsequent fiction.[26]

Since Ellen cannot make the wood nymph "mind," she shoos her away as she would shoo a stray chicken from the porch; and she tries to dismiss the troubling thoughts provoked by her presence. When George crosses the girl's path, however, assuming his godlike prerogative and fulfilling Ellen's prophetic warning, he accepts her as a gift of the forest; takes her, he tells Ellen, "over to the old Argyle gin and [sleeps] with her" (*DW*, 79); then he discards her as unconsciously as the train that soon kills her and flings her "off in the blackberry bushes" (*DW*, 218). Thus we, with Ellen, see the dangerous side of George that sometimes prompts him, "the kindest of them all, [to] say a deliberate wounding thing . . . which was the same as a wild, free kind of self-assertion" (79).

Although George is "intimate" with the forest spirit, as he is with the forest itself, Ellen comes to understand that he is "not intimate with [the Fairchild] houseful at all, and that they did not know it" (81). Perhaps his serene detachment prevents real intimacy with anyone, and it

26. Peggy Whitman Prenshaw, "Woman's World, Man's Place: The Fiction of Eudora Welty," in *Eudora Welty: A Form of Thanks,* ed. Louis Dollarhide and Ann J. Abadie (Jackson, 1979), 48; J. A. Bryant, Jr., "The Recovery of the Confident Narrator: *A Curtain of Green* to *Losing Battles,*" in *Eudora Welty: Critical Essays,* ed. Prenshaw, 72; Virginia Woolf, *The Waves* (1921; rpr. New York, 1978), 240.

may explain an anguish in Robbie that seems more profound than can have been caused by the train incident alone. George moves easily, independently, between worlds and people—the forest spirit and his wife not excepted. The novel's resolution confirms George's intermediary, life-giving/taking function by the suggestion that he will move back to the Delta, taking over the Grove from the resident aunt hearth goddesses, and replacing cotton with new crops to forge a new wedding between the Delta wilderness and the family. His partnership with his new brother-in-law in the venture will be one of equals in many ways, for George is no more a stranger to brutal passions than is the lower-class plantation overseer, whose job includes mediating knife fights among the black field hands. The enigma of George may derive from the fact that only part of him attempts to be the calm, heroic figure that the Fairchilds expect of him. In terms of the paradigm of the southern "figural" hero they wish him to be, and whose duty, as Michael Kreyling has pointed out, is "wise mating," he is flawed by his intimate commerce with the mundane world, including his uncontrolled mating. He fails in this not because of his "unwise" copulation with the wild and indifferent forest girl but because of his marriage to the lower-class Robbie, the latter a fact that threatens to adulterate the clan's "pure" bloodline by mixing it with that of the "wild life" he has trapped, or who has perhaps trapped him: the "catch" of the Fairchild clan.[27]

When Robbie penetrates the labyrinth of family where her husband is "lost" to her, she lets in a bird; and its beating wings in the artificial wilderness of the house are symbolic of Robbie's own inarticulate fury at the Fairchilds' cool appraisal of her passionate love. The incident has been foreshadowed by the bird's counterpart in George's flying words, which "shot out like one bird, then beat about the walls, [and] struck in the rooms upstairs," a trope that extends the wilderness imagery even to the speech of the characters (*DW,* 102). These pervasive comparisons of the family to the wilderness and its various manifestations amount to an extended metaphor in *Delta Wedding.* The family as a whole determinedly ignores the mystery in all of life, and its members worry each other with trivia as though they were rattling bones to frighten away evil spirits in an almost petrified forest of tradition. The novel's setting in a clearing of the Mississippi woods forces the comparison of the family's stubborn indifference to individual need with the nonmanipulatory indifference of the real wilderness and, by extension, with those characters who are in tune with that more elemental order of things.

27. Kreyling, *Figures of the Hero,* 109.

Dabney senses that her Uncle George knows "another way to be" (*DW,* 33); but she only briefly imagines this other, freer, lifestyle before entrusting herself to a traditional female role in the bonds of marriage. In the same way, Nina, in "Moon Lake," momentarily contemplates the relative freedom of orphans, using an expression Welty had made memorable in *Delta Wedding:* "The other way to live" (*CS,* 361). The ironically named Shelley, however, fears the confining world her sister is entering and perceives marriage to be "like a door closing to her [from which] her desire fled . . . to an open place—not from one room to another room with its door, but to an opening wood, with weather—with change, beauty" (*DW,* 220). Welty foregrounds the contrasting images of place as either monotonously ordered or excitingly varied when Ellen, a transplanted Virginian, meditates on the maze of dancers at the wedding in which her daughters seem lost to her because they "all looked alike . . . [in this] season of changeless weather, of the changeless world, in a land without hill or valley. How could she ever know anything of her own daughters, how find them, like this?" (*DW,* 221).

Both Shelley's longing for escape from familial entanglement to an open and uneven terrain and Ellen's enigmatic but clearly fond memory of the hills of home are images of female assertion through landscape that have many historical precedents in women's writing. Ellen Moers sees the female landscape as a sexually suggestive but complicated topography that no simple image such as phallus or vagina can describe. She recognizes fictional settings of high ground and open expanses as signifying self-assertion to the woman writer, citing the moors of Emily Brontë, the prairies and mesas of Willa Cather, and the high African desert plateaus of Isak Dinesen as examples of landscapes that give expression to the kind of "oceanic feelings" of universal oneness that are often experienced on the open seas. Moers finds only one such female landscape in Welty's fiction, that of Laura's view from the train in *Delta Wedding;* but there are many others, such as the equally wide expanse Laurel views from the train in *The Optimist's Daughter* and Gabriella's vision of a high place even while she is in the belly of the ship in "Going to Naples."[28]

Thus Ellen's vision at the wedding dance articulates one of the most consistent contrasts in Welty's fiction: that of stultifying conformity opposed with an ideal of self-confident identity that makes possible the heroic separateness that is not alienation, as the live oak is separate from and yet integral to the forest. Many of Welty's male characters drift in and

28. Moers, *Literary Women,* 255–63.

out of family or community, but they remain essentially outsiders and thus are either fantasized ("pin-up") heroes or anti-heroes. More often it is her female characters who achieve, or show promise of achieving, varying degrees of success at heroic balancing of private integrity with communal ties, as John Alexander Allen has shown; and, significantly, such balance is best accomplished by the female characters in her most recent, and most feminist, novels, *Losing Battles* and *The Optimist's Daughter*.[29]

Of all Welty's longer fiction, *Delta Wedding* is perhaps the most concentrated, most in need of being read, as John Edward Hardy says, "close, like a poem." Its simple surface narrative—a lush pastoral, rich with mythic possibilities—is endlessly enriched when read with full knowledge of the early Natchez Trace stories that depend upon Gothic romance conventions, legend, and folk traditions. And, likewise, the other stories bear reexamination in the light of the concentrated poetic force of this novel. In Welty's *Losing Battles,* for example, the circle is the basic image for the family; and that too is related to the forest in the growth rings of the giant *bois d'arc* tree which, as Michael Kreyling notes, "record the lives and events of the family and hold all generations in permanent and equal relation." This use of the image is reminiscent of W. J. Cash's description of the South itself as a tree with age rings, and thus as continuous with the past, and of Cash's extension of that concept of continuity to "the mind of the South."[30] The complicated and imprisoning family memories of *The Optimist's Daughter* also are better understood if viewed in the light of the family wilderness metaphor. Even the bird-in-the house scene, used again by Welty in *The Optimist's Daughter,* takes on a more complex significance than the popular folk belief that it is symbolic of death, when it is considered in the context of *Delta Wedding* and the bird that symbolizes Robbie's terror in the forest of Fairchilds.

In *Delta Wedding,* Welty extends the image of the wilderness in ways that acknowledge their ancestry in Cooper's and Faulkner's seminal complexities; but the most striking characteristic of *Delta Wedding* may be that underneath the veneer of the familiarly patterned southern novel of manners is that sense of ambivalence that haunts the modern novel. Noel Polk cannot express without oxymora what he calls the "tender savagery

---

29. John Alexander Allen, "Eudora Welty: The Three Moments," in *A Still Moment: Essays on the Art of Eudora Welty,* ed. John F. Desmond (Metuchen, N.J., 1978), 19.

30. Hardy, "*Delta Wedding* as Region and Symbol," 406; Michael Kreyling, "Myth and History: The Foes of *Losing Battles,*" *Mississippi Quarterly,* XXVI (1973), 641; W. J. Cash, *The Mind of the South* (New York, 1941).

of family relationships" and the "ferocious possessiveness of love" in the novel; and Michael Kreyling speaks of the family in terms of a "double-edged weapon." *Delta Wedding* provides a prime example of what Sara McAlpin calls the deceptive surface of Welty's fiction, which conceals at first view the negative functioning of family. From a narrative that is at best enchantingly poetic and at worst hypnotically deceptive, we see modern man and woman glossing over or succumbing to that rapacious element in human nature that can harden into the intractable rings of family. Realist that she is, Welty includes this characteristic as a basic unit of her representation of human society as a highly organized, tenacious life form, protected, and perhaps buried, under a shelly mound of tradition, which is occasionally startled and invigorated by the penetration of other, more primitive, incorrigible life forces.[31]

Delta Wedding (1946) is an early pivotal work in Welty's development, her first full-length novel, coming after two volumes of stories and her book-length fable, *The Robber Bridegroom.* After the first volume of stories, *A Curtain of Green* (1941), when publishers were already begging Eudora Welty for a novel, Katherine Anne Porter said that there was no reason that she should write one, no reason that she should not simply concentrate on her obvious talent for the short story. But, as Michael Kreyling tells us, at the repeated urging of editors and, finally, of her agent, Welty finally did turn to the novel to develop greater networks of theme. *Delta Wedding* is significant not only as the first of Welty's novels of family, but also for its influence on her subsequent short-story cycle, *The Golden Apples* (1947), which turns around the MacLain family of Morgana, Mississippi. Welty has, then, created in her stories a microcosm of relationships in which to carry out what amount to experiments in the techniques of modern fiction, including the use of narrative designs that implement the theme of the family as an ambivalent wilderness, of family, even in its role of nurturer, as society's most basic instrument for imposing closure on individual freedoms and narrative control of an individual's own story.[32]

Such narrative control is accomplished by the carceral network of "walls, space, institutions, rules, discourse," as described by Foucault, a

31. Noel Polk, "Water, Wanderers, and Weddings: Love in Eudora Welty," in *Eudora Welty: A Form of Thanks,* ed. Dollarhide and Abadie, 99; Kreyling, *Welty's Achievement,* 156; Sara McAlpin, "Family in Eudora Welty's Fiction," *Southern Review,* XVIII (1982), 480–94.

32. Katherine Anne Porter, Introduction to *Selected Stories of Eudora Welty* (New York, 1954), xviii–xix; Michael Kreyling, *Author and Agent: Eudora Welty & Diarmuid Russell* (New York, 1991), 95–111.

network that works at every hierarchic level of society and makes of a community, then, a sort of ward or prison which, by coercing behavior, forces human beings into preestablished roles. It is perhaps especially prevalent in societies in transition and desperately trying to hold on to a communal coherence that is disappearing, as Andrew Lytle said that the "coherent view of life" began to disappear with the coming of the automobile; but it also works in ordinary times as the force of *communitatus,* "the state of recognizing shared humanity," as Carey Wall has demonstrated in terms of "June Recital." [33] Although the family is the basic unit in which proper relationships and corresponding behavioral limits are learned and enforced, the concept of the extended family of community as a discrete and conscious agent of this carceral network is validated in southern literature by the many communal representations of point of view—like, for example, that in Faulkner's "A Rose for Emily." Following in this tradition, Eudora Welty establishes the community voice at the outset of *The Golden Apples* through the first-person narrative in "Shower of Gold" of Katie Rainey, the self-appointed *porte-parole* of the town of Morgana, Mississippi. Through her we become aware of the community's received wisdom about what constitutes an orderly society and what threatens it. The major tension in the stories of *The Golden Apples* is that between the confinement of individuals to expected patterns of behavior that results in a homogeneous community and the several human passions that exceed the approved limits and threaten the comfortable status quo of the town and its official representatives. In terms of the contemporary linguistic theory of discourse analysis, which examines the grammar of a text to determine whether a character acts as, or is viewed as, subject (self-controlled) or object (other-controlled), one might say that the community sees itself as subject—that is, as self-evidently authorized to exert control over its own text, or narrative, and hence of the subtexts of each individual life story within the circle of its influence. To illustrate the concept in terms of the kind of graphic physical images more consonant with Welty's practice, one might use Kepler's and Newton's "two-body" scientific theory; that is, in the case of a satellite body (an individual's small mass) in the orbit of a larger body (the large mass of a community), the two exert equal and opposite influences resulting in a relatively unchanging relationship. The satellite would need an impetus from another source to achieve escape velocity. When such

33. Andrew Lytle, *The Hero with the Private Parts* (Baton Rouge, 1966), 173; Carey Wall, "'June Recital': Virgie Rainey Saved," in *Eudora Welty: The Eye of the Storyteller,* ed. Trouard, 17.

impetus is provided and the larger body's control fails, the human community will tend toward the unnatural (in terms of the natural laws of the universe) response of refusing to acknowledge that failure, preferring instead to preserve the façade of "normality" to which it subscribes. This imagined "normality," then, ironically reveals the point at which the scientific analogy fails when applied to the human situation.

The community may secretly experience some vicarious pleasure in the forbidden adventures of its renegades, but it officially denies the existence of all who cannot be neatly accommodated within the carefully ordered society. The conscious self-delusion inherent in this attitude is evident, in "Shower of Gold," from Katie Rainey's early comment about Morgana's view of the errant King MacLain's lifelong wanderlust, sexual antics, and consequent neglect of his wife, Snowdie: "nobody wanted to think, around her, that he treated her that way" (CS, 263). King is a Zeus-like womanizer who is always described in terms of his dazzling gold-white appearance, while Snowdie is a gentle albino whose weak eyes cannot abide even the light of day. The common expectations and beliefs about their unlikely union are apparent in Katie's speculations that, before their marriage, "people more or less expected [Snowdie] to teach school: not marry" (CS, 265) and that, during King's perpetual wanderings, "we heard things from out in the world that we listened to but that still didn't mean we believed them" (CS, 267). King's personality is as mysterious as any Welty has created; and commentators have not agreed upon whether his character is designed to reflect the transcendent potential of all Morgana "beholders" of his antics, as Merrill Skaggs believes, or to show him as a catalyst on the community, as Danièle Pitavy-Souques asserts. Of Katie's narration, Mme Pitavy says that "sa fonction est en effet moins d'éclairer la personalité de l'homme, que de montrer l'effet qu'elle produit sur la communauté." [34]

Katie herself may have been one of King's conquests, and certainly her (their?) daughter, Virgie, seems his spiritual descendant. In "June Recital," set ten or twelve years later than "Shower of Gold," flashbacks reveal that, by her unkempt appearance and her "airs of wildness," Virgie has consistently rebelled against the town's conforming spirit. Her musical virtuosity (as well as her determined effort not to care about it), her dirty neck, and her stewed peach sandwiches equally mark her as "exciting as a gypsy" (CS, 291). And by the time she is a teenager, her sexual

34. Merrill Maguire Skaggs, "Morgana's Apples and Pears," in Eudora Welty: Critical Essays, ed. Prenshaw, 232; Pitavy-Souques, "'Shower of Gold,' ou les ambiguités de la narration," 73.

exploits begin to resemble King's. The single-minded character of the Morgana community, intent on maintaining order through its concern for coherence (and also intent on ignoring what it cannot control) is apparent in what young Loch Morrison perceives as the noisy "drowning out [of] something" by the women in the "duck-like line" hurrying to the Rook party (*CS*, 280, 281). What their noise obliterates is the sound of "Für Elise" being picked out on the piano next door by an aged and outcast Miss Eckhart just before she sets fire to the piano in the room of the vacant MacLain house, where her hopes had been confined before she was consigned to the county poor farm.

The ladies are also officially oblivious to the tryst going on upstairs above Miss Eckhart between Virgie and the young sailor Kewpie Moffitt. They ignore both transgressions, as they have previously ignored Virgie's inexplicable musical talent. Although Miss Eckhart has said that her star pupil should leave Morgana and develop her extraordinary gift, the provincial community is incredulous that Virgie should escape her place in their scheme: "How could Virgie be heard from, in the world? And 'the world'! Where did Miss Eckhart think she was now?" (*CS*, 303). The Presbyterian church's college music scholarship is awarded to the less talented but hard-working (and Presbyterian) Cassie Morrison, who rationalizes her luck by remembering that "the Raineys were [only] Methodists" (*CS*, 306). Both Miss Eckhart and Virgie seem indifferent to community approval; and the punitive community reaction, according to Katie, is that "perhaps nobody wanted Virgie Rainey to be anything in Morgana any more than they had wanted Miss Eckhart to be, and they were the two of them still linked together by people's saying that" (*CS*, 306).

Miss Eckhart, the German piano teacher of unknown origin, who has never "allowed herself to be called by her first name. . . . Or . . . belonged to a church that had even been heard of. . . . Or . . . been married to anybody at all, just the awfullest man—like Miss Snowdie MacLain, that everybody could feel sorry for," and who goes "down out of sight" once her pupils leave her, is a mysterious affront to a community in which "most destinies were known to everybody" (*CS*, 308). Even Miss Eckhart's personal life is tragically regulated by Morgana's sense of decorum. When she falls in love with Mr. Sissum, the relationship is foredoomed: "What could they either one have done? They couldn't go to church together; the Sissums were Presbyterians from the beginning of time and Miss Eckhart belonged to some distant church with a previously unheard-of name, the Lutheran. She could not go to the picture show with Mr. Sissum because he was already at the picture show. He played the music there every evening after the store closed" (*CS,* 297). Nothing in the community's scheme of order provides an acceptable outlet for her emotion; and although we are not privy to Mr. Sissum's thoughts, we learn that he "was drowned in the Big Black River one summer—fell out of his boat, all alone" (*CS,* 297). Even the gentle Snowdie, who plays a virtuous Penelope to King MacLain's Odysseus, acts as enforcer of decorum when Miss Eckhart's emotion erupts at Mr. Sissum's funeral. The grieving teacher's silent scream and headlong rush to the edge of the grave suggest a feeling that "failed to match the feelings of everybody else. It was not the same as sorrow" (*CS,* 299).

The emotion revealed by Miss Eckhart's silent scream is indeed "not the same as sorrow"; it more nearly suggests the gothic terror of long confinement, the pain of her every bondage: to mother, to music, to Virgie, and to a society that has held her without admitting her. The unvoiced scream may also symbolize her unspoken love, a love that "never did anybody any good" (*CS,* 307), and her analogous yearning to release her passion for music to an equally passionate disciple. But Virgie, the only qualified candidate, refuses this commitment as she has refused all bonds. In fact, Miss Eckhart's despairing grimace is related to the open-mouthed yearning after the water of life Eugene MacLain exhibits in "Music from Spain" (*CS,* 409), and to the horrible "silent yell" that the aged King MacLain makes "at everything—including death, not leaving it out," in "The Wanderers" (*CS,* 446). Even in this inarticulate protest, however, Miss Eckhart is controlled by Snowdie, the official community martyr, whose "grip tightened on her hand and stayed tightened until Miss Eckhart got over it" (*CS,* 299). But Snowdie's ministrations cannot save the music teacher's place in Morgana; for, notwithstanding Miss Eckhart's long service to the community, afterward "some ladies stopped their little girls from learning any more music" (*CS,* 300). Her public display has reminded them of her thinly veiled, and potentially subversive, difference from them.

In addition to her unorthodox passions, Miss Eckhart, as victim of another's violent eruption, bears the stigma of an unforgotten attack on her that makes her presence a continuing embarrassment in Morgana. When a "crazy Negro had jumped out of the school hedge and got Miss Eckhart, . . . [who] had been walking by herself after dark . . . [,] people . . . wished she had moved away. . . . But Miss Eckhart stayed, as though she considered one thing not so much more terrifying than another" (*CS,* 301). Morgana cannot tolerate her *indifference* to the personal affront of rape, because her attitude makes impossible the community's patronizing tolerance. Further, Morgana cannot forgive Miss Eckhart's *difference,* including *her* tolerance of a racial/sexual outrage that has been a fear of white southerners since the days of slavery. Miss Eckhart is a mystery who makes the entire town uncomfortable, and thus she is doomed to remain an outsider. Conversely, the "freedom" implied by the several sexual affairs of the ironically named Virgie, while not condoned, must be ignored as part of the community's attempt to hold the native Virgie within bounds.

The fact that Virgie and Miss Eckhart are musicians is important to a special facet of Welty's theme of enclosure and escape: that of the artist's position in society. In "Music from Spain," Eugene seems a likely *porte-parole* for the author when, in an interior monologue, he asserts that "the life of an artist, or a foreigner, or a wanderer, [are] all the same thing" (*CS*, 409). But another facet of the artist's alienation is presented symbolically, and with more immediacy, in "June Recital" in "the smell of new sheet music [that comes] out swift as an imprisoned spirit" from the cabinet during music lessons (*CS*, 289). With these two images, Welty shows the danger of both exposure and enclosure to the independent personalities she makes the protagonists of her fiction; and the use of the word *swift* suggests a connection to other imprisoned wild spirits—for example, those symbolized by images like the chimney swift caught in the McKelva home in *The Optimist's Daughter.* The release of the "imprisoned spirit" in the music through the energy of the artist, as she plays what is apparently Beethoven,[35] is depicted in the passion that transforms Miss Eckhart's face into "a sightless face, one for music only." Inspired by a sudden violent morning storm, she gives such an impromptu performance only once, alarming her pupils, who think "something had burst out, unwanted, exciting, from the wrong person's life . . . [,] some brilliant thing too splendid for Miss Eckhart" (*CS*, 301). Thus Miss Eckhart's story, like that of the adult Virgie, represents what has been called the "negative" of the romance narrative: one in which "all avenues of apparent freedom—including adultery and the artist's life, which is itself half an expression of sexual freedom—[lead] to the dead end of oppressive ties."[36]

The alarm of Miss Eckhart's students is representative of the general attitude toward the flash of any passion that disturbs the calm surface of culture, and it is an attitude that results in the defensive stance of the music pupils' mothers. At the June recital that provides the name for the second story in *The Golden Apples,* the threat of the community's inhibiting sense of order is evident in such passages as that which describes

35. Rubin, "Art and Artistry in Morgana, Mississippi," 66.
36. DuPlessis, *Writing Beyond the Ending,* 17.

the annual event as one attended "in full *oppression* [by] . . . all female Morgana" (*CS*, 311, emphasis added). It is not that they do not appreciate music, or at least the "cultural" idea of it; rather, the target of their purposeful oppression is the passionate spirit that seeks no sanction from the guardians of culture, a spirit especially exemplified by the artist, who is represented in Welty's fiction as a wandering outsider but also as a creative life-affirmer who attempts to energize a cultural and/or social wasteland. The artist in Welty's fiction, who in most cases is female, is not only inevitably set apart from society because she actually cannot be known and explained; she is also self-enclosed by the singular focus of her own aims. The resident outsider is a role Welty herself knows well; as James Gray Watson points out, "Like a stranger within the gates of her village worlds, [Welty] sees the resources and the risks of shared community more clearly than those [southern writers] who have gone away."[37] Ironically, a female life-enhancing outsider seems to threaten the established order that tries to contain her, while an errant male with similar qualities may be viewed by the same community with amused tolerance or even vicarious pleasure.

Welty depicts both males and females, in some measure, as victims of the various confinements and estrangements of the human community. The adolescent Loch Morrison, confined to his room with malaria, dreams of a time "when his sister was so sweet, . . . when they loved each other in a different world, a boundless, trustful country all its own, where no mother or father came, either through sweetness or impatience—different altogether from his solitary world now, where he looked out all eyes like Argus, on guard everywhere" (*CS*, 280). Loch, an adolescent artist figure like the young girl in "A Memory," turns his upstairs sickroom into a vantage point from which he frames and narrates to an imagined audience some important scenes of the story—both Virgie's lovemaking and Miss Eckhart's firemaking. His status as outsider is confirmed in "Moon Lake" where he is the lone white male—the vaunting fifteen-year-old Perseus, a "Boy Scout and Life Saver" (*CS*, 342)—in a camp of adolescent girls. In "The Wanderers" we learn that the adult Loch lives in New York City and "likes it there" (*CS*, 449). Welty does not follow him to the city, but we can speculate on his fate by the light of the tragic stories of other characters who dwell in, "escape" to, or travel through cities. An early example from *A Curtain of Green* is Howard, in "Flowers for Marjorie," who murders his young wife out of his sheer desperation at being unable to find work in the city to provide for her and their

37. James G. Watson, "The American Short Story: 1930–1945," in *The American Short Story, 1900–1945: A Critical History,* ed. Philip Stevick (Boston, 1984), 144.

coming child. We will perhaps refrain from presuming too much about Loch's "liberation" from Morgana if we remember the plight of characters in, for example, "Death of a Traveling Salesman," "The Hitchhikers," and "Music from Spain." Attesting to the urban malaise of Welty's characters is Albert Devlin, who believes that Loch settles in New York after the war to "nurture his discontent." Similarly, Jan Nordby Gretlund, while pointing out that, for good or ill, the small town is interested in the affairs and conversations of all its citizens, notes that "in his San Francisco exile among the living dead of the City, Eugene MacLain is in the most frightening of worlds."[38] In addition, Laurel, in *The Optimist's Daughter,* after twenty years in Chicago, has escaped neither the hold of memory nor that of the unrealistic ideals fostered by cultural mythology about the proper "place" of women.

Welty devotes two stories in *The Golden Apples* to the twin sons of King MacLain, each of whom experiences a different type of confinement from which he attempts to escape. In "The Whole World Knows," Randall "Ran" MacLain's marriage to Jinny Love Stark, the daughter of the town's leading family, has devolved into a painful tangle of emotions. Jinny is openly unfaithful to Ran, and he has left her. Frankly unhappy, he cannot stay away from Jinny, but he often brings eighteen-year-old Maideen Sumrall with him to visit in the Stark home. The situation puts him at the mercy of the town's blame and pity. With great economy in this brief story, Welty suggests the complexity of human entanglement by multiple points of view: Ran's own interior monologue, which frames the story and is addressed to his wandering father, and the views of three women. Miss Perdita Mayo's view sounds like the voice of human reason and charity, but it disguises Morgana's habit of ignoring, and thus devaluing, the "thing[s] of the flesh" that have always entrapped human beings. She compares Ran's case with that of his father and urges him to forgive Jinny: "Your mother never bore your father a single grudge in her life, and he made her life right hard. . . . We're all human on earth. . . . Ah, I'm a woman that's been clear around the world in my rocking chair, and I tell you we all get surprises now and then. . . . It's a thing of the flesh not the spirit, it'll·pass" (*CS,* 376). Miss Perdita, whose astute observations about human nature are aided by her position as the local telephone operator, prophetically cautions Ran not to "ruin a *country* girl in the bargin" simply because he himself is unhappy (*CS,* 381, Welty's emphasis).

Glossing over the hurt of the lifelong unfaithfulness of her own husband, Ran's mother, Snowdie, ironically expresses the historical double

38. Devlin, *Eudora Welty's Chronicle,* 135; Gretlund, "Out of Life into Fiction," 53.

standard of the community in words that provide the title of the story. As he is driving with Maideen down into the dark, "deep as a tunnel" riverfront world, a surrealistically described landscape much like those of "No Place for You, My Love" and "At the Landing," Ran's mind tunnels back to the memory of his mother's warning against going back to his wife. He recalls the words of her argument: "The whole world knows what she did to you. It's different from when it's the man" (*CS,* 390). But his mother-in-law, Miss Lizzie Stark, suggests the true complexity of the situation and her own feeling of helplessness to untangle it when, telling Randall about a hand of cards she played, she begins, unaccountably, to weep: "You men," she says, "You got us beat in the end. . . . We'd know you through and through except we never know what ails you. . . . Of course I see what Jinny's doing, the fool, but you ailed first. You just got her answer to it, Ran." Confirming her analysis is Ran's immediate unspoken response, directed to the always absent King MacLain: "And what ails me I don't know, Father, unless maybe you know" (*CS,* 385). Ran points to what may be Jinny's ostensible imperviousness to, or perhaps inability to admit to, any specific problem as instrumental to the trouble in their marriage: "When I couldn't give her something she wanted she would hum a little tune. In our room, her voice would go low and soft to complete disparagement" (*CS,* 385). Since her own family, the Starks, are the leading benefactors of the community, it is more likely personal, perhaps sexual, than material needs that distress Jinny. Certainly Ran does not possess the sexual "magic" for which his father is notorious.[39]

In her own way Jinny reflects the community's customary refusal to face life's uncouth passions; she "escapes" the bonds of culture, such as marriage, through an extramarital affair that means no more to her than does Ran's love, and through her inexplicable detachment from life. Thus she is a parody of Welty's resident artist outsiders. Like Miss Eckhart, she finds "one thing not so much more [meaningful] than another," a fact that enrages her passionate husband, as George's detachment enrages Robbie in *Delta Wedding.* Jinny assumes the distance of an artist but has not the artist's moral passion; Ran, on the other hand, attempts to escape the reality of his passion's failure by fantasizing the murders of his wife, her lover, and himself, and by his ambiguous prayer that is at least partly addressed to King MacLain: "Father! Dear God wipe it clean. Wipe it clean, wipe it out. Don't let it be" (*CS,* 386). Thus, when he cannot possess Jinny even within marriage, the agony of separateness within love

39. Vande Kieft, *Eudora Welty* (1987), 105; Julia L. Demmin and Daniel Curley, "Golden Apples and Silver Apples," in *Eudora Welty: Critical Essays,* ed. Prenshaw, 248.

transforms Ran, in the words of Danièle Pitavy-Souques, from the "fascinated" into the "fascinator" whose gaze "kills," as Perseus killed the Medusa.[40]

Ran's inability to act to restore his marriage and his feeling of being "cornered" by the kindness of Maideen lead him to take her, while she sleeps, across the "nineteen miles . . . and the thirteen little bridges and the Big Black" River (*CS*, 387) to Vicksburg, where he forces her to drink rum and Coke and then rapes her. As she sobs "for herself," he simply goes to sleep, unaware that she feels violated. Even in Ran's retrospect it seems not guilt but annoyance that makes him complain, "How was I to know she would go and hurt herself?" (*CS*, 392). Like his father, he acts only out of his own need, dropping Maideen after using her, as the swan drops Leda from his great beak in Yeats's poem, and as George Fairchild discards the wood sprite in *Delta Wedding*. But whereas King MacLain's Zeus-like adventures always seem to engender life, Ran's touch brings death; thus he is a failed life-giver, although he is still attributed mythic status by the community. Ironically, Ran even benefits from the tragedy: it lends him an aura of mystery like that of his legendary father. In "The Wanderers," he has become the mayor of Morgana, elected because "once he had taken advantage of a country girl who had died a suicide. . . . They had voted for him for that—for his glamour and his story, for being a MacLain and the bad twin, for marrying a Stark and then for ruining a girl and the thing she did. . . . They voted for the revelation; it had made their hearts faint, and they would assert it again. Ran knew that every minute, there in the door he stood it" (*CS*, 433).

Maideen has been caught in the clichéd romantic triangle and plays out the role of the sentimental heroine who, once dishonored, must die. But Ran, like George of *Delta Wedding*, is caught too, in the mythology of the community that honors him for playing a role that feeds its fantasies—that of a demigod despoiler of women. Unlike his infamous father, whose bravado is apparently part of a consciously assumed persona, Ran is an uneasy hero-villain; but unable or unwilling to escape his community-ordained destiny, he has simply "stood it."

Eugene MacLain, whose story is told in "Music from Spain," is the sensitive MacLain twin who, as a child, had taken piano lessons from Miss Eckhart. His own sense of displacement because of his father's constant absence may have prompted his move to San Francisco, where he has married his landlady. Eugene and Emma's little daughter, Fan, has

---

40. Danièle Pitavy-Souques, "Technique as Myth: The Structure of *The Golden Apples*," in *Eudora Welty: Critical Essays*, ed. Prenshaw, 264–65.

recently died of a sudden fever, precipitating a crisis in his marriage that has caused him unaccountably to slap Emma one morning at breakfast. Later, as he walks toward the jewelry store where he works at repairing watches, he ponders the act that has stopped time for him: the slap that he now personifies as "a part of him [that has] slipped loose from him, turned around and looked at him in the form of a question" (*CS*, 394). He tries to answer that question as he skips work and wanders the streets of San Francisco all day in the company of a Spanish guitarist he has heard in concert the night before, and whom he has happened upon once again just in time to pull him from the path of a streetcar. The two have no language in common but seem to need none; ironically, Eugene is more in tune with the Spanish musician, whose name he does not know, than with his own wife. The strangely silent odyssey of the two men through the city allows for Eugene's story to unfold by means of his interior monologue, set against a background of mysteriously silent "music" that he "hears" as if the silent Spaniard were some mythic Pan or legendary pied piper.

The displaced Mississippian is caught in a double bind in which he feels both locked in and locked out. His claustrophobia is apparent when he surveys the city that "often . . . [looks] open and free"; and yet he sees the very hills and clouds as "any man's walls still" (*CS*, 407). Although he has "escaped" the confines of Morgana and its communal family, he is caught in the prison-world. Like Aldo Scampo, who is seasick and confined to his cabin on the open sea in "Going to Naples," Eugene is an example of the failures to which humans are "probably doomed," because "the essence of their nature [is] frail" (*CS*, 584). The absolute isolation in which Welty places Eugene—virtually incommunicado in an urban wilderness—is a situation like that which some penal experts believe to be conducive to an individual's confrontation of his own conscience, especially if attended by the minimal attentions of someone with a sympathetic posture. The monastic Auburnian prison system, for example, is characterized by individual cells with work and meals in common, but all activities are conducted in absolute silence except for minimal conversation with a warder.[41] Eugene's Spanish "warder," who indeed assumes the lead role in their day's wandering, is too enclosed in his own pain to give any more comfort than his physical presence offers. But that is enough, for Eugene confronts his conscience through the reflection of himself he imagines in the Spaniard.

Eugene is at once a prisoner and an outcast in relation to his wife also, because although he has mourned "the same thing she mourned, he was

41. Foucault, *Discipline and Punish*, 238–39.

not to be let in" (*CS,* 399) to share Emma's grief. As Eugene and the Spaniard escape the city's boundaries and climb high into the hills overlooking the ocean, his ambivalence is clear when he rapturously breathes the sea air and watches "the birds fly out, blow back" (*CS,* 419). At this point in the 1949 version of the story, a long parenthetical paragraph of Eugene's meditations make his ambivalence, and his spiritual incarceration, even more explicit. The passage is omitted from the text printed in *Collected Stories,* presumably for reasons of geographical accuracy; for if Eugene had been looking out over the Pacific from San Francisco, he would have been unable to see Alcatraz. Geography aside, however, in the earlier version, as he looks out over Alcatraz, he thinks the prison-island in San Francisco Bay looks as "light as a lady's hat afloat on the water, looking inviting," even though he has "a horror of closed-in places" (*GA,* 218).

Eugene not only suffers from claustrophobia but from gynophobia. His inability to understand how a mother could neglect to "watch a fever, while you were at the office," compounded by his inability to confront Emma with his accusation, is somehow entangled with his disgust at his wife's obesity, which Emma calls "Woman's Sacrifice" and blames on her pregnancy (*CS,* 413). Eugene's fear extends to all things intricate: "The laddered, tricky fire-escapes, the mesh of unguarded traffic, coiling springs, women's lace, the nests in their purses—he thought how the making and doing of daily life mazed a man about, eyes, legs, ladders, feet, fingers, like a vine. It twined a man in" (*CS,* 413–14). This list includes two references to fears of specific female intricacies, suggesting his general dread of female sexuality, and perhaps even of female physiology, a dread that Juliann Fleenor says has been "a constant gothic theme" in fiction by both men and women, and which may also afflict Eugene's brother, Ran. It is a theme that has its roots in what Judith Fetterley calls the "biological mythology . . . [that] women's power derives from their possession of a womb." Fetterley's remarks, which are part of her analysis of Norman Mailer's *An American Dream,* include quotations from Mailer's *The Prisoner of Sex,* the language of which is uncannily like the language with which Eugene MacLain describes his wife in "Music from Spain." Mailer describes the womb as that "mysterious space within," that *"purse of flesh"* where there are "psychic tendrils, waves of communication to some conceivable source of life, some manifest of life come into human beings from a beyond."[42]

42. Juliann E. Fleenor, Introduction to *The Female Gothic,* ed. Fleenor, 14; Judith Fetterley, *The Resisting Reader: A Feminist Approach to American Fiction* (Bloomington, 1978), 172; Norman Mailer, *The Prisoner of Sex* (New York, 1971), 47 (emphasis added).

Eugene MacLain's, like Norman Mailer's, is a contemporary male's complaint, not one from an outmoded romance genre. In the classic Gothic, as well as in contemporary patriarchal society, such dread may prompt a man to react by imprisoning or otherwise abusing women; but Eugene, after one perfunctory slap of Emma, exhibits anxieties consonant with his having had no male role model and thus no patriarchal power base. In this he is like Mary Shelley's creature in *Frankenstein,* without any real sense of identity; and thus he roams the earth, as does Shelley's creature, exposed and vulnerable. His complicated plight exemplifies the two chief manifestations of Gothic terror: fear of confinement and an equal fear of exposure to an inhospitable world; for, he thinks, "it would be terrifying if walls, even the walls of Emma's and his room, the walls of whatever room it was that closed a person in in the evening, would go soft as curtains and begin to tremble . . . [,] if they would threaten to go up. That would be repeating the Fire—of course. That could happen any time to San Francisco. . . . But the thing he thought of wasn't really physical" (*CS,* 407–408). Eugene's inner maze of emotions is thus externalized by metaphors generated from the features in the landscape through which he walks. Here the technique Peter Brooks has called the "same-but-different . . . double operation upon time" is apparent in Welty's juxtaposition of Eugene's memory of the tangles he has already experienced with the imagined chaos of the historical San Francisco holocaust.[43]

Throughout his day, at the side of the foreign musician whom he has saved from certain death and who now seems to be ravenous for life—for exotic beauty, sumptuous food, and violent actions—Eugene remembers his youth in Mississippi. The sweet scent of the Spaniard's cigarette smoke recalls the mimosa flowers outside the window of the room where he had played for Miss Eckhart. As he holds his glass to be filled, he sees himself in an attitude that suggests a silent scream at his living death as well as a longing for rebirth. He is, he thinks, "the kneeling Man in the Wilderness in the engraving in his father's remnant geography book, who hacked once at the Traveler's Tree, opened his mouth, and the water came pouring in. . . . That engraving itself, he had once believed, represented his father, King MacLain, in the flesh, the one who had never seen him or wanted to see him" (*CS,* 409).

All of the individual motifs of the enclosure-escape theme in *The Golden Apples,* as well as many from previous stories, come together in the final story, "The Wanderers." At the funeral of Katie Rainey, the commun-

43. Brooks, *Reading for the Plot,* 91–93.

ity's "circling" whispers (*CS*, 429) about the incorrigible Virgie continue even as the women gather to "lay out" her mother. And in spite of the fact that she has lived with her mother for most of her forty years, Virgie senses one aspect of the community's double-edged power—to ignore and to know all—when "people who had never touched her before" now presume to tell her: "Honey, you just don't know what you lost, that's all" (*CS*, 435). Although Virgie's fling in wicked Memphis had ended when she returned home at age seventeen, one evening "at the right time to milk" (*CS*, 452), she has kept the town at bay with her stance as an independent, single working woman who never apologizes for her series of love affairs. There is even the suggestion that Virgie has enjoyed her difficult life, which has included working at the bank and doing the rough work of the farm as well. According to her mother, Virgie liked "struggling against a real hard plaid" (*CS*, 430). The image—the last of Katie's life—is appropriate; for her dying call interrupts Virgie's cutting out a dress from some plaid material, a domestic metaphor for Virgie's struggle against the fate to which she has returned in Morgana. As Elizabeth Bowen once wrote in a draft of an article on Welty's work, comparing her characters to the Wessex people of Thomas Hardy, "locality . . . can be destiny. Nothing more shows fatality than the returns of natives. (There is a struggle against Morgana in *The Golden Apples.*)"[44]

In spite of Virgie's having assumed such household duties as milking and sewing, however, the women of Morgana ostracize her even in her own kitchen as they fry the funeral chicken; and they speculate greedily about who will get Katie's possessions: "Her pretty quilts, she can't ship those to the Fair no more. What does Virgie care about housekeeping and china plates without no husband, hm? Wonder what Virgie'll do with the chickens" (*CS*, 436). When they look at her as though "something . . . should prevent her from knowing at all how to cook—the thing they knew," as if in silent response to their excluding appraisal, Virgie purposefully "went to the stove, took a fork, and turned over a piece or two of the chicken, to see Missie Spights look at her with eyes wide in a kind of wonder and belligerence" (*CS*, 434). Even in the act of consoling Virgie, Jinny Stark MacLain looks at "the burns and scars on Virgie's hands, . . . making them stigmata of something at odds in her womanhood"; and Jinny begins at once, "out of the iron mask of the married lady . . . [to try] to drive everybody . . . into the state of marriage along with her" (*CS*, 444–45). Jinny, as a proponent of marriage, thus reveals herself as a pillar of society in the most basic sense of that metaphor; for

44. Bowen, Rejected pages for the Welty article, in Bowen Collection.

in the twentieth-century American world of *The Golden Apples,* as in Victorian England, marriage is still, as Tony Tanner has said, "the structure that maintains the Structure" of society. Literary critiques of the "structure," and of "pillars" like Jinny Love Stark, have existed since early in the twentieth century; for example, one of Dorothy Richardson's heroines complains about society's inevitable romance plots, in which "one would go on . . . making happy matches for other girls or quietly disapproving of everybody who did not believe just in the same way . . . ; keeping such people outside."[45]

Virgie Rainey will not stay on in Morgana, and apparently will not be a party to maintaining "the structure." The last night that she milks her mother's cows before leaving, she contrasts her old dream of freedom with a new goal of "the blindness that lay inside the beast, inside where she could have a real and living wall for beating on, a solid prison to get out of, the most real stupidity of flesh, a mindless and careless and calling body, to respond flesh for flesh, anguish for anguish. And if, as she dreamed one winter night, a new piano she touched had turned, after the one pristine moment, into a calling cow, it was by her own desire" (*CS,* 453).

The "solid prison" of flesh represented by the cow seems the perfect antithetical image of her old desire of creative artistic freedom. But perhaps the fleshly walls she conjures here are but a form of Jean-Paul Sartre's concept of a body-prison necessary to the attainment of existential freedom: a transcendence of our condition through an exercise of consciousness, which has particular meaning to artists in isolation, according to Mary Ann Frese Witt.[46] For at this crucial moment of exhaustion, grief, vulnerability, and seeming despair, Virgie experiences a Weltian "assault of hope" like that which Dr. Strickland experiences in "The Demonstrators" (*CS,* 618). Virgie has "never doubted that all the opposites on earth were close together, love close to hate, living to dying; but of them all, hope and despair were the closest blood—unrecognizable one from the other sometimes, making moments double upon themselves, and in the doubling double again, amending but never taking back." She can even enjoy the natural beauty of the "ripe afternoon [when] all about her was that light in which the earth seems to come into its own, as if there would be no more days, only this day—when

---

45. Tanner, *Adultery in the Novel,* 15; Dorothy Richardson, *Backwater* (1916; rpt. New York, 1976), 284, Vol. I of Richardson, *Pilgrimage,* 4 vols.

46. Jean-Paul Sartre, "La République du silence," in *Situations III,* by Sarte (Paris, 1949), 11; Witt, *Existential Prisons,* 110–11.

fields glow like deep pools and the expanding trees at their edges seem almost to open, like lilies, golden or dark. She had always loved that time of day, but now, alone, untouched now, she felt like dancing; knowing herself not really, in her essence, yet hurt; and thus happy." It is a timeless moment for Virgie: "The chorus of crickets was as *unprogressing and out of time* as the twinkling of a star" (*CS,* 452–53, emphasis added). The language of this long, meditative passage, which describes the fact that "moments double upon themselves," seems virtually a fractal coda of the technique of the "double operation upon time" that pervades Welty's narratives, in miniature as well as in the larger elements of plot construction.

The image of being enclosed in the mindless cow's skin is one of several in "The Wanderers" that oppose the idea of release to that of confinement. Before the funeral, for example, Virgie takes a moonlight swim, and like King MacLain (who may have been her father), she leaves her clothes on the bank of the Big Black River and opens her arms to the wide, natural world. She is uncertain but hopeful, like Delilah in the same river in "The Burning." The scene repeats the same centrifugal, outward-flinging motion that characterizes Delilah's frenzy, as well as that which marks the climatic crowd scenes in "Lily Daw and the Three Ladies" and "Going to Naples." And in the latter story, Gabriella's defiant stance has been prefigured by Virgie's ecstatic confirmation that she is "not really, in her essence, yet hurt; and thus happy" (*CS,* 453). Such epiphanic expansions of consciousness in Welty's fiction are mirrored by dispersions that, ironically, it might seem, imply cyclic returns to natural chaos; for, to be sure, images of the futility of human attempts at order are everywhere apparent in the stories. At Katie Rainey's funeral, for example, the carefully arranged flowers fall prey to "the tumbling activity and promptitude of the elements. . . . Already, tomorrow's rain pelted the grave with loudness . . . , already settling the patient work of them all; not one little 'made' flower holder, but all, would topple; and so had, or might as well have, done it already; this was the past now" (*CS,* 451).

Although there is no logical connection between the fact of uncontrolled natural processes and that of self-determined intellectual liberations such as those that Virgie and Gabriella experience, the conclusion of "The Wanderers" suggests some mysterious, but felicitous, elemental harmony between the free human spirit and the untamable energies of the universe. The final image of "The Wanderers" is that of Virgie, on her way out of town, sitting on a stile under a tree with "an old black thief"—a Negro woman with a red hen under her arm. To Virgie's imagination, still that of the artist unbound by the communal designs of human society, the sound of the rain calls up images that antedate all human community, and thus all human confinement: "the running of the horse and bear, the stroke of the leopard, the dragon's crusty slither, and the glimmer and the trumpet of the swan" (*CS*, 461)—images of unfettered natural passions, together with their violence and their triumphant beauty. For Virgie, this epiphanic experience, like that of her night in the Big Black River, has the intensity of one of Martin Buber's "uncanny moments," which can penetrate the mundane "I-It" world with "strange lyric and dramatic episodes, seductive and magical, but [which tear] us away to dangerous extremes, loosening the well-tried context, leaving more questions than satisfaction behind them, shattering security."[47] In fiction, this kind of moment evinces a lyric poetics; that is, it constitutes a subjective instead of rational appeal—what Buber would call an "I-Thou" appeal.

The river and the rain at the end of the final story in *The Golden Apples,* which represent natural processes, are also universally recognized symbols that Welty appropriately employs to mark a character's rebirth or entry into a new phase of life. But here and elsewhere, Welty complicates initiation scenes by repeated depiction of images of violent centripetal and centrifugal human forces that play havoc with other human attempts at creating order. Indeed, although the image of water often adds mythic force to literature, in Welty's fiction water is either secondary to the wild, spiral motions made by individuals or crowds, as the sea is secondary in "Going to Naples," or it is absent altogether, as in "Lily Daw and the Three Ladies." Welty's more sophisticated technique relies heavily on the ancient symbolism of initiation that Mircea Eliade cites as involving a reenactment of Creation, which is "preceded by a symbolic retrogression to Chaos."[48] An essential part of Welty's vision can be perceived in her validation of characters who can courageously accept the dangerous freedom that accompanies such chaos, involving, as it does, a unifying melange of opposites. Virgie understands it in terms of love and hate, living and dying, and of "hope and despair [which] were the closest blood." Welty externalizes such inner states by mysterious yet realistic images of the merging of natural elements: by means of a cone of light from the moon in "The Wanderers," by "a crucible of sun-filled water" in "Moon Lake" (*CS*, 357), and by the mixture of land and water that Welty describes so vividly as the "strange . . . amphibious"

---

47. Buber, *I and Thou,* 34.
48. Mircea Eliade, *Rites and Symbols of Initiation: The Mysteries of Birth and Rebirth,* trans. Willard R. Trask (New York, 1958), 78.

Louisiana delta country of "No Place for You, My Love," where the muddy Mississippi River "looked like the earth" (*CS,* 479, 470).

In the latter passage Welty's writing closely parallels that in a letter to Elizabeth Bowen, in which she describes her 1951 visit to Venice, Louisiana, in the company of Carvel Collins, then a young professor at Harvard. Welty writes to her friend that their drive took them "lower than the river, beside the levee . . . [where they] crossed the river on a good ferry at Pointe a la Hatche [*sic*], full of Cajuns combing their hair and giving each other baskets of shrimp . . . , into a remarkable cemetery that . . . was two rows of elevated graves, like bureau drawers . . . [with] the raging sound of all those crickets and locusts and what-all in the jungle around it. Crawfish scuttled across the road in front of us. . . . lots of little fishing boats right at any break in the forest—the water. . . . Huge catfishes were lying on people's front porches. The whole place was amphibious."[49]

Welty's letter to Bowen, which is the apparent raw material for her story, depicts the scene—the tangled bank the couple enters in "No Place for You, My Love"—as one that Barbara Harrell Carson has recognized as "straight from scenes of primordial chaos . . . , the original condition before division into parts." Carson alludes to Mircea Eliade's theory that access to the "Other World" is found only "where Sky and Earth embrace," since entry to "Reality" comes only at a point of union of opposites.[50]

Thus Welty calls upon an archetypal image of the mysterious, multitudinous nature of the Real for a story that suggests the difference between the realities of the mundane, separate worlds from which the couple in "No Place for You, My Love" have come, and the ephemeral world of experience they find together when they open themselves to it. They find, only *because* of their relationship, what Welty calls "the mystery [that] waits for people wherever they go, whatever extreme they run to." For Welty considers "No Place for You, My Love" a "realistic story in which the reality *was* mystery" (*ES,* 114, Welty's emphasis). This latter comment of Welty's has been well noted, but what has not been recognized is that in her explanation of this mysterious reality she utilizes the language of the literary Gothic when she says that her story concerns "the heart that has expected, while it *dreads . . . exposure*"; and, further, that what they are exposed to is "*something demoniac*

---

49. Eudora Welty to Elizabeth Bowen, 17.8.[1951], in Bowen Collection.

50. Barbara Harrell Carson, "Eudora Welty's Tangled Bank," 10; Mircea Eliade, *The Two and the One,* trans. J. M. Cohen (Chicago, 1965), 82.

[*sic*]" (*ES,* 113, emphasis added). Further, in presenting a character who achieves a new "birth" from a primordial plasma—essentially a womb—Welty creates an exhilarating but also potentially terrifying image, one symbolic of female sexuality, which is known to her fictional character Eugene MacLain but also to actual men like Norman Mailer, who called it a "mysterious space . . . [with] psychic tendrils . . . to some conceivable source of life . . . from a beyond." Such spaces usually inspire gothic fear in Welty's male characters, as they do in Eugene MacLain, while they may be the scene of energetic "births" or "rebirths" for women.[51]

When we connect Welty's theme of initiation, by which a cultural unit binds an individual unto itself, with her depiction of the terror of human finitude and vulnerability before primordial chaos, or primeval wilderness, or some human counterpart (family or community), we can see how far her "comedies of manners" are from Jane Austen's novels of family and how much more closely her landscapes align with the wild and barren heaths of Emily Brontë and the frozen steppes of Mary Shelley, but especially with the mysterious forest-psyche tangles of Hawthorne and Faulkner. In *Delta Wedding,* for example, the frightening whirlpool deep in the woods that is revealed when Dabney, just before her wedding, parts vines "like legs" and feels the vertiginous pull of the motion of roots that float "like hair" (*DW,* 123) is remarkably suggestive of the complex sexual imagery of William Faulkner. In his *Sanctuary,* for example, Horace Benbow describes nature as "a she"; and, in terms also reminiscent of the fears of Welty's Eugene MacLain and of writer Norman Mailer, Benbow fears nature "because of that conspiracy between female flesh and female seasons . . . the reaffirmation of the old ferment [that is] the green-snared promise of unease." And there is much more at stake than an Austenian initiation into family in the Beecham-Renfro's gang "rape" of Gloria (with its prophetic warning for her daughter, as Lady May watches with "her mouth wide open and soundless"), by their vicious cramming of watermelon "swarming with seeds" down her "little red lane" until she lies prone and "exposed" (*LB,* 269–70). Such an attempted mind rape through physical force is a challenge to human integrity in its most basic sense—one far beyond the challenges faced by Jane Austen's protagonists. And it is this kind of punitive enforcement of the communal bond that corroborates Joyce Carol Oates's judgment that Welty sees the "seams of the world, through which a murderous light shines."[52]

51. Mailer, *The Prisoner of Sex,* 47.

52. William Faulkner, *Sanctuary* (1931; rpr. New York, 1958), 13; Joyce Carol Oates, "The Art of Eudora Welty," *Shenandoah,* XX (1969), 54.

Welty's outside-versus-community tensions are also less like those of Flannery O'Connor, in which society is disrupted by the intruder, and more like those of Faulkner, in which the community assimilates the outsider without being itself essentially altered, as Jefferson subsumes Lena Grove in *Light in August.* Although assimilation is a realistic component of the character of American communities, as Manz-Kunz has shown, its treatment in literature involves an archetypal pattern. Northrop Frye describes community outsiders as figures that appear in various kinds of romance and represent "partly the moral necessity of the intermediate world of nature and partly a world of mystery which is glimpsed but never seen, and which retreats when approached." The lost girl Ellen meets in the woods in *Delta Wedding* is an example. In that novel, the mysterious intruder figure impresses only the consciousness of Ellen, but Welty will often utilize the pattern.[53]

One result of such carefully controlled assimilation is its frustration of those it subsumes, whose resultant behavior often takes the form of eruptions. In *The Golden Apples,* Welty reveals it in Mr. Voight's flashing, Cassie's mother's suicide, Maideen's suicide, Virgie's beating her head against the wall, and Miss Eckhart's singularly violent performance at the piano. All are evidences of the passional self in bondage to the double-edged, purposefully indifferent but carceral community.

To be lost in the family wilderness or caught in the network of the carceral community is, in Welty's fiction, to be faced with the ultimate danger to individual human identity. The manner in which Welty's characters respond to such challenges determines whether they be victim, mock-hero, or hero. Victims like Ran and Eugene MacLain are known by the closure of life options: either death or spiritual defeat. Mock-heroes like King MacLain may be seen as actual heroes by their culture but are marked by character deflations such as being caught in unheroic positions (asleep or dependent in old age, as in "Sir Rabbit"). Welty's true heroes are not the paragons of perfection—the figural heroes—of the traditional southern romance or the narrative of nostalgia, though they are easily identifiable because of selected traits they share with them. Neither are they blind optimists; they are frankly flawed, perhaps beleaguered, but undaunted pessimists who are vulnerable to "assaults of hope." Like George Fairchild and Virgie Rainey, they are intellectually detached from family or community. And they are open to historic change, although they attempt to elude the regulating beat of time. Thus

53. Manz-Kunz, *Eudora Welty: Aspects of Fantasy,* 197; Frye, *The Anatomy of Criticism,* 197.

131

Virgie Rainey's refusal to play to the metronome has been recognized as evidence of her passing of a boundary that "the true hero must be able to pass."[54] Such limited heroes may accomplish nothing more remarkable than the knowledge of themselves, but it is enough to tempt them to escape from their personal prison-worlds into promising and treacherous futures.

54. Demmin and Curley, "Golden Apples and Silver Apples," in *Eudora Welty: Critical Essays,* ed. Prenshaw, 250.

IV

Character Role Reversals and Confluent Genres
The Female Hero

Eudora Welty has often mentioned her enjoyment of the classic romantic tales of heroes and villains, of fairy tales and ghost stories, the latter an interest that manifests itself ephemerally in her many book reviews of modern ghost stories[1] and substantively in the subversive intertextuality of her own fiction. In *Losing Battles,* this interest is seen in creatively devious transformations of the many faces of the heroic romance. In developing her important canonwide themes of human limitations versus possibilities, and of safe enclosures versus perilous freedoms, Welty utilizes some significant narrative devices that can be identified with a variety of sources, from the "female Gothic" to the classical heroic epic. Since it is clear from Welty's published statements that what she admires about other writers often sheds light on her own work, we should not overlook the mention of some of Welty's favorites in Ellen Moers's discussion of the "literary feminism" implicit in women writers' uses of the Gothic. Moers distinguishes between the classic Gothic novel, which entertains by inciting fear and causing physiological sensations through the devices of fantasy and the supernatural, and the more serious fiction she terms the "female Gothic," which employs similar devices to provide a psychologically, and often literally, realistic picture of the cultural confinement and persecution of women. The female Gothic had its inception, Moers says, in Anne Radcliffe's concept of "traveling heroism," in which female picaresques, while in the power of villains, perform extraordinary feats, paradoxically exhibiting both power and powerlessness. She traces the "literary feminism" implicit in women writers' uses of the Gothic through the nineteenth-century British tradition exempli-

---

1. See, for example, Welty's Introduction to *Hanging by a Thread,* by Joan Kahn (Boston, 1969).

133

fied by Austen and Brontë to some of its modern exponents like Dinesen, Cather, and McCullers.[2]

Eudora Welty knows these writers, of course, but she has also had the example of a near contemporary in Evelyn Scott, a Mississippi writer whose *The Narrow House,* a modernist novel of family, depicts every member, but especially its women, as suffering under intolerably constricting circumstances. Images of drowning, torpor, darkness, and entombment permeate the work. The central image of the novel is that of Winnie Laurence, who at one point is described as walking "into a narrow marble doorway [whereupon the] . . . stone rolled back and the angel went into the tomb." The treatment of enforced sexual abstinence as well as the mental and physical inactivity imposed upon the female protagonist of *The Narrow House* resembles that in Charlotte Perkins Gilman's *The Yellow Wallpaper,* and it results in Winnie's illness, rage, and rebellion. Finally, she is "lost in pain as in a wilderness." Ironically more powerful after her death in childbirth than she had been in life, she entraps her husband even more firmly than she had been trapped; and the capitalized personal pronouns indicate his posthumous deification of her: "He threw himself into the vortex of Her terrific quiet. It caught him and twisted him and bore him to its center." Although the initial impression of Eudora Welty's fiction is very different from the work of all these writers of the female Gothic, the extent of the literary devices she shares with them is impressive. Most basic is the theme of confinement, especially the confinement of women "for their own good" in family and/or community; but also significant, in this example from Scott, are the metaphors of the wilderness and the "vortex": the image of a spiral from the discipline of physics.[3]

Welty creates (especially female) characters who suffer various physical and psychological constraints, and she depicts them through narrative codes and conventions (of image, structure, character) that both she and her readers recognize from lifetimes of reading across a wide spectrum of literary traditions and genres, including the several forms of Gothic. Welty knows, as Robert Scholes asserts, that "genres persist like any convenient codification of cultural behavior [and that] a responsible poetics . . . must function to . . . encourage in readers a freedom that comes from understanding, offering writers audiences that are sophisticated enough about literary coding but unprejudiced about the value of particular codes [such as those of the Gothic]."[4] Staple conventions for

2. Moers, *Literary Women,* 90–112.
3. Evelyn Scott, *The Narrow House* (1921; rpr. New York, 1977), 61, 173, 181.
4. Scholes, Introduction to *The Fantastic,* by Todorov, viii–ix.

Welty include the narrative pattern of the centripetal spiral around a still center, one that she has relied upon throughout her writing career, along with concomitant images of entanglement, entrapment, enclosure, and exposure. Not least are her utilization of picaresque characters—in Weltian terms, "wanderers"—and the tone of irony that results from their status as both powerful and powerless.

In addition to a female author's concern with enclosure, exposure, and escape, women are constantly sensitive to their own lack of economic and political authority, a fact that has undermined their general sense of themselves as *authors* in any sense, according to Sandra Gilbert and Susan Gubar. This "anxiety of authorship" results in a "disease," the primary symptom of which Gilbert and Gubar see as woman's continual imaging of herself as entrapped, as mad, as paradoxically dispossessed because she is so well possessed. Thus the female author, from the earliest known samples of her work, has represented woman's anxiety about spatial constrictions and obsession with escape, contributing to the subgenre of "female Gothic." It is true that male writers make use of the same kinds of images, but Gilbert and Gubar believe that male metaphors of imprisonment have a different aesthetic and philosophic function because men have historically exercised a freedom of expression that female writers have often lacked, women seeming constrained to refer to the literal realities of their confinement. Anne Goodwyn Jones does not find such anxiety in women writers of the Southern Renaissance, an observation that, at first glance, seems to corroborate Welty's sense of her easy entry into the literary establishment. However, Jones is quick to point out that women's seeming advantage was closely related to the South's low literary expectations as well as to the "feminization" of the southern gentleman and his idea of beauty, including literary beauty, especially after the Civil War.[5]

It is impossible, however, to attribute to low expectations the relatively quick critical success of Welty's fiction, given the fact that her early recognition came from those Vanderbilt "fugitives" from the lax standards of the sentimental fiction Jones describes. And although Welty would perhaps disagree with Gilbert and Gubar about women writers' anxiety of authorship (*C,* 59), her own acceptance by the southern literary elite did not obviate her depiction of the broader scope of women's realities. Thus, in her fiction we see women as confined in many ways, both physically and mentally. Delilah, in "The Burning," has been born

---

5. Gilbert and Gubar, *Madwoman in the Attic,* 84–85, 87–88; Anne Goodwyn Jones, *Tomorrow Is Another Day: The Woman Writer in the South, 1859–1936* (Baton Rouge, 1981), 41.

into slavery. Livvie, in the story that bears her name, is essentially carried into captivity, however benign, at age sixteen by her aged husband. In "At the Landing," Jenny Lockhart is held, with locked heart, in a similar prison-home by her father until his death releases her into a dubious sexual freedom with Billy Floyd, which, in turn, only betrays her into a new kind of thralldom as a riverfront prostitute. In "Clytie," the title character walks freely about the town, but her spirit is enclosed in a Gothic mansion with the rest of her proud but moribund family. In *The Robber Bridegroom,* Rosamond is captured by her bandit-lover, who tries to keep her, literally and figuratively, in the dark of his forest hide-out. The initial sense of the romantic in these stories soon proves to be part of the negative romantic thralldom plot, in which such confinements are accompanied by the sexual trauma of rape, or by a kind of spiritual death, or even by actual death for Clytie, and for Maideen Sumrall in "The Whole World Knows."

In her two most recent novels, *Losing Battles* and *The Optimist's Daughter,* Welty imagines two roles for women that usurp traditional masculine character functions and force comparison of the historical *bildungsroman* with stories of women's comparatively narrow path to individuation. Mary Anne Ferguson traces the *bildungsroman* from the archetypal journeys of both father and son in the Homeric epic, a genre in which a given is that women "simply *are,* their existence a part of the world which men test in their own search." Yet she reads Jenny Lockhart in Welty's "At the Landing" as a questing hero who must experience through rape the "grim but preferable alternative to arrested development." This "either/or" analysis may have some merit here, but the female's choices are wider in Welty's more recent fiction. Ferguson's argument for Jenny's "sense of *self-worth* as a woman seeking love" while being used by the fishermen is not persuasive, except in the negative terms of "romantic thralldom," a phenomenon that is central to the sentimental romance plot.[6]

Because it applies so well to several Welty protagonists, especially Jenny and Rosamond, Rachel Blau DuPlessis' articulation of the phenomenon is worth quoting at length:

> Romantic thralldom is an all-encompassing, totally defining love between apparent unequals. The lover has the power of conferring self-worth and purpose upon the loved one. Such love is possessive, and while those enthralled feel it completes and even transforms them, dependency rules. The eroticism of romantic love, born of this unequal relationship, may de-

6. Mary Anne Ferguson, "The Female Novel of Development and the Myth of Psyche," *Denver Quarterly,* XVII (1983), 58–74.

pend for its satisfaction upon dominance and submission. Thralldom insists upon the differences between the sexes or partners, encouraging a sense of mystery surrounding the motives and powers of the lover. Because it begins and ends in polarization, the sustenance of different spheres is both a cause and an effect of romantic love. Viewed from a critical, feminist perspective, the sense of completion or transformation that often accompanies such thralldom has the high price of obliteration and paralysis. This kind of love is socially learned, and it is central and recurrent in our culture.[7]

Welty's depiction of a love relationship in "At the Landing" that amounts to romantic thralldom seems ironic and not intended to valorize this ingredient from a sentimental romance.

Psychologists like Carol Gilligan have argued that male models of maturation, which would certainly include epic heroes and enthralling lovers, depend upon distance from intimate relationships of family, while models of female development show that women have defined their identities more within or through family than by separation from it. Welty, however, depicts many female characters who seek "masculine" separation, yet who do not exhibit the explicitly grotesque masculine attributes of other modern fictional loners, such as those created by Carson McCullers in the subgenre known as the Southern Gothic. The perversion of McCullers' "member of the wedding"—her lack of self-acceptance in terms of female maturation—provides a sharp contrast to healthy adolescent androgyny as it is described by Patricia Yaeger in Welty's "Moon Lake." Yaeger demonstrates Welty's theme of patriarchal suppression of overt normal female sexuality that results in "the tensions between the young girls' desires and the society which tries to reshape their desires." Yaeger analyzes Loch's rape-like resuscitation of Easter, concluding that as a result of his assault, Easter learns "'feminine' passivity" as she passes from "an active, androgynous life to the stunted and conventional life defined by a masculine hierarchy."[8]

At least until this point, however, Easter/Esther, the self-named orphan whose private world is the still center of "Moon Lake," has held aloof from the hold of any family or community, as do many other Welty characters: Shelley, the Europe-bound daughter in *Delta Wedding;* Miss Eck-

7. DuPlessis, *Writing Beyond the Ending,* 66–67.

8. Carol Gilligan, *In a Different Voice: Psychological Theory and Women's Development* (Cambridge, Mass., 1982), 154–64; Patricia S. Yaeger, "The Case of the Dangling Signifier: Phallic Imagery in Eudora Welty's 'Moon Lake,'" *Twentieth-Century Literature,* XXVIII (1982), 431–38. See also Appel, *A Season of Dreams,* xiv, 73–103. Appel asserts that Welty's *isolatos* transcend the grotesques of the "village" genre of Sherwood Anderson and E. A. Robinson, and he compares the grotesque and the Gothic in Welty.

hart, the mysterious stranger of "June Recital"; Sister, who declares her "freedom" from family by installing herself behind the bars of the "P.O."; and Fay Chisom McKelva, who has tried to disown her Texas family in *The Optimist's Daughter.* In the list of such characters, Peggy Prenshaw includes Becky McKelva, because of her "aggressive, masculine advance against monstrous Nature, which brutishly accepts or forgives, or ignores individual victory or death." Franziska Gygax, in a recent study of the novels only, includes Virgie Rainey, who epitomizes what Gygax sees as Welty's transformation of the "male image of creativity [in the quest myth] to the image of a woman's desire and 'fire.'" Each of these demonstrates a role reversal of the kind perhaps best exemplified by the female hero of *Losing Battles.* By imagining such role reversals, Welty addresses a manifestation of women's rebellion against confinement that is directly related to gender-specific cultural expectations: their self-confinement or self-isolation. When women seek personal integrity apart from family, they must distance themselves, and often cloister themselves, from a frankly indignant, even if reluctantly admiring, community.[9]

In *Losing Battles,* the professional woman, pariah of both patriarchy and matriarchy, opts for the authoritarian but lonely existence of schoolteacher instead of the cultural confinement of marriage. Here Welty has realistically portrayed the situation of teachers in the first few decades of the twentieth century; for in Welty's Jackson, Mississippi, they were not allowed to marry. Julia Mortimer is modeled closely after Welty's own teacher, Miss Duling, who was considered "almost supernatural . . . [and] all-powerful" (*C,* 328). In *The Optimist's Daughter,* Laurel has for most of her life remained trapped in a self-spun web of idealism, even though, as a contemporary professional woman, she has ostensibly escaped the limitations of a traditional, gender-specific role. Both Julia and Laurel, however, are hero-victims of "romantic imprisonment" in the same sense that Nina Auerbach describes Jane Austen's Fanny Price of *Mansfield Park:* they are Byronic *isolatos* who strive and suffer in a world apart from community. The classic examples of the character are male heroic outcasts such as Byron's Manfred and Childe Harold, Maturin's Melmoth, and Mary Shelley's creature in *Frankenstein.*[10]

Like those Gothic heroes and like Austen's Fanny Price, Welty's female

9. Prenshaw, "Woman's World, Man's Place," in *Eudora Welty: A Form of Thanks,* ed. Dollarhide and Abadie, 68; Franziska Gygax, *Serious Daring from Within: Female Narrative Strategies in Eudora Welty's Novels* (Westport, Conn., 1990), 46.

10. Nina Auerbach, *Romantic Imprisonment: Women and Other Glorified Outcasts* (New York, 1986), 20–21, 25–33.

Byronic characters, although not as obviously grotesque as McCullers' Frankie, in some way lack fully balanced humanity. In *Losing Battles,* Julia's scientific insistence upon having "everything brought out in the wide open, to see and be known" (*LB,* 432) also recalls Hawthorne's amoral scientists while it conflicts with the family's very human reluctance to face some painful truths. Laurel, throughout most of *The Optimist's Daughter,* is so incomplete a character—so lacking in will that her passion is ineffectual—that Welty has created for her an "evil" alter ego as dramatic foil, an equally incomplete but willful and energetic antagonist who plays the "villainous" reflection of Laurel. Thus Fay/Laurel constitutes what is essentially a split protagonist. Both *The Optimist's Daughter* and *Losing Battles* expand Welty's continuing concern with individuals who, at great personal cost in terms of human nature and nurture, eschew the intimacy of family in favor of some self-ordained model of integrity. In the case of *Losing Battles,* a measure of the success that Julia Mortimer achieves is apparent from her bearing of some distinguishing marks not only of the Byronic hero but also of the southern figural hero that Michael Kreyling describes as "erect, slender, tall, commanding of eye," a hero whose very person constitutes the icon of "the people's holy self-image." [11]

"I feel like we've *been* to her wake," Maud Eva Moody offers to the discussion of the imminent funeral of "Miss Julia" in Welty's *Losing Battles* (*LB,* 307, Welty's emphasis); and Mrs. Moody's perception of the extent of attention being given to Julia confirms that the Banner community sees itself in terms of the life of the woman who has taught most of them. The scene is the evening farewell of participants in the Beecham-Renfro family reunion—the ostensible subject of the novel. We have good reason to agree with Mrs. Moody, however: to perceive the true subject not in the reunion but in the wake it has become, and to see its protagonist not in Jack Jordan Renfro, the prodigal and favorite son who breaks out of prison a day early to grace the annual gathering, but rather in Julia Mortimer, the self-appointed schoolmistress and bane of Banner community whose death has been the central topic of the day. That she, in death, should paradoxically be relieved of her mundane power, yet newly empowered in the community's imaginations, is evidence of the novel's convergence with Gothic forms of literary power.

As is appropriate to the story of a very lively ghost, *Losing Battles* is haunted with traces of the Gothic novel. Into a wastelandian setting in

11. Kreyling, *Figures of the Hero,* 13, 110.

the poor Mississippi hill country, where locusts are heard just before sunrise, Welty introduces, in a novel that has been highly acclaimed for its comic sensibility, numerous gothic images, including maimed and tortured victims and enigmatic figures. However, these images will serve not the ends of the Gothic, but rather the depiction of harsh reality. The chief enigma is, of course, Julia Mortimer, a female hero-villain.

The novel begins with what is on the surface a celebratory creation scene, but which is sobered by subtle negatives that suggest a less-than-perfect dawn, when "the moon had still *not* left the world but was going *down* on flushed cheek, one day *short* of the full. A long *thin* cloud crossed it slowly, drawing itself out like a name being called. . . . Mists, *voids, patches* of woods and *naked* clay, flickered like live *ashes*" (*LB,* 3–4, emphasis added). Repeated references in the novel to the failure of crops are punctuated by wastelandian refrains analogous to the ominous "long thin cloud like a name being called," the most suggestive of which is: "a long sound like a stream of dry seed being poured into an empty bucket, the song of the locusts" (*LB,* 271). Both of these ghostly images recall the silent screams that "echo" throughout Welty's fiction. One author of the hill country's devastation is Mr. Dearman, an ironically named villain whose apparent seduction and desertion of Rachel Sojourner resulted in the birth of the orphan Gloria Short and whose saws ravaged the formerly nurturing wilderness. "Those forest pines," relates Uncle Noah Webster, "he took right in his maw"; and, Mr. Renfro adds, he left "a nation of stumps" (*LB,* 342). The figure includes the stump of the hand of Nathan Beecham, who killed Dearman on Rachel's behalf and then maimed himself as an act of penance. Toward the novel's end, "distant thunder" (355) is heard, suggesting the relief promised at the conclusion of T. S. Eliot's *The Waste Land,* but it rains only enough to spoil what hay has already been cut (*LB,* 374).

The novel is permeated with ghost images, which complement a landscape that is the ghostly remnant of a formerly fecund forest setting. Birdie wants to be excused when "Miss Julia's ghost" (*LB,* 292) commands the community to mourn her. A "ghost of a dog" runs in the moonlight (311). The picture of Beulah's wedding seems to be "filling up with the dead" even as they look at it. It includes not only a newly noticed second image of the family hero, Sam Dale Renfro, who "evidently by racing the crank of the camera and running behind backs . . . had got in on both ends of the panorama," but also a ghostly blur identified as Rachel Sojourner, whose face Beulah has not seen there before and whose "ice cold" fingers she now recalls. The Renfro house is "haunted" by an unseen raccoon that frightens the children by pulling on the light cord from the attic (329–30). Guests come and go in "ghostly dust" (355). Walking to Julia's funeral, in a landscape "empty like an empty room, exhausted of sound like a schoolroom in summer," Jack and Gloria notice "a smell that had steeped for years, of horses and leather and waiting and dust, and the *ghost-smell* of mulberry leaves and wet mustard belonging to the tables that had gone to yesterday's reunion" (*LB*, 426, emphasis added).

The image of Julia Percival Mortimer that emerges from this perilous landscape is that of a combination Percival/Perseus: an "overreaching," courageous quester, a "Saint George" who fights the invisible "dragon" of Ignorance, as Peggy Prenshaw has shown, and whom Beulah, significantly, mistakes for the dragon itself in Gloria's metaphor (*LB*, 245). Julia is "Byronic" not only in the sense of her Manfred-like opposition to what she considers the powers of evil but also in the sense of her own self-exile and, as author of the impassioned "public" work that her last will becomes, in the sense of her stance as a social critic. For her will reveals a public spirit in Julia not unlike that of Lord Byron, who was, as Howard Jones asserts, a "noble liberal commenting with sympathy and scorn upon men." The dramatic dawn setting is not to emphasize the hill country as a wasteland, however; far from it, as the bounteous reunion feast will try to deny. Rather, it provides an appropriately desolate backdrop for the reciting of an elegy for a dead hero.[12]

Julia is known in Banner as the repository of worldly knowledge as well as of sibylline prophecy; and she is the "tyrant . . . for others' own good" (*LB*, 325), the lawgiver, and the scourge to all who "suffered under her" (234). She is the self-created, admirable villain who sows her own dragon's teeth that germinate in Lexie, Gloria, the Judge, Vaughn, and others. Julia Mortimer seems to fit several of the important criteria Peter Schmidt, in his discussion of Welty's short fiction, has identified as characteristic of sibyls, chiefly because of her designation as an enigmatic persona who is also an instructor and because of the many horrified allusions by Banner citizens to Julia as to a Medusa, the mythic character that is called "the sibyl's dark alter ego." It is true that Julia is more closely related to written than oral tradition and that she is not the empowering "link between an independent older woman and a young heroine," as Peter Schmidt describes the sibyl. She is, rather, the link between the entire tradition of intellectual knowledge and her students, especially

---

12. Prenshaw, "Woman's World, Man's Place," in *Eudora Welty: A Form of Thanks*, ed. Dollarhide and Abadie, 68; Howard Mumford Jones, "Lord Byron," in *Atlantic Brief Lives: A Biographical Companion to the Arts* (Boston, 1973), 122.

Gloria. Nevertheless, the community's false appraisal of her as a Medusa-like figure, her passing on of knowledge that empowers, and her cryptic messages would seem to relate Julia to the sibylline tradition. Although Schmidt's study concentrates on the short fiction, it briefly mentions *Losing Battles,* connecting it to the tragic mode.[13]

Julia is still trying to pass on a secret message in one of the last scenes of her life, which is presented in terms of gothic incarceration. In her last illness, when Gloria has deserted her and Lexie confiscates her pencil and paper and ties her in bed, Julia's final look at Lexie "with living dread in her face" (*LB,* 280) is the tragic gaze of a hero who perceives at last the consequences of human limitations (perhaps both her own and Lexie's), chief of which is the scandal of mortality. Julia knows that death will end her personal assault on a cultural adversary that has much in common with what has been described in Jane Austen's fiction as only a modern version of the Gothic terror of the labyrinth in "Maturin's Inquisition." As Nina Auerbach has shown, that old terror was based upon "the institutionalization of mediocrity, a tyranny of the normal," the same tyranny Julia Mortimer has always seen as her foe.[14] Even Jack, who never knew her but has "heard [her] life," recognizes her last confinement as having been worse than his in prison: "That sounds about like the equal of getting put in the Hole!" he declares; "Kept in the dark, on bread and water, and nobody coming to get you out! . . . I'd rather have ploughed Parchman" (*LB,* 312–13). What he could never understand is that her greatest dread—and one that has gothic overtones—has been realized in the forced intimacy that, for Julia, constitutes a kind of rape by Lexie, her controlling warder. Jack is actually the antithesis of the traditional hero in Western culture, because he has a more conventionally feminine belief in the value of community than does Julia. Jack has led "a sheltered life" (81), and he will "make a wonderful little mother" (94); and thus he is an appropriate foil for his fiercely independent wife, Gloria, who has been Julia's protégée.

The strong protagonist whose self-constricting single-mindedness is necessary to a sense of moral integrity is epitomized in Welty's fiction not by Jack Renfro but by Julia Mortimer, an avatar of the romantic, isolated artist who chooses distance over intimacy, who works, as Welty said of Willa Cather, "without help or need of help from another" (*ES,*

---

13. Peter Schmidt, "Sibyls in Eudora Welty's Stories," in *Eudora Welty: The Eye of the Storyteller,* ed. Trouard, 80; Peter Schmidt, *The Heart of the Story: Eudora Welty's Short Fiction* (Jackson, 1991), 49, 223.

14. Auerbach, *Romantic Imprisonment,* 20.

55), a practice that she also sees as central to her own work (*C,* 63). Moreover, it is not beside the point here that in the original version of her essay on Cather, Welty added the observation that the writer's accomplishment is "not without tragic cost."[15]

Miss Julia, magnificent in her self-sufficiency, distributes her benison of truth (book knowledge) and beauty (flower seeds), but also of food (milk for pupils and fruit-tree cuttings mailed out with directions) and service (practical lessons in homely crafts), to mostly unwilling and indignant recipients. Her own idealistic vision is symbolized by her stance in Beulah's wedding picture, "turned away from the crowd . . . , looking off . . . as from her own promontory to survey the world" (*LB,* 330). The pose suggests a landscape of female assertion in the same vein as that imagined by Gabriella in "Going to Naples" or remembered by Ellen in *Delta Wedding.* And the narrator's accompanying description of Julia suggests not only the ethereal southern (historically male) figural hero in Kreyling's paradigm but also a melancholy eyed, Mississippi hill country Byronic "Childe Julia": "The full throat, firm long cheek, long-focused eye, the tall sweep of black hair laid with a rosebud that looked like a small diploma tied up in its ribbon, the very way the head was held, all said that the prospect was serious" (*LB,* 330). And complementing the lofty isolation of Julia and those characters whom she influences is a narrative technique that Robert Heilman calls Welty's "Joycean . . . [method of] the artist as distant divinity, electing an air of Olympian independence from all the scrabble and pother and sound effects he has plunged his reader into. He interprets nothing."[16]

Most of the characters in Welty's fiction that critics such as John Alexander Allen have called "demigods" are male; and indeed Jack Renfro, the quixotic young adventurer of *Losing Battles* who was Welty's stated reason for extending what began as a short story into her longest novel (*C,* 50), seems at first glance to be cut from that pattern. Certainly he satisfies many of the requirements of the mythic southern hero, even to his making of a wise marriage (in spite of himself) that will ensure the pure heritage, if the mysterious parentage of Gloria proves them to be cousins. Yet although his family accords him heroic status, and although he enters the tale as a weary knight with a "torn sleeve that flowed free from his shoulder like some old flag carried home from far-off battle" (*LB,*

15. Eudora Welty, "The Physical World of Willa Cather," *New York Times Book Review,* January 27, 1974, p. 20.

16. Robert B. Heilman, "*Losing Battles* and Winning the War," in *Eudora Welty: Critical Essays,* ed. Prenshaw, 272.

72), his quest for the ring has led only to the mundane test he endured when he "ploughed Parchman" (313), his only escape an easy ride out of the penitentiary field on a mule. The returning challenge in which he is represented as a "knight" is only that of the younger brother who has, literally and metaphorically, worn Jack's pants for two years. What Carol Manning has shown to be Jack's true mock-heroic stature is apparent from the playful action involving "a pair of dried cornstalks . . . [with which] the brothers jousted . . . , shaking them like giant rattles, banging them about like papery clubs" (*LB,* 72).[17]

Although Jack, as long-awaited savior, "might as well be coming back from the dead" (*LB,* 72) to "resurrect something out of nothing" (326) in the drought-ruined fields, throughout the novel he is "ever out of sight when most needed" (331), while others do the saving. And, of course, he loses the ring that he tried to save in the altercation that led to his conviction and incarceration in Parchman prison. The real "demigod" in the novel is, rather, Julia, who "taught the generations" (240) and filled Gloria "so full of inspiration" (244), and whom Lexie "worshipped" (275). Even Nathan Beecham emerges as one of Julia's Byronic protegés when we learn that, after murdering Dearman, he had confided in her and she had instigated his lonely, wandering life by the advice that "even when there's nothing left to hope for, you can start again from there, and go your way" (344). In life and in death, Julia has seemed more than human to the folk of Banner. She has "spent her life in a draught," which would have caused a lesser person to "die of pneumonia," Birdie relates. And Beck adds, "What other mortal would know the way to die like she did? Just met her end and all by herself—what other mortal would succeed?" (295). Noah Webster recalls that she "had a might of sweetness and power locked up in her voice. To waste it on teaching was a sin" (295). But Julia is no sinner; on the contrary, Beulah attests that "she's never made a mistake, on purpose or otherwise" (316).

All of Banner acknowledge her as hero of the cyclone; and her image as a female Goliath (and hence champion of her people) is suggested obliquely when, hearing that her mentor "dropped dead this morning," Gloria identifies so strongly with her that she herself "stood as if she had been struck in the forehead by a stone out of a slingshot" (*LB,* 157). In keeping with Welty's use of dual image patterns, Julia's superhuman strength as well as her triumph against formidable odds—as Goliath's opponent and thus a female David—is suggested by the reflection of these qualities in another disciple, Lexie, when that "little bantie" lifts a

17. Allen, "The Other Way to Live," in *Eudora Welty: Critical Essays,* ed. Prenshaw, 48; Manning, *With Ears Opening Like Morning Glories,* 158.

heavy, potted century plant (*LB,* 18). But whatever their images of her, those who follow her coffin in the funeral procession agree that death has not diminished their venerable teacher's power. Responding to Julia's "last words" in the will, "And then, you fools—mourn me," Uncle Dolphus voices the uncanny feeling that Julia's ghost will haunt them: that she is "following *us* to our graves," he complains; and Beulah adds that Julia "may be dead . . . , but she hasn't given up yet" (292, emphasis added).

To the Banner community, Julia seems not only omnipotent but omniscient; and the merging of the two qualities is apparent in Judge Moody's reminiscence about yet another field of expertise in what has become a virtual catalog of Julia's virtues: she was his rhetoric coach. His appropriate example is a quotation from Archimedes: "Give me a standing place and I will move the world" (*LB,* 302). Willy Trimble, who has made a coffin for Julia in tribute, says that she could have made her own, because "her *eye* was true." He credits her with his skills as an artisan: "I'm the artist because she put a hammer in my hand," he testifies. Yet he confirms the "villainous" methods others have ascribed to his hero by his admission that she "rammed a good deal down me" (*LB,* 233, Welty's emphasis). Beulah admits that Julia "is responsible for a good deal I know" (234), although she can't resist reminding the reunion that the teacher "never did learn how to please" (293). Homer Champion arranges for her burial plot, in gratitude, he says, for Julia's having "made me what I am today" (339). Even old Captain Billy Bangs, "too old to rise," is moved to confess, "'She taught me. She taught her elders. Because after the Surrender, they didn't leave us no school to go to' . . . [, as he] touched one trembling finger to the brim of his hat" (424). Thus, one by one throughout the book, the folk of Banner make their final salutes to the paragon who has been to them the fountain of all worldly knowledge.

But she has also been a repository of secret knowledge, an oracle of prophecy, and a writer of enigmatic texts. The reunion has its first glimpse of this side of Julia when Gloria reveals that her mentor had warned her not to marry Jack:

> The pupils of his shocked eyes nearly overflowed the blue. "*Why?*"
> "She said it promised too well for future trouble."
> "She came out with the bare naked words?"
> "Trouble and hardship." (*LB,* 169, Welty's emphasis)

Gloria goes on to relate that Julia had asked her, "Just who are you? You don't know," and had told her that, in Gloria's words, "there was a dark thread . . . running through my story somewhere . . . [and that] she hated to think of it being unravelled by unknowing hands, and after it's too late" (*LB,* 251). The "dark thread[ed]" story of Gloria's parents is only one of the mini-Gothic romances subsumed in the text of *Losing Battles;* another is the story of Ellen Vaughn and Euclid Beecham, the children of "rival preachers" and the maternal grandparents of Jack. Long ago, these two young parents of seven small "good as gold" children had mysteriously fled their large family early one morning only to drown in the Bywy River (*LB,* 216ff.).

Jack, of course, has never had a "dark thread" run through his sunny mind. When he admits to Judge Moody that he had never suspected his possible blood relation to Gloria, the comparison of Julia with Jack Renfro deflates his character and inflates hers; for Jack's family ridicules the notion that *he* should be knowledgeable:

> "Jack," [Judge Moody] said . . . , "the thing that strikes me strongest is that you didn't know you were marrying your cousin—if you *were* marrying your cousin."
> "No sir," Jack stammered, "I wasn't worrying about who she used to be before I married her!"
> "Jack, you didn't know?" Aunt Birdie asked.
> "Jack? Jack know?" they chorused at her all around, as Miss Beulah gave a short laugh.
> "No, but *she* did. *She* had knowledge," Miss Beulah said. (*LB,* 316, Welty's emphasis)

Not to be overlooked here in Welty's glancing narrative is Jack's unconscious reflection of male obliviousness to a woman's identity before she becomes legitimized (*authorized*) as his wife. Jack provides an example of the general tendency in males that Leon Edel ascribes to male authors (as he compares Henry James's unusual ability to understand women): "Women look at women as persons; men look at them as women." [18] Just so; in Welty's novel, Jack Renfro has seen his wife *only* as a woman, and one whose hegemonic definition he thinks he knows. His own "feminine" qualities give him the potential for human growth that allows him to empathize with Julia in the abstract but not to alter deeply ingrained habits of mind fostered by the traditions of his culture that prevent his full acknowledgment of either Julia or his wife as a *person.* On the other hand, the powerful articulation of female intelligence (both book-knowledge and intuition) in this novel, and its juxtaposition with Jack's stammering admission of innocence, imply the shortsightedness of his

---

18. Leon Edel, *Henry James: The Conquest of London, 1870–1881* (New York, 1962), 359.

view. Thus Jack's ostensible liberality with regard to his wife ("I wasn't worrying about who she used to be") is undercut not only by Welty's creation of female characters intent upon their own identities but also by Jack's own family's estimate of his intellectual acuity. In addition, his statement that he was not "worrying about who she used to be" is evidence that, with respect to conscious intent, he fails the controlled-mating test of the southern figural hero.

And yet, the fact that Jack is not expected to *know* has a positive connotation in terms of his characterization as a figural knight; and it is consistent with Welty's valorization of the ambiguous, a narrative strategy that, according to George Haggerty, "heightens the Gothic power" of Hawthorne's "The Minister's Black Veil." Haggerty is distinguishing between Poe and Mrs. Radcliffe, who insist upon explaining away mystery, and Hawthorne, who, like Welty, emphasizes the mysterious as a given in human life. Ambiguity was integral to a medieval knight's quest, part of which was a search for knowledge—for the meaning of the marvels he experienced; and in the economy of *Losing Battles* as a heroic epic, Jack's function is to *do,* not to *know,* as compared with Julia's function as a tragic hero, which is both "doing and knowing," as Peggy Prenshaw notes in her seminal work of feminist criticism on Welty. Tzvetan Todorov has explained that, in the heroic fantasy, "possessors of meaning form a special category among the characters: they are 'sages,' hermits, abbots, and recluses. Just as the knights could not *know,* these latter cannot *act.*" There is no denying that, notwithstanding Jack's ragged-shirtsleeve banner and ersatz jousting lance, Welty has portrayed him as a knight errant, no doubt with great delight in the ambiguous implications of the word *errant;* and as such he is, in Todorov's terms, the one who "acts." [19] He is dependent upon Granny, the "sage," who is too old to act but who is able to ascribe meaning to his deeds; for while the gathered family ponders the mystery, Granny has known the answer all along. Gloria was "Rachel's *secret*" (*LB,* 256, Welty's emphasis), the illegitimate child of the girl Mr. Dearman had seduced as surely as he had taken the virgin forest "in his maw." The family speculates that Rachel's father, who had turned her out once before, had probably rejected her again after the baby's birth, when Miss Julia found her "fixing to die" (257) in the cold on Banner bridge, and that he had later soothed his guilty conscience

19. Haggerty, *Gothic Fiction/Gothic Form,* 111; Prenshaw, "Woman's World, Man's Place," in *Eudora Welty: A Form of Thanks,* ed. Dollarhide and Abadie, 68; Tzvetan Todorov, *The Poetics of Prose,* trans. Richard Howard (Ithaca, N.Y., 1977), 122–23 (emphasis Todorov's).

with the lamb tombstone he could not afford. The association of tombstones (and thus death) with the sexual experience of women is a recurrent image accompanying that theme in Welty's fiction, from the early "Magic," an uncollected story about a first sexual encounter, to a passage that was cut from the *New Yorker* story "The Optimist's Daughter."[20]

The mystery of Gloria's parentage, which is clarified through the dialogic process of the family's conversation, contributes to the binary narrative pattern that is found throughout the novel, as Welty continually juxtaposes knowledge with other values that battle for ascendancy. In the telling, factual knowledge is contrasted with the orally transmitted, sustaining but much "embroider[ed]" (*LB*, 129) narratives of family history. For, in the South, according to Welty, where such history is also entertainment, "the tales get taller as they go along" (*C*, 183). Further, factual knowledge consistently fights losing battles against a highly validated and powerful opponent: human feelings. That this theme is one that continues to interest Welty is borne out by her subsequent creation of the dueling protagonists of *The Optimist's Daughter.* Thus, defending the character that Welty has drawn most sympathetically in that novel, Vande Kieft asserts that Laurel's antagonist, Fay, "lacks the survivor's virtues" because she has "no capacity to feel."[21]

In many passages of *Losing Battles,* it is the visual shape of Welty's dialogic narrative on the page that reflects the conflict of Julia's embattled, bittersweet existence. When Gloria begins to tell her own story, for example, Julia's adversarial relationship with the world is suggested by Lexie's antiphonal responses:

> "It was the last time I went across to see Miss Julia," said Gloria. . . . "The Silver Moon rose was already out. . . ." "It's about to pull the house down now," said Miss Lexie.
> "The red rose too, that's trained up at the end of the porch—"
> "That big west rose? It's taken over," nodded Miss Lexie.
> "She'd filled the cut-glass bowl on the table," said Gloria. "With red and white."
> "She didn't cut 'em any longer," Miss Lexie said, as if she were bragging on her (247)

Here, in the gaps between the innocuous words of Julia's two chief protégées, is an unspoken elegy not only to a beloved woman but to a pow-

---

20. Eudora Welty, "Magic," *Manuscript* (September/October, 1935), 3–7; Eudora Welty, "The Optimist's Daughter," *New Yorker,* March 15, 1969.

21. Ruth M. Vande Kieft, "Looking with Eudora Welty," in *Eudora Welty: Critical Essays,* ed. Prenshaw, 255.

erful human force as it gives way before the recovering chaos of the natural world. As it reveals Julia's further retreat into herself, Welty's dialogic imagination depicts two women, representing two generations in the life of Julia Mortimer, who together chant unawares the devotion to her they had withheld while she lived.

Patricia Yaeger has demonstrated the dialogic process in *The Golden Apples*. The narrative technique was developed by Mikhail Bakhtin to explain the plural nature of novelistic discourse. To illustrate the technique at work, Yaeger points up Welty's rhetorical and ideological strategy of appropriating Yeats's poem "The Wandering Aengus," a tactic that enables Welty to write, Yeager says, "in a culture that suppresses her." Although Welty would perhaps disavow as extreme Yaeger's premise that she (Welty) is writing what Bakhtin calls a subversive "heteroglossia that rages beyond the boundaries of such a sealed-off cultural universe," Welty does write narratives that open and extend a protagonist's possibilities "beyond the ending" in several of Rachel Blau DuPlessis' categories of that concept. And Welty would certainly acknowledge her own continual dialogue with other cultures and literatures. Welty's images do, in fact, set up the dialogue of gendered discourses, as Yaeger shows; moreover, the dialogues of her characters create what Bakhtin would call their own "authentic environment of . . . utterance[s]." [22]

One such environment for the utterances actually printed on the page in *Losing Battles* is the silent text of Julia that takes shape in the gaps of Gloria and Lexie's antiphon. We hear faintly the truth they cannot speak, if we approach the text in the manner Welty imagines for an ideal reader of her work—a manner that would, curiously, place the reader in the role of a "traveling" Gothic heroine entrapped in a dungeonlike maze of words that, as Welty says, "follow the contours of some continuous relationship between what can be told and what cannot be told." To the reader, Welty believes, such words will be "in the silence of reading the lightest of the hammers that tap their way along this side of chaos" (*ES*, 143). To a writer who, by depicting the reader as feeling his or her way along the mysterious passages of the text, seems to conceive of reading as a daring and solitary quest, the conventions of the literary Gothic would seem to present themselves naturally as part of the raw materials of her fiction. Further, through such narrative techniques as the antiphonal "tapping" around the unsaid in the dialogue about Julia's roses, Welty

22. Yaeger, "'Because a Fire Was in My Head,'" 956–58; Mikhail M. Bakhtin, *The Dialogic Imagination*, trans. Caryl Emerson and Michael Holquist, ed. Michael Holquist (Austin, 1981), 272, 368.

seduces readers into sharing the disconcerting sense of limitation experienced by Julia, Lexie, and Gloria. For throughout the novel these women, like Julia before them, have been wandering through a landscape as limiting as the one in which Mrs. Marblehall seems "cruelly trained" in Welty's early story with its Gothic mansion; and the Banner women have seemed ironically fated to limit each other as well. Indeed, as Gloria attempts to tell her story—to have the last word—she is countered by Julia's story, which overshadows the conversation as the teacher had dominated Gloria and Lexie in life, and dominates the novel.

After a life of heroic but, as she perceived it, losing battles, Julia's last days of seeming madness resemble the wild ranging of Frankenstein's heroic monster over an inhospitable terrain. Lexie chases Julia "over . . . tangly old beds, stumbling over 'em like graves . . . and down into those old white flags spearing up through the vines all the way down her bank as far as the road, thick as teeth" (*LB,* 278). Where a traditionally forceful male protagonist would have progressed naturally into a life's work, Julia Mortimer has begun as a "gothic" hero and has ended as a "gothic" victim, in a literal and psychological wilderness. Although "all she [had] wanted was a teacher's life" (*LB,* 294), to follow her dream in a rigidly divided patriarchal/matriarchal society she has had to choose a life of Byronic isolation, "fighting kind hands" (271) and refusing to give in, as has Gloria, to being "struck down by tender feelings" (250).

One of Julia's losing battles has apparently been with Gloria, who has chosen to give up teaching and marry. And yet (and readers of Welty must continually say "and yet"!), there is the possibility, as Aunt Beck says, that Julia's "words must still be in letters of fire on [Gloria's] brain" (*LB,* 250). Indeed, Gloria has steadfastly refused to be swallowed up in Jack's "mighty family" (*LB,* 320), even after the women's laughing, brutal initiation of her with watermelon: "the red hulk shoved down into her face, as big as a man's clayed shoe, swarming with seeds, warm with rain-thin juice . . . as hands robbed of sex spread her jaws open" (269). The scene recalls the behavior of Welty's Grandmother Carden's "over-familiar" pigeons, who feed each other by placing their entire heads in each others' mouths, an act that caused "agitation and apprehension" in the young Eudora (*OWB,* 57, 56), and the essence of which Welty has recreated in various ways in her fiction. Welty's deliberate use of sexually rapacious images emphasizes the gang-rape effect of their assault on the girl, in spite of their laughter about what was supposedly a good-natured southern face-washing with a melon, a ritual that has been called a "leveling" process. Robert B. Heilman believes the object of the family's initiation of Gloria, "the outsider, the teacher, the individual who felt apart," is to "cut [her] down to community size. Community survival would demand that." Nina Auerbach bases a similar argument about nineteenth-century fiction partly on Mary Wollstonecraft's observation that women together are "too intimate." In Auerbach's words, they violate "the right to private distance [and] the laws of isolation and self-containment, . . . the norm of need." The women who initiate Gloria constitute just such a community of women.[23]

After being thus tortured "in the bosom of . . . family" (*LB,* 270) until she loses her breath, Gloria recovers to deny she is a Beecham and also, significantly, to refuse to wash off the signs of the struggle: "I'm standing my ground," she declares (*LB,* 271). Thus "bloodied" by the red stains but undaunted, she makes a heroic stand, worthy of her mentor, her dishevelment and her demeanor meant (though unperceived by her audience) as a reproach to the family's symbolic invasion of individual privacy.

Thus Welty leaves ambiguous the fact of Gloria's "losing" battle with the family: physically, they have won, but mentally, she has resisted their overfamiliar, pigeonlike presumption to "feed" her their name. Welty herself has pointed out that "you can look at 'losing' in two ways: the verb or the participle. Even though you are losing the battle, it doesn't mean that you aren't eternally fighting them and brave in yourself. And I wanted to show indomitability [in Julia Mortimer]. I don't feel it's a novel of despair at all. I feel it's more a novel of admiration for the human being who can cope with any condition, even ignorance, and keep a courage, a joy of life, even, that's unquenchable" (*C,* 52). Welty was quoted in the Jackson *Daily News* as saying that *Losing Battles* is about battles we only "*seem* to be losing." In addition, Vande Kieft asserts that "losing battles implies not only fighting them but also dropping them off, emerging from a state of destructive conflict to one of at least temporary reconciliation, peace, union," since many battles are "lost" during the course of the novel because of enemies who are forgiven whether or not they wish to be.[24]

One who makes her own separate peace, having lost, in terms of Julia's standards, is Lexie. While Gloria dramatizes her defiance, a quieter but

---

23. Heilman, "*Losing Battles* and Winning the War," in *Eudora Welty: Critical Essays,* ed. Prenshaw, 298; Noel Polk, "Going to Naples and Other Places in Eudora Welty's Fiction," in *Eudora Welty: The Eye of the Storyteller,* ed. Trouard, 156; Nina Auerbach, *Communities of Women: An Idea in Fiction* (Cambridge, Mass., 1978), 15; Mary Wollstonecraft, *A Vindication of the Rights of Woman,* ed. Charles W. Hagelman, Jr. (1792; rpr. New York, 1967), 194–95.

24. Welty's comment quoted from the Jackson *Daily News, April 5, 1970,* by Seymour L. Gross, "A Long Day's Living: The Angelic Ingenuities of *Losing Battles,*" in *Eudora Welty: Critical Essays,* ed. Prenshaw, 328; Vande Kieft, *Eudora Welty* (1987), 152.

equally determined stand is made by this other principal disciple of Julia. Lexie long ago "fell down on Virgil, and wasn't shown any mercy" (*LB,* 276); thus, she could not advance as a teacher. Lexie, however, remains independent of family and, after nursing her old teacher, will take up the position of live-in nurse to old Mr. Hugg, combining "masculine" independence with her own version of "feminine" nurture. When approaching dark threatens "putting out [Lexie's] eyes" (*LB,* 281) as she repairs Gloria's dress torn in the "rape," Beulah's command that someone "take away [Lexie's] needle" (284) may seem analogous to Lexie's depriving Julia of pen and pencil. However, it more appropriately cautions the failed teacher who "fell down on Virgil" against the classic fate of Virgil's heroine, who "fell down" on a sword for love of hardhearted Aeneas. However, Lexie the practical nurse will not "impale" herself in the manner of Dido the romantic heroine, but instead will accept the unsympathetic (for females) role of the hardened entrepreneur. However much she lacks the stature of Julia or the drama of Gloria, Lexie is a true disciple of her determined mentor and a more realistically heroic figure than Jack Renfro. Lexie is another strong woman who, as Beulah says of Julia, "never did learn how to please" (*LB,* 293). Julia, Lexie, and Gloria are more alike than different, because they all refuse the romance plot as DuPlessis has described its postures of "yearning [and] pleasing." Thus the subtexts of these characters exemplify Welty's narrative strategy of "writing beyond the ending" in *Losing Battles,* each subtext constituting a literary critique of the society that valorizes such postures.[25]

Pleasing or not, female characters consistently overshadow and deflate the male protagonist in *Losing Battles;* yet it is apparent why Jack Renfro's story is of such interest to Welty that she sees him as the sympathetic center of the novel (*C,* 50). Again, the determining factor is Welty's narrative technique of gender role reversal. Although Jack's "heroic" exploits are generally nonproductive, his sensitive attempts to understand his wife and Julia are portrayed as positive. Welty deflates only Jack's masculine vaunting and blind optimism, never his "feminine" nurturing traits. There is irony but not a trace of condescension in his portrayal as a "wonderful little mother"; thus Jack assumes the supporting (and limited) role traditionally assigned to a romantic heroine.

As elsewhere, Welty emphasizes human limitations by pairing two "halves" that together constitute one whole human character—here, Jack and Gloria, a nurturing, family-oriented father and an independent, authoritative mother. Not only are the protagonists' roles reversed, but the character of this "comic epic" novel, as it has been called, differs in

25. DuPlessis, *Writing Beyond the Ending,* 2.

more than its comedy from the masculine genre of Virgil's heroic epic, which valorizes action over character.[26] For in spite of the dramatic structure of the narrative of *Losing Battles* and the frenetic automobile rescue scenes, the novel's emphasis is on character, especially the character of Julia, who is not the heroine but the female hero-villain. Even her last poignant and enigmatic cry, "What was the trip for?" recalls the Byronic hero; and Julia Mortimer, a modern champion of knowledge, ends her life in an "ignorance" that is perhaps like that which the Destiny attributes to Manfred in Byron's dramatic poem:

> This man
> is of no common order, as his port
> And presence here denote; his sufferings
> Have been of an immortal nature, like
> Our own; his knowledge, and his powers and will,
> As far as is compatible with clay,
> Which clogs the ethereal essence, have been such
> As clay hath seldom borne; his aspirations
> Have been beyond the dwellers of the earth,
> And they have only taught him what we know—
> That knowledge is not happiness, and science
> But an exchange of ignorance for that
> Which is another kind of ignorance.
>
> (*Manfred*, IV, 53–63)

If we substitute feminine pronouns in this excerpt, we can recognize an apt description of Julia Mortimer, a description that signifies a more complex (trans-generic) understanding of a novel that is somehow both epic and elegy. And if we count the potential Julias "awakened" by the hero-villain of the story, we may perhaps justify a Joycean removal of the apostrophe from "Julia's wake," suggesting a more complex understanding of the multivalent and subversive concept of the word *wake*, which, from its hiding places in the conversation of even minor characters, haunts the entire novel. For it is present in spirit even in the opening scene, where the "baby bolt[s] naked out of the house" followed by her mother, Gloria, whose "curl-papers, paler than the streak of dawn" (*LB*, 3), identify her as a contextual symbol of some significant awakening.

Both *Losing Battles* and *The Optimist's Daughter* involve family rituals and incorporate ghostly settings; in both, the stories of several complex lives are spun out, weblike, from the still center of a corpse; and, in both,

26. Mary Anne Ferguson, "*Losing Battles* as a Comic Epic in Prose," in *Eudora Welty: Critical Essays,* ed. Prenshaw, 305ff.

female protagonists are measured against the community, especially against those complementary characters with whom they are paired because of things that separate yet link their lives. Michael Kreyling has pointed out that the field of group conflict in *Losing Battles* narrows to that of the individual in *The Optimist's Daughter,* in which Laurel "is herself the battlefield."[27]

Each of Welty's stories has its own primary metaphoric base: Greek myth in *The Golden Apples* and the heroic epic in *Losing Battles,* for example. But these freely interact with other image systems and narrative patterns, among which Welty relies upon none more faithfully than those suggested by her "lifetime of fairy-tale reading" (*C,* 2). Significant strands in Welty's favorite web of ideas and images are spun from fairy tales, "the bedtime stories of our collective consciousness," which serve as metaphors of the human "psyche's struggle to be free of fear and compulsion," according to Madonna Kolbenschlag. That such fairy-tale conventions are compatible with those of the Gothic "drama of enclosure and escape" is evident from Rosamond's adventure in *The Robber Bridegroom.* The serious use that Gilbert and Gubar's *Madwoman in the Attic* attributes to this "female Gothic" theme is, I believe, attributable also to Welty's fiction, although Donna Landry demurs in the case of *The Optimist's Daughter.* Landry asserts, for example, that Welty's omission of significant passages, which establish "metaphorical strategies," from the early *New Yorker* version of the novel anticipates "the demands of a less sophisticated, more 'popular' reader." She argues that the short story "The Optimist's Daughter" is of higher literary quality than the novel. In fact, she not only suggests that the novel is not serious literature but also derogates the cover of the Fawcett-Crest edition for its look of a popular paperback romance.[28]

At first glance, the pattern of enclosure and escape seems to be sketched lightly in *Losing Battles,* in terms of the auburn-haired Gloria's Rapunzel-like enclosure in the Mississippi hill country "tower" of Banner top; yet careful readers will not miss the psychic terror that has haunted the bride in that novel, an emotion that to someone with a reading background like Welty's might very well be reminiscent of Gothic terror, and that strikes out from the novel's dark passages. As Joyce Carol Oates notes, at first "we are so charmed by family that we are shocked to see

27. Kreyling, *Welty's Achievement,* 154.

28. Madonna Kolbenschlag, *Kiss Sleeping Beauty Good-Bye: Breaking the Spell of Feminine Myths and Models* (Garden City, 1979), 3; Donna E. Landry, "Genre and Revision: The Example of Welty's *The Optimist's Daughter,*" *Postscript,* I (1983), 95.

Gloria . . . desperate in this web of love." Her comment recalls John Alexander Allen's about *Delta Wedding* that, "having skillfully seduced the reader with the Fairchild charm, Welty brings Robbie onto the scene . . . [through whom] the reader gains . . . a new perspective on the Fairchilds. Her vision is as direct, unsparing and relentless as a battering-ram, and its effect is devastating." Thus, in spite of her obvious fondness for the leading male characters she has created in George Fairchild of *Delta Wedding* and Jack Renfro of *Losing Battles,* both of whom are ornaments upon the bosoms of their adoring families, when Welty shifts to the perspectives of their wives, Robbie and Gloria, we are indeed "shocked" and "devastated" by the opposing blade of her dual-edged vision, which slices through the chimeric web of family storytelling in these novels as decisively as do these two female web-breakers.[29]

From *The Robber Bridegroom* to *The Optimist's Daughter,* in the latter of which she says she treats "an imprisoned spirit" (*C,* 269), Welty brings full circle both the theme and narrative pattern of enclosure, exposure, and escape. In *The Optimist's Daughter,* she creates fairy-tale "Sleeping Beauty" and "Wicked Stepmother" characters: a reticent heroine and a strident (female) hero-villain, the latter of which is also a female version of the legendary robber of the Natchez Trace that she had earlier transformed into a robber bridegroom.

Various affinities between *The Robber Bridegroom* and *The Optimist's Daughter* have been noted. Albert J. Devlin points out that Clement Musgrove and Laurel McKelva Hand are two sensitive evaluators of cultural change, both of whom face strong-willed agents of that change. Bev Byrne sees *The Optimist's Daughter* as renewing the theme announced in *The Robber Bridegroom* that "all things are double" (*RB,* 126) and shows that both Clement and Laurel are victims and beneficiaries of times "when all is first given, then stolen away" (*RB,* 143). Further, Byrne acknowledges Welty's pattern of double vision that splits reader reaction (and again the verb *to devastate* describes the emotion involved): she reads Fay as a "kind of Jungian shadow self for Laurel at the moment Laurel knows her own emotional truth to be as *devastating* as Fay's action in laying hands on the judge."[30]

In *The Robber Bridegroom,* life's ambiguity is set forth in bold, fairy-tale style in dual day-night worlds peopled with "two-faced" characters,

29. Oates, "Eudora's Web," 177; Allen, "The Other Way to Live," in *Eudora Welty: Critical Essays,* ed. Prenshaw, 39.
30. Devlin, *Eudora Welty's Chronicle,* 196–97; Bev Byrne, "A Return to the Source: Eudora Welty's *The Robber Bridegroom* and *The Optimist's Daughter,*" *Southern Quarterly,* XXIV (1986), 84 (emphasis added).

principally Rosamond as both Beauty (innocent lover) and Witch (deceitful liar) and Jamie Lockhart, the titular robber bridegroom, as both Beast and Handsome Prince. Byrne's argument can be extended by the recognition of another parallel between the books: the male source, in Jamie Lockhart, of Welty's female robber brides. Like Gloria, who plans to reverse the sexual roles and steal Jack away from the clan in *Losing Battles,* and like the significantly named Robbie in *Delta Wedding,* who came out of nowhere to capture George Fairchild, the mischievous Wanda Fay (wand/fairy) of *The Optimist's Daughter* has stolen away Clint McKelva, the "delicate" (*OD,* 74, 146) "fair child" of Mount Salus. And in a further doubling of roles, reminiscent of Rosamond's complicity with Salome, Fay is not only the replacement of the "good" wife of Judge McKelva; Maureen Howard calls her Laurel's "cruel stepmother."[31] Most importantly, Welty develops a pattern, established by Rosamond's awakening in *The Robber Bridegroom,* of the transition from female heroine to female hero, from romantic imprisonment to more realistic release toward the fullness of human potential.

Welty's strong women characters generally take one of two forms: either they are maternal administrators such as Ellen Fairchild of *Delta Wedding,* Edna Earle Ponder of *The Ponder Heart,* Beulah Renfro of *Losing Battles,* and Miss Lizzie Stark of *The Golden Apples;* or they are artistic loners such as Miss Eckhart of *The Golden Apples.* Julia Mortimer of *Losing Battles,* like Laurel, and in her own way Fay, of *The Optimist's Daughter,* are of the latter type. They have all established lives independent of family and community. They act alone, unlike, for example, the female heroes of Charlotte Brontë's *Villette* or Henry James's *The Bostonians,* who are part of the vital female communities Nine Auerbach has described. Welty's Fay and Laurel are, as Auerbach has said of Jane Austen's Fanny Price, "closer to the Romantic hero than to the heroine of romance" in the solitude of their conditions and in their animosity to "the intricacies of the normal."[32]

Laurel is a designer of fabrics who has practiced her profession for twenty years in Chicago. A contemporary woman, she has not been forced by patriarchal expectation to a choice of career *or* marriage, as had Julia Mortimer in *Losing Battles.* Laurel has had them both. Her romantic isolation is, rather, a result of her pietistic attempt to keep her

31. Maureen Howard, ed., *Seven American Women Writers of the Twentieth Century: An Introduction* (Minneapolis, 1977), 23.

32. Auerbach, *Communities of Women,* 119; Auerbach, *Romantic Imprisonment,* 24, 33.

memories inviolate. She has wanted to have it all, but she has refused to define a self apart from her past and is thus psychologically immured in that past. It is, in fact, Welty's narrative entrapment of her characters in memory that most reflects the influence of her friend and mentor Katherine Anne Porter, whose Miranda, for example, in "Old Mortality" and *Pale Horse, Pale Rider,* is caught in a similar bind.

As *The Optimist's Daughter* opens, Laurel is a kind of fairy-tale heroine—a Beauty character involved in a passive period of "concentration on the self," which Bruno Bettelheim says is often as necessary to maturation as is overt action. As if in training for the role of Beauty, that is, for being appalled and overcome by some Gothic villain, some Beast or Bluebeard, some wicked stepmother, or some evil fairy, Laurel, since childhood, has been as horrified by the grotesque bestiality of human intimacy as by the pigeons she has seen "eating out of each other's craws" (*OD,* 140). The same reaction to over-familiarity is registered in the early story "A Memory," and it recurs throughout Welty's fiction. Laurel has avoided the crude realities of adult life by dwelling in a self-imposed "glass coffin" of gentility and naïveté; and she has avoided as well the fact of her father's marriage until forced by his death: "It was still incredible to Laurel that her father, at nearly seventy, should have let anyone new . . . walk in on his life, that he had even agreed to pardon such a thing" (*OD,* 26). The novel's dramatic tension is due to the psychological crisis provoked when Laurel's memory of her beloved dead—both husband and father—is challenged in confrontations with two female heroes, both more powerful presences than she and both avatars of the Terrible Mother: her young stepmother, who, like the pigeons, is hungry for life, and her dead mother, "the brave one" (*OD,* 144). Indeed, the overpowering presence of Becky McKelva is an image like that which Claire Kahane has described as "repeatedly locked into the forbidden center of the Gothic which draw[s the reader] inward." It is the "spectral presence of a dead-undead mother, . . . all encompassing, a ghost signifying the problematics of femininity which the heroine must confront."[33]

The story of a virtuous but enclosed "princess" would be dull reading without an evil, and very lively, antagonist. Thus the felicity of Welty's creation of what John Edward Hardy has called a "bad fairy" as foil for Laurel. Wanda Fay McKelva makes up in willful activity what her genteel counterpart lacks, and she adds dramatic intensity to the book. In fact, the juxtaposition of "good" Laurel and "evil" Fay, however clichéd a surface construct, essentially constitutes the sophisticated narrative device

33. Bettelheim, *The Uses of Enchantment,* 226; Kahane, "The Gothic Mirror," 335–36.

of the split character, one that may be said to function also in *The Robber Bridegroom*. In that early novella, where the story proposes two characters, the structure of the narrative suggests one. The story is set in a transitional time and place between the wilderness and civilization; and Clement, not unlike Mr. Marblehall, has a wife for each world. Salome, his "bad" second wife and Rosamond's wicked stepmother, is perhaps only his perception of his "good" first wife, who has developed—as he has not—into the kind of shrewd and enterprising economic realist who is able to meet the challenge of the frontier. Clement himself suggests the split character when he wonders "if even my own wife has not been the one person all the time, and I loved her beauty so well at the beginning that it is only now that the ugliness has struck through to beset me like a madness" (*RB*, 126). In fact, as Barbara Carson has noticed, the names of Salome and Amalie are "practically anagrams."[34]

Welty's characterization of the complexity of the human psyche in this way suggests Bettelheim's interpretations of fairy tales, in which, he explains, evil characteristics of an otherwise good character are assigned to a witch or other vixen (literally, a "she-fox," and thus a beast-villain). One human crisis expressed by such a strategy provides a pattern that Bettelheim recognizes in "Hansel and Gretel": a child, unable to assimilate the mother's unwillingness "to meet all his oral demands . . . , believe[s] that suddenly Mother has become unloving, selfish, rejecting."[35] And indeed, Clement, the trusting, "innocent planter," is remarkably childlike (perhaps Welty's prototypical "fair child").

In the pairing of Laurel and Fay as functional alter egos revealing conflicting human impulses, Welty demolishes the vixen and heroine stereotypes of female characterization even as she affirms the psychological validity of the underlying mythic pattern of the "wicked stepmother" plot. The split protagonist is largely responsible for the complexity of *The Optimist's Daughter* since, in addition to their complementary roles, Laurel and Fay are partial reflections of strong mothers from whom each has declared her independence. Further, they are realistic contemporary characters as well as avatars of beauty and the beast. The novel's strong ties to the Gothic tradition are apparent in each protagonist's confinement in a situation of unreality and exile, as well as in the threatening presences that rise up to penetrate each one's solitary defenses. It is suggested as well by the use of the gothic language, as Fay is identified as

34. Hardy, "Marrying Down in Eudora Welty's Novels," in *Eudora Welty: Critical Essays*, ed. Prenshaw, 108; Carson, *Two Pictures at Once in Her Frame*, 56.

35. Bettelheim, *The Uses of Enchantment*, 159.

"Becky's own *dread*" (*OD*, 172, emphasis added); for, in a surreal tele-scoping of past and future time (and in a passage that echoes Clement Musgrove's musings about whether Amalie/Salome "has not been the one person all the time"), Laurel sees that the betrayal that Fay has come to personify "might have existed [as a ghostly, unrealized presence] right here in the house all the time" (*OD*, 172).

As the novel opens, Laurel and Fay are seen equally as exiles—strangers in a strange land: in New Orleans, a city that is "out-of-town for all of them" (*OD*, 3). The two women are also virtual strangers to each other, not having met since the judge and Fay were married over a year before. They seem to have nothing in common except their relationships to the ailing Clinton McKelva. The novel's multilayered irony derives, however, from the traits that characters unwittingly share and the unper-ceived gaps between ostensible intimates. For example, Laurel does not know her father nearly so well as she thinks, since she has not come to terms with his sexual (normal human) life. Thomas Daniel Young sees the novel as a whole as an illustration of "why it is important for anyone to be absolutely certain that he fully understands the nature and impor-tance of human actions and experiences." In Michael Kreyling's discus-sion of the psychological distances between characters in this novel, he notes Laurel's shock at seeing her father after surgery "naked of [his] aura of permanence and invincibility." Kreyling also recognizes the "auto-matic conspiracy" between Laurel and the physician, an old family friend, "to keep Fay at a distance." Their tacit exclusion of the interloper is apparent from Dr. Courtland's comment to Fay, "My family's known [Clint McKelva's] family for such a long time," a remark characterized by the narrator as "a sentence never said except to warn of the unsayable" (*OD*, 8).[36]

For the two women, and for the patient who will soon withdraw into his own enigmatic solitude, the "lime-white glare of New Orleans" (*OD*, 12) at Mardi Gras season provides a grotesquely unreal setting for the opening scenes of the novel. The tangled wilderness landscape that serves as a projection of the psychological dilemmas of characters in other Welty stories is here, in Laurel's conflicting feelings, replaced by "the atmospheric oppression of a Carnival night, of crowds running wild in the streets of a strange city" (*OD*, 31). The festival, which shows to Fay "a man . . . dressed up like a skeleton and his date . . . in a long white dress, with snakes for hair, holding up a bunch of lilies" (*OD*, 43), forms

36. Thomas Daniel Young, *The Past in the Present: A Thematic Study of Modern Southern Fiction* (Baton Rouge, 1981), 87; Kreyling, *Welty's Achievement*, 158, 167.

an ironic background for the serious business of optics and optimism, of life and death, taking place in the judge's hospital room. It serves, perhaps, as an oblique reflection of the dying judge and his younger, "gorgon" wife. Through the temporary madness of Mardi Gras, Laurel and Fay come and go between the hospital and their rented rooms in a "decayed mansion" (*OD,* 17).

Even the hospital itself is as ghastly as a moonlit Hawthornian "neutral territory, somewhere between the real world and fairyland, where the Actual and the Imaginary may meet." In addition, the image of a gothic labyrinth is suggested in the "strange milky radiance [that] shone in a hospital corridor at night, like moonlight on some deserted street. The whitened floor, the whitened walls and ceiling, were set with narrow bands of black receding into the distance, along which the spaced-out doors, graduated from large to small, were all closed. Laurel had never noticed the design in the tiling before, like some clue she would need to follow to get to the right place" (*OD,* 31). To Laurel, through whose eyes we view the story, New Orleans viewed from the "grayed-down, anonymous room" is "like a nowhere. . . . [It could have been] any city" (*OD,* 14). Even the weather is equivocal: too cold for the judge's panama hat but too warm for Laurel's "wintry" Chicago suit (*OD,* 11, 3). And the scene of the judge's death is presented as a surreal collage of air and water, chimera and substance, where "inside the room's darkness a watery constellation hung, throbbing and near. [Laurel] was looking straight out at the whole Mississippi River Bridge in lights." After retina surgery, the judge lies for weeks "full of effort yet motionless," "such a distance away," self-exiled in concentration on "time passing"; and he, "who had been the declared optimist, had not once expressed hope." As he is dying, he makes a "mysterious response" to Laurel: "His whole, pillowless head went dusky, as if he laid it under the surface of dark, pouring water and held it there" (*OD,* 19–33). Here, in a contemporary setting, Welty creates a gothic space of bewildering unreality, where characters are lost and alone, "blundering" (43) through frightening mazes—wildernesses—of feeling, as are the Mardi Gras crowds who throng the streets of New Orleans. Reminiscent of the "neutral territories" of previous stories—the no-man's land of the Natchez Trace wilderness in *The Robber Bridegroom* and the amphibian Mississippi River delta world of "No Place for You, My Love"—the opening section of *The Optimist's Daughter* presents a fantastic urban landscape in which borders are ambiguous and anything can happen.

Fay is the mysterious stranger who has penetrated the community of Mount Salus, Mississippi, and made off with its favorite son. She had left her family in Madrid, Texas, to make her way as a typist; and it was in the typing pool at a meeting of the Southern Bar Association that she had met Clinton McKelva. "None of 'em living," Fay lies to Laurel about her family. "That's why I ever left Texas and came to Mississippi" (*OD*, 27). And again, as the two women bring the judge's body home to Mount Salus, Fay complains of the mourners who surround Laurel that "it's evermore unfair. I haven't got anybody to count on but me, myself, and I . . . *I haven't got one soul*" (*OD*, 54, emphasis Welty's). But the plea for sympathy seems merely a ploy for attention when members of the Chisom family materialize at the funeral. Mrs. Chisom's own powerful personality may have provoked the self-exile of her daughter, as it had apparently caused her son Roscoe to flee before committing suicide. Yet Fay has deliberately chosen the role of the outsider, and will again. After the funeral, when her mother hints that the McKelva house is big enough "for the whole nation of [Chisoms]" and that it would "make a good boarding house," Fay decides to go home with them to Texas for a visit; "Just long enough," she says (*OD*, 97), implying that she means to keep her relatives at "enough" of a distance to maintain her independence of them.

Welty forces comparison of the orphaned status of Fay and Laurel when Mrs. Chisom's language at the funeral echoes Fay's earlier complaint. The mother whom Fay had denied now accuses Laurel, "So you ain't got father, mother, brother, sister, husband, chick nor child. *Not a soul* to call on, that's you" (*OD*, 69, emphasis added). And there are other accusations that link the two women as Laurel is harshly judged for her self-exile from Mount Salus. Although the extended family of community gathers to share her grief, old Mrs. Pease warns that Laurel's place in the group is precarious: "Once you leave after this, you'll always come back as a visitor . . . [,which] people don't really want." Miss Tennyson Bullock tries to coerce Laurel into staying by appealing to sentiment. "You still might change your mind if you could see the roses bloom, see Becky's Climber come out," she coaxes; when Laurel replies that she "can imagine it, in Chicago," Miss Tennyson argues, "But you can't smell it" (*OD*, 112–13).

Laurel had been educated at the Art Institute in Chicago, where she had married Ohioan Phil Hand. After his death at sea in World War II, she has remained there; and she has tried to extend the "brief protection" of that marriage by living constantly not only in the memory of its perfection but also in "the guilt of outliving those you love" (*OD*, 160). Laurel, as Marilyn Arnold shows, is only one of the characters in this novel who seek various protective mechanisms to shelter their lives from reality;

and her own brief experience with marriage has ill-equipped her for understanding the realities of a longer intimacy in which humans, like her grandmother's pigeons, "could not escape each other and could not themselves be escaped from" (*OD*, 140).[37] Certainly, it has not prepared her for what seems her father's betrayal of her mother by his marrying Fay; she has judged him to be at once more and less perfect (thus, less human) than he actually is. Neither has it prepared her for Fay's "betrayal" of Clint McKelva in what Laurel perceives as a virtual assault on the gravely ill judge, but which Fay had meant "to scare him into living" (*OD*, 173). In her anger at Fay for "making a scene" at the hospital and again at the funeral, Laurel thinks that death "in its reality passed her [Fay] right over" (*OD*, 131). But a great deal of reality has passed Laurel over, too, as she holds tight around her a mantle of pious tradition that belies the supposed freedom of a modern woman.

Her equivocal stance is illustrated by her simultaneous dependence upon the funeral ritual and the exceptions she takes to specific details of it. Her father's wake will not be at the funeral parlor but "at his home" (*OD*, 50), Laurel directs, as aghast at the alternative as she is at Fay's choice of the new section of the cemetery for the judge's burial. Yet she finds equally offensive both Major Bullock's traditional lionizing eulogy and the bridesmaids' factual but humorous stories about her parents. She is as grotesquely limited in her excessive "sensibility" as is Fay in her materialistic "sense." Thus, Welty's dual protagonists recall the contrasting characteristics of Jane Austen's Marianne and Elinor Dashwood in *Sense and Sensibility*. In fact, because of "feelings," Laurel has lived for twenty years in the unreal world of idyllic memory, a choice that has exiled her from the reality of her parents' private lives, and actually from life itself, from having a full life of her own. Ironically, because of her almost obsessive feelings about what constitutes filial loyalty, she does not sense that Major Bullock's mythmaking patriarchal oration is the only way he knows "to say for a man that his life is over" (*OD*, 82); nor is she sensitive to the fact that the matrilineal storytelling tradition of the bridesmaids, the soothing human voice more than the content, which I have elsewhere called "the ritual of the word," is their way of "grieving *with*" her (*OD*, 127, Welty's emphasis).[38]

The limited nature of human understanding and of human freedom is

37. Marilyn Arnold, "Images of Memory in Eudora Welty's *The Optimist's Daughter*," *Southern Literary Journal*, XIV (1982), 28–38.

38. Jane Austen, *Sense and Sensibility* (1811; rpr. New York, 1961), 8; Ruth D. Weston, "The Feminine and Feminist Texts of Eudora Welty's *The Optimist's Daughter*," *South Central Review*, IV (1987), 82.

seen in the lives of all the principals of *The Optimist's Daughter,* but in none so poignantly as in that of Becky McKelva. By nature a courageous and independent woman, Becky had singlehandedly rafted her own father down a freezing river to a Baltimore hospital when she was but a girl, although she had failed to save him, as Laurel has failed to save her father. Further, she had chosen to leave her Virginia home when she married Mississippian Clint McKelva. In Becky's old desk, Laurel finds letters that her grandmother had written to Becky, "her young, venturesome, defiant, happily married daughter as to an exile" (*OD,* 153). But when a stroke left Becky blind and her mind confused during the last five years of her life, her self-exile had seemed to her an involuntary incarceration; she came to believe "that she had been taken somewhere that was neither home nor 'up home,' that she was left among strangers, for whom even anger meant nothing, on whom it would only be wasted. She had died without speaking a word, . . . in exile and humiliation" (*OD,* 151). Before her final silence, however, her tirades recall the wild extravagance of Salome's browbeatings of Clement Musgrove in *The Robber Bridegroom,* and thus transform her into a second, "bad," wife and mother even before Fay appears. Ironically, Judge McKelva, recognized as a "public figure" as he lies in state at the funeral (*OD,* 63), dies in similar isolation, confirming the pathos of human contingency, the truth of which underlies the actions of many fairy tales and all of Welty's fiction.

A sense of the romantic isolation of Becky, a proud soul in mortal terror, attends Laurel's final confrontation with memory in the cold upstairs room "where her mother's secretary had been exiled" (*OD,* 132). The scene, haunted as it is by ghostly vestiges of Becky's dying "madness," unavoidably suggests the Gothic confinement of Bertha Rochester, Charlotte Brontë's madwoman in the attic in *Jane Eyre.* Sorting through old letters on the night after the funeral, Laurel comes to realize the truth of her mother's final desperation and her sense of "betrayal on betrayal" (*OD,* 150) when her husband and daughter could neither help nor admit the truth of her despair. It was that very helplessness that had turned the judge into "what he scowlingly called an optimist"; and Laurel finally admits to Fay that she and her parents "were a family of comparatively helpless people—that's what so bound us, bound us together" (*OD,* 174). It is partly the effect of Becky's still echoing words ("Lucifer! . . . Liar!" [*OD,* 149]), which rise up to penetrate Laurel's shell of idealistic remembrance of her parents' marriage, that allows her to reexamine her own marriage to Phil Hand and, finally, to allow the tragedy of life's inevitable betrayal to qualify the memory of that brief happiness: "Now, by her own hands, the past had been raised up, and *he* looked at her, Phil himself—here waiting, all the time, Lazarus. He looked at her out of eyes wild with the craving for his unlived life, with mouth open like a funnel's. . . . 'Laurel! Laurel! Laurel!' Phil's voice cried. . . . 'I wanted it!' Phil cried. . . . His voice rose with the wind in the night and went around the house and around the house. It became a roar. 'I wanted it!'" (*OD,* 154, Welty's emphasis). Phil's ghostly silent scream, like many such screams that reverberate throughout Welty's fiction, is a literary equivalent of post-impressionist Edvard Munch's painting *The Scream* (1893); and, as it rises "around the house and around the house," it also describes a ghostly spiral of silent "sound," the shape of which approximates the spirals, whirlpools, and other cone shapes of memory with which Welty, throughout the canon, links other characters to their pasts, their futures, and their inner selves. To realize that Laurel's image of Phil's silent scream is a vision like that, which has been described in the context of painterly art, of "the mind cracking under prolonged anxiety" is to understand the difficulty of Laurel's *rite de passage* before she is able to experience a healing grief.[39]

Although her encounter with Becky's spirit begins the process, the decisive impetus to Laurel's reintegration of identity is the puncture of her false sense of imperviousness, an ironic deflation of this sympathetic protagonist that is accomplished in two stages by the female "villain" of the story. The first stage has involved Fay's penetration of Laurel's community and family. Laurel believes that when Fay crudely "laid hands on" (*OD,* 32) Judge McKelva in the hospital, she caused his death. Her aristocratic sensibility is further outraged when, at the funeral, Fay "burst[s] from the hall into the parlor" (*OD,* 84) in black satin, running, throws herself upon the corpse in the casket, "driving her lips without aim against the face under hers" (86), and must be dragged screaming from the room. The scene is a *tour de force* of the manipulation of eclectic traditions. In Fay's character, Welty smoothly integrates female versions of the prince who attempts to awaken Sleeping Beauty (Miss Tennyson declares that he is "lovely" in his coffin [63]) and the Gothic vampire (for Fay, as her sister warns, "bites" [86]). However, instead of waking the "sleeping" judge, Fay has, at least in Laurel's view, put him to sleep forever.

Laurel wants the coffin closed in a final attempt to protect her father, as she herself wishes to be protected, from life's crude intimacies; but

39. Helen Gardner, *Art Through the Ages,* ed. Horst de la Croix and Richard G. Tansey (6th ed.; New York, 1975), II, 707.

she is overruled by Miss Tennyson Bullock, the self-appointed funeral director, who cites the priority of public over private grief, never mind that Fay's having lined the coffin with peach satin is a ludicrous affront to the dignified occasion Miss Tennyson envisions. (Laurel knows, as Miss Tennyson does not, that the bedroom is done in the same fabric!) Of course, the propriety-conscious matriarch could not have foreseen the opportunity that the open casket would afford Fay to act out what she perceives to be her role in the proceedings. Paradoxically both an outsider and the primary bereaved, Fay writes her own script for the occasion, ignoring her mother's interpretive narration that compares Fay's actions to her own.

In a novel teeming with "authors" who routinely create "texts" for (feel *for,* think *for*) one another, Fay is, for good or ill, a self-created character secure in her own identity. Her mourning erupts in what is a virtuoso performance that is, as only Miss Adele realizes, "Fay's idea of giving a sad occasion its due . . . [, of] rising to it, splendidly.—By her lights!" (*OD,* 109). But it is also a violation that constitutes a symbolic (and gothic) rape of the corpse, and an act that codifies her character as the penetrating aggressor. In terms of the poststructuralist literary theory of the metaphysics of presence in Western philosophy and, as Jacques Derrida explains it, in Freudian psychology in particular, both of which assume that *being* in general means physical *presence* that is countered by an *absence,* Fay represents the presence of sexual expression in the story, while her aging husband portrays the lack, the passive patient.[40] Thus, the Freudian penis-as-positive, vagina-as-negative code is reversed in Wanda Fay and Clinton McKelva. Although the critical consensus about Fay's character is overwhelmingly negative, such evaluations are based entirely upon her lack of "feeling" and her materialism instead of upon her literal behavior and its symbolic consequences: her violent assaults on her husband in his bed and coffin. The role that Welty has actually designed for Fay is more radical than has been recognized, since it inverts conventional female/male sexual roles.

Wanda Fay is a wonderfully symbolic name for a character seen as a "bad fairy," but the semiotics of that name suggests a more important feminist context. Fay's "wand," her clitoris, is the female sexual organ that no other character in the novel would be "common" enough to admit having (and, to be sure, Fay would not know its name). Yet it is an appropriate image, for she represents unbridled female sexuality. What-

40. Jacques Derrida, *Of Grammatology,* trans. Gayatri Chakravorty Spivak (Baltimore, 1976), 234.

ever else Fay is, she is a woman who is committed to life. As the robber bride of *The Optimist's Daughter,* Fay is the female version par excellence of Welty's life-force characters. Such Dionysian characters are mostly male, both historically and in Welty's fiction, and they are usually seen as sympathetic *only* if male, the prime example being King MacLain in *The Golden Apples.* Carol Manning has pointed out that Welty's sensual female characters, such as Virgie Rainey in that novel and Fay in *The Optimist's Daughter,* suffer the negative connotations that result from the double standard.[41] And the fact that a female sexual force like Fay is presented as "evil" perhaps reflects Welty's perception of what was possible in fictional characterization when she first wrote the story in the late 1960s that became the novel in 1972.

When Laurel asks why she "struck" the judge in his hospital bed, Fay replies, "I was trying to scare him into living! . . . I tried to make him quit his old-man foolishness. . . . I was being a wife to him! . . . Have you clean forgotten by this time what being a wife is?" (*OD,* 173). A good question, since Laurel's husband died after their brief honeymoon long ago. Fay has a self-serving, even crude, view of marriage; yet it is she, not Laurel, who breaks through Clint's coma-like trance by offering him a brief sensual experience: neither Laurel's reverent attendance upon her father nor her dutiful reading to him elicit as much response as the physical act of Fay's inserting her cigarette into his mouth. The "whole solid past" (*OD,* 176) of genteel tradition that has been Laurel's protective shield "isn't a thing" to Fay (177); it is, rather, the concrete present that interests Fay and, it seems, at a brief moment toward the end of his life, has also interested Clinton McKelva. In addition to demonstrating uncharacteristically frank sensuality in a female character, Fay represents what has historically been the masculine ethic of progress, which always conflicts with what Peggy Prenshaw has identified as the "vast . . . ordering, protecting, domestic realm . . . of the fertile world . . . of the mothers," and which, Madonna Kolbenschlag asserts, also conflicts with the traditional feminine role of primary "transmitter and preserver of values." Fay even buries her husband in "the new part" of the cemetery (*OD,* 90); for, as she says, she "belong[s] to the future" (*OD,* 177).[42]

Fay usurps another male role, for her feminine penetration of the circle of tradition (and of the patriarchal family) is essentially an inversion of the rape theme in traditional literature. The judge is symbolically

41. Manning, *With Ears Opening Like Morning Glories,* 192.

42. Prenshaw, "Woman's World, Man's Place," in *Eudora Welty: A Form of Thanks,* ed. Dollarhide and Abadie, 60; Kolbenschlag, *Kiss Sleeping Beauty Good-Bye,* 127.

"raped" in several ways by Fay, who leaves unsightly scars on his material possessions and invades his sickbed and coffin. Conversely, the patriarch who suffers her attacks has himself been unable to penetrate the passionate but private despair of his first wife, or to penetrate only with weak, useless words, pitiful spurts, and not with enough deep love. Thus another aspect of the pattern of contrasts in the novel is "the rivalry . . . between too much love and too little" (*OD*, 151–52). As Fay has inserted herself into Mount Salus society and inscribed herself in the McKelva home in peach satin on Becky's bed, red nail polish on Clint's desk, and green stiletto heels on the mantel, so she penetrates the last wall of Laurel's defense against change.

The climatic scene in which she and Laurel struggle over the breadboard that Phil had made for Becky marks the second phase of the assault made by this "hero-villain" of the future on the blindly optimistic daughter of the past. Having penetrated Laurel's community and family, Fay now rudely interjects herself into Laurel's most intimate thought processes, essentially forcing Laurel into personal control of a value system that has been operating at least partly on automatic. For, ironically, although Laurel has chosen a nondomestic lifestyle, she now clings unrealistically to an old southern ideal for self-validation: she makes an issue of the breadboard that Fay claims as part of her widow's inheritance. Appalled that Fay has defaced it with cigarette burns and with a hammer, used to crack walnuts, Laurel seizes the finely crafted artifact. Very much her father's daughter, in desperation she optimistically vows to restore it and "have [her own] try at making bread . . . [from her] mother's recipe." Fay, who thinks bread "all tastes alike," taunts her, "And then who'd eat it with you?"; and Laurel's habitual retreat into her glass coffin of memory produces the only mental response possible for her: "Ghosts" (*OD*, 175).

She holds the contested board over Fay's head in a timeless moment of reverie, an "uncanny" moment that Welty has marked with signature spiral images resembling those in the epiphanic scenes of Delilah before the mirror in "The Burning" and Virgie in the river in "The Wanderers," and which has also marked Laurel's telling vision of her husband's ghostly longing for the life he was denied. To Laurel, the board "seemed to be what supported her, a raft in the waters, to keep her from slipping down deep, where the others had gone before her" (*OD*, 175–76), and she escapes the whirlpool of her emotions only when a striking clock recalls her into time and into the presence of Fay, a representative of time's changes. Laurel now experiences the final spasm of letting go of the bonds by which she has been held. She has already repudiated the blindly optimistic fictions she had created about her parents' relationship and about her own short, idealized marriage. Since the emotional blindness was inherited from her father, as Carol Manning notes, her disavowal of it constitutes a belated move out of the Oedipal syndrome and toward maturity for the forty-year-old woman.[43] And now, in a further development of her own identity, she lets go of traditions that hold no relevance for her own life. In Laurel's hands the breadboard is neither a work of folk art nor a traditional tool of feminine creativity; it is a weapon. Its relinquishment, no less than a similar relinquishment for Faulkner's Ike McCaslin in "The Bear," allows her to vanquish a larger-than-life adversary. Letting go of this final mundane symbol of the past's hold on her, and thus approaching the past with "freed hands" (*OD*, 177), allows Laurel a flexible and nonmanipulatory self-authority over memory that was impossible for the self-exiled and, like Fay, grandstanding "heroine" she has been. And with those "freed hands," she can assume control of her own narrative: she can write the text of her life. She now can distinguish between the past, which cannot be changed, and the memory, which can—which must—be adjusted by those who live on. She thinks,

> The past is no more open to help or hurt than was Father in his coffin. The past is like him, impervious, and can never be awakened. It is memory that is the *somnambulist.* It will come back in its wounds from across the world, like Phil, calling us by our names and demanding its rightful tears. It will never be impervious. The memory can be hurt, time and again—but in that may lie its final mercy. As long as it's vulnerable to the living moment, it lives for us, and while it lives, and while we are able, we can give it up its due. (*OD*, 177, emphasis added)

Welty's use of *somnambulist* to describe the haunting apparition of memory recalls the Gothic villain Dr. Caligari, who is associated in Welty's own memory with the term, again confirming the pervasive gothic "haunting" of this contemporary writer's language (*OWB*, 36).

As the principal agent of Laurel's awakening "to the living moment," Fay functions not only as villain but also as hero, confirming the hidden virtue in her fairy-tale "Beast" character. For she is also the unlikely "Prince Charming" who has released Laurel from her living sleep. It has been possible finally because of Laurel's recognition that Fay is her mirror image. The horror Laurel experiences with Fay is related to the Perseus/Medusa syndrome that Danièle Pitavy-Souques has identified in *The Golden Apples:* a mirrorlike reflection that is a sign of the "near identity of opposites"; and it engenders perhaps the most frightening crisis an

---

43. Manning, *With Ears Opening Like Morning Glories,* 184–85.

artist can face: the confusion of identity. Laurel has been "making a scene," like the actual tantrums Fay had staged and the mental "scene" she herself had made as she, needing "to be released . . . to tell, unburden it," contemplated "reporting" Fay's supposed guilt to her dead mother. Even then, Laurel had been granted the beginning of new vision as, horrified, she had thought, "who am I at the point of following but Fay? . . . The scene she had just imagined, herself confiding the abuse to her mother, and confiding it in all tenderness, was a more devastating one than all Fay had acted out in the hospital. What would I not do, perpetrate, she wondered, for consolation?" (*OD,* 132). Now, at the end of her ordeal, her vision is again enlarged as she sees herself "pursuing her own way through the house as single-mindedly as Fay had pursued hers through the ceremony of the day of the funeral" (*OD,* 175). She sees that she has been as self-centered as Fay. The Medusa mirror that Fay provides enables Laurel to see another side of herself, to open her heretofore closed self-text enough to identify with the Other, and thus to revise her own narrative. She is now able to see her story from a new point of view and thus "alter its core assumptions," in a method that constitutes one of the narrative techniques of "writing beyond the ending." One significant aspect of the Fay/Laurel climax, then, is a further validation of openness to the Other, or marginal, point of view, a Weltian theme which has recently been analyzed in studies by Robert H. Brinkmeyer, Jr., and Elaine Orr. In "Circe," for example, Welty rewrites Homer's narratives from the sorceress's perspective.[44]

As the two women face each other in the McKelva kitchen, Fay mocks Laurel's pretension to superiority and to the self-appointed task of preserver of tradition: "I'll tell you what: you just about made a fool of yourself . . . trying to hit me with that plank. But you couldn't have done it. You don't know the way to fight" (*OD,* 176). Fay, who does know how to fight, and who knows her own strengths, is victorious on her limited scale. She has even earned the Chisom family's admiration for the quality of the judge's funeral:

> "Well, you've done fine so far, Wanda Fay," said old Mrs. Chisom. "I was proud of you today. And proud for you. That coffin made me wish I could have taken it right away from him and given it to Roscoe."

44. Pitavy-Souques, "Technique as Myth: The Structure of *The Golden Apples,*" in *Eudora Welty: Critical Essays,* ed. Prenshaw, 265; DuPlessis, *Writing Beyond the Ending,* 109; Robert H. Brinkmeyer, Jr., "An Openness to Otherness: The Imaginative Vision of Eudora Welty," *Southern Literary Journal,* XX (1988), 69–80; Elaine Orr, "'Unsettling Every Definition of Otherness': Another Reading of Eudora Welty's 'A Worn Path,'" *South Atlantic Review,* LVII (1992), 57–72.

"Thank you," said Fay. "It was no bargain, and I think that showed."

. . . .

"You drew a large crowd, too," said Sis. "Without even having to count those Negroes."

"I was satisfied with it," said Fay. (*OD,* 95)

But Laurel gains more. She acknowledges her common humanity with her alter ego, who, like the rest of the Chisom family, as Miss Adele says, is only "a trifle more inelegant" (*OD,* 109) than Mount Salus society. But she also achieves individuation and confirmation of her true superiority to Fay, which is not so much due to her sensitive "feeling" as to the power of her imagination, now released with the relinquishment of the prized breadboard, the last of her material and symbolic ties to an idealized past. She will not have the board that her husband made and her mother used, any more than she will smell the fragrance of Becky's Climber, but she "can imagine" them both.

She has broken out of confining cultural circles to make possible her creation of an authentic self, and thus a fuller life. For in *The Optimist's Daughter,* Welty fully acknowledges the gap that is growing between the contemporary woman who will define herself and the woman caught in what Michael Kreyling has called the circular time of the southern family's mythic consciousness that comes with built-in definitions. As Kreyling argues, Laurel's life will henceforth be enriched by memory but not "ordered" by it. Her time will perhaps be more like Julia Kristeva's concept of "woman's time," based on the woman's biological cycles or on the concentric circles of her various passions, expanding outward in all directions, toward life, toward "women's desire for affirmation."[45] Unlike Fay's straightforward acts of penetration, Laurel's more sophisticated accomplishment, however delayed, represents more than the simple inversion of male semen that penetrates. Her feminine seminal energy is nonlinear: it dives in, breaks out, flowers profusely but not on any schedule, like Becky's Climber ("If it didn't bloom this year, it would next" [*OD,* 114]). It is an energy like that which Laurel associates with Becky herself, whose powerful presence, like that of Julia Mortimer's in *Losing Battles,* is as much evidence of the inefficacy of the historical (linear) closure of death as one could hope for this side of a Gothic novel.

The catalyst for Laurel's maturation has been a virtual rape of her virgin psyche by a powerful "fairy," an attack that, however crude and painful, has been necessary to engender new life. The pattern is the same as

45. Kreyling, *Welty's Achievement,* 145; Julia Kristeva, "Women's Time," *Signs,* VII (1981), 31.

that in Welty's stories of rapes by violent but life-giving male "demigods"; however, as with them, there is no guarantee of success. Fay's catalytic action is also analogous to Judge McKelva's crude but necessary pruning of Becky's rose, which will thrive in spite of, perhaps even because of, his unfeeling touch. In *The Optimist's Daughter,* through adaptations of gothic conventions and fairy-tale structures, then, Welty has demonstrated a distinctly feminist ideology, one that valorizes female wholeness: both the realistic sexual penetration of Fay and the imaginative intellectual passion of Laurel. Although Laurel is the sympathetically presented protagonist, the critical action has been performed by Fay as unorthodox but heroic antagonist. She may have failed with Judge McKelva; but just as, according to Birdie, the reunion scares the century plant into blooming in *Losing Battles,* Fay, operating almost as an uncontrolled natural force, finally scares Laurel into living. Welty gives both Fay and Laurel new options for life; yet, as she did with Gloria in *Losing Battles,* she stops short of combining the professional and the sensual woman into a truly whole female hero. She has shown in both novels that, alone, either half of the split protagonist represents a grotesque limitation of human nature. Still, the resolution of *The Optimist's Daughter,* more than that of *Losing Battles,* implies the most basic and yet most avant garde (and optimistic) of contemporary feminist hopes: that women can reach beyond what Peggy Prenshaw has called the "lonely separateness of patriarchs and heroes," and also beyond what I have called the matrilineal "ritual of the word," toward a more enlightened humanity. Like Alice Walker's heroine in *Meridian,* Welty's Laurel McKelva Hand comes to wear the past lightly, to accept humanness gracefully, to redefine heroism as something more flexible and unpretentious than tradition has taught. The novel's resolution is not so different from that of *Wuthering Heights* in the sense that, as George Haggerty says of Brontë's Cathy and Hereton, Welty's Laurel will face the future "neither haunted by private meanings nor trapped within public ones." [46]

Like other Welty protagonists, notably Virgie Rainey and Gabriella Serto, Laurel is able to walk away from stultifying security, reversing the spin that has held her in an orbit of sameness. The pattern is also the same as that in "The Bride of the Innisfallen," in which the young American wanderer feels fully able to go from the ship into the village "without protection into . . . lovely [places] full of strangers" (*CS,* 518). The

---

46. Prenshaw, "Women's World, Man's Place," in *Eudora Welty: A Form of Thanks,* ed. Dollarhide and Abadie, 76; Weston, "The Feminine and Feminist Texts of *The Optimist's Daughter,*" 82; Haggerty, *Gothic Fiction/Gothic Form,* 49.

thoughts of that un-bride on board the Innisfallen, who has apparently fled a dead marriage, could well be Laurel's thoughts as she prepares to leave Mount Salus, having let go of some illusions: "Love with the joy being drawn out of it like anything else that aches—that was loneliness, not this. *I* was nearly destroyed" (*CS,* 517, emphasis Welty's).

Conclusion

Psyche, the Great Mother,
and Marriages of Death
A Structural Coda for Female Liberations

Among the many image systems Welty blends to energize her fiction are the Gothic, because of its suggestive images of confinement and its dependence upon the mood-defining possibilities of place, and the mythic, both of which often overlap the themes and patterns of fairy tales in terms of their common structures of enclosure and escape and of emergence from darkness into light. The result of the blend is that an affective style supports an intellectual engagement with ideas, contrary to Joyce Carol Oates's conviction that there are "no ideas" in Welty. In Mark Schorer's familiar terms, form achieves content: Welty's fictional confining lines and spaces portray baffling human limitations and isolation as well as tenuous human relationships. She surrounds her protagonists with a sense of dread that has its source in Gothic tradition, but in the Gothic as it was modified by the Brontës, Austen, Eliot, Dickens, Lawrence, and others in the English novel, and by Hawthorne and others in the American romance. In the novels of George Eliot, for example, Judith Wilt asserts that "dread is the infallible sign . . . [of] the formidable claim by the intenser life" for characters who find themselves, as does Eliot's Rosamond, "walking in an unknown world which had just broken in upon her." For one can live in a protective shell, or one can, if "broken in upon, . . . repel . . . dread like an . . . enemy [and] sit all [one's] days 'at this great spectacle of life and never . . . be fully possessed by [life's] glory.'" But in order to "join the feast [of life], the soul must bring its dread along, its 'garment of fear,' like a wedding garment."[1]

Welty modifies both the English and American Gothic traditions by

---

1. Oates, "Eudora's Web," 171; Wilt, *Ghosts of the Gothic,* 174–75; George Eliot, *Middlemarch* (1872; rpr. Boston, 1956), 206, 583.

173

her unsentimental approach; by her treatment of both male and female confinement; and by her appeal to myth and codes of other genres that "persist like any codification of cultural behavior," codes that writers know readers will recognize.[2] Her most memorable characters are captive and captivated women who honor the claims of "the intenser life" and who welcome unknown worlds that break in upon them and energize them, enabling them to rush out to partake of the "feast of life," whatever the cost.

The pervasive patterns of enclosure and escape that emerge from the study of Welty's narrative techniques demonstrate a clear relation to the Gothic that complements her equally pervasive use of the mythic and other primitive and classic literary traditions in her development of themes that represent the most basic human fears and longings. It is her instinctive reliance upon these cultural mythologies that makes her female characters' attempts at escape from confinement intelligible not only in Gothic terms but also in terms of the quintessential myth of female liberation from cultural bondage: the myth of Psyche, as Mary Anne Ferguson has shown.[3] Welty's knowledge of the protean archetypes of this ancient story, in classical mythology and in the folklore and fairy tales of many cultures, is impressive. This myth, including its complement of codes and character types, exerts significant force throughout the Welty canon, appearing most fully in Welty's own adult fairy tale, *The Robber Bridegroom,* in which Rosamond Musgrove is captivated by love in her dark encounter with Jamie Lockhart in the forest. Especially here, the mythic and Gothic reinforce each other as mutually revealing keys to the fiction. I wish to consider Welty's use of the myth of Psyche in the light of female psychic development, especially in terms of the influence of a mother figure in that development; but more than that, as a credible coda for female liberations throughout the fiction, one that informs her most characteristic narrative techniques.

In the myth of Psyche, Aphrodite is angry because men venerate Psyche's beauty, so she conspires with her son, Eros, to sexually enslave the mortal woman without revealing his divine beauty. Although at first Psyche submits, her natural human curiosity about her lover is sparked by her "evil" sisters. While Eros sleeps, Psyche lights a lamp, which dispels the mystery of his godliness but which also—and significantly—*awakens* him with a drop of hot oil. Although he loves Psyche, he withdraws his love to punish her for daring to know him. Through the heroic

2. Scholes, Introduction to *The Fantastic,* by Todorov, viii.
3. Ferguson, "The Female Novel of Development and the Myth of Psyche," 58–74.

actions of Psyche, and the psychic awakening of Eros, however, they are happily reunited in love, but now in full consciousness. Erich Neumann explains the myth's implication that only *through* a love relationship (and not apart from one) in which equals freely give of themselves can a woman achieve a true and satisfying maturity. Although Neumann's thinking unrealistically limits women to a maturity in terms of the heterosexual union of marriage, it is helpful in understanding cases where such a love relationship is a woman's choice. Many implications of the following theory of Neumann's, at any rate, seem to be borne out by research such as Carol Gilligan's on women's affinity for relationship in general. Neumann writes: "The embrace of Eros and Psyche in the darkness . . . impersonally bestows life but is not yet human . . . Psyche's individual love for Eros as love in the light is . . . *the* essential element in feminine individuation [which is] always effected through love. Through . . . her love for him, Psyche develops not only toward him but toward herself." [4] The most interesting aspect of Neumann's study for contemporary feminist criticism is his recognition of patriarchal and matriarchal assumptions about their respective rights to collaborate in control of, and in subsequent misappropriation of, a woman's role in such a relationship.

Not only Ferguson but several other critics have investigated the various manifestations of the Psyche model throughout the wider spectrum of the literature. The captivating love of Eros for Psyche and the primordial abduction of Kore/Persephone by Hades are the mythic archetypes of what Neumann calls the "marriage of death"—that is, the rape and enslavement of the female, which reappears in romantic form in the Gothic seduction of the heroine. There is blame enough to go around in such destructive relationships, which can involve not only the lover, but also fathers, mothers, and other community members, including the female victim herself. For as Mary Anne Ferguson points out, a woman's "unknowing consent, her passive acquiescence is tantamount to accepting rape, to denying her human need for knowledge." Various elements of this story appear in Eudora Welty's fiction, the most important of which is the female protagonist who is encased in an actual or symbolic "marriage of death," a liaison that subsumes and in some cases destroys her. Ferguson's example is that of Jenny Lockhart in "At the Landing," but marriage and analogous entanglements with godlike males are clear threats to the identities of many of Welty's other female protagonists,

---

4. Erich Neumann, *Amor and Psyche: The Psychic Development of the Feminine: A Commentary on the Tale by Apuleius,* trans. Ralph Manheim (New York, 1962), 109–10.

including Livvie, in the story that bears her name, Snowdie, in *The Golden Apples,* and Miss Sabina, in "Asphodel." In *Delta Wedding,* Welty leaves the reader to wonder whether Dabney's marriage, like her mother's, will result in some loss of her identity or other component of personal integrity. In fact, however, John Alexander Allen has identified her field-god husband, Troy Flavin, as playing the part of "the ravished maiden's gloomy Dis."[5]

In the myth, Aphrodite is the archetypal dualistic Great Mother. As the insidious element of female complicity in the marriage of death, she is a man-hating Terrible Mother, who must consign her daughters to the sexual domination of mysterious but necessary males. But she is also a Good Mother, who aids her daughters by demanding of them tasks that develop their powers. In the latter role she enables them either to escape or, to use Neumann's phrase, to bring "love [into] the light": to transform liaisons of unconscious sensuality with mysterious bridegroom demigods into unions of equality. It seems not to matter whether the mother is actual or symbolic, or even whether her influence is positive or negative, for her to be a catalyst to psychic growth for the daughter. What is necessary is that she be *powerful,* that she provide the way and the impetus, and that *the daughter* then have the initiative and fortitude to achieve true separation from her and to assume power for herself. Psyche would not have achieved maturity had she not accomplished the tasks set for her by the Terrible Mother and thereby shown that she was competent to accept the real world on its own terms. However, her acceptance was not—could not be—blind; otherwise the light and the awakening cease to be meaningful symbols for the liberation of either Psyche or Eros.

Part of the richness of Eudora Welty's interpretation of the Psyche myth is that she presents not only Psyche and Eros characters but also Great Mother and sometimes lesser characters in the Psyche paradigm. And part of the reason she says that her fiction "has something to do with real life" is, I believe, that she allows the myth to play out in the lives of mother avatars who command differing degrees of will and power and thus have differing abilities to initiate daughters in the ways of the world: abilities that may *empower* them to develop independent ego-structures. We may often infer from the daughters' degrees of success or failure which ones have had what post-Freudian psychologists call "good

5. Prenshaw, "Woman's World, Man's Place," in *Eudora Welty: A Form of Thanks,* ed. Dollarhide and Abadie, 72; Allen, "The Other Way to Live," in *Eudora Welty: Critical Essays,* ed. Prenshaw, 40–41; Westling, *Sacred Groves and Ravaged Gardens,* 77–86; Neumann, *Amor and Psyche,* 61–75; Ferguson, "The Female Novel of Development and the Myth of Psyche," 6.

enough" mothers; that is, mothers who are "good enough," as Nancy Chodorow asserts, "to socialize a non-psychotic child." Among the Great Mothers in Welty's fiction are Miss Lizzie Stark in *The Golden Apples,* who supervises the violent life-saving in "Moon Lake" that seems to transform Easter into a docile "ravished maiden"; and the trio of irritable old women who silently witness the fishermen who "come in to" Jenny in "At the Landing." The intolerance toward any resistance to what Robert Heilman calls the "leveling" operations of community that is evident in these matriarchs, as well as in matriarch-to-be Jinny Love Stark in "The Wanderers," in her conspiracy to "drive everybody . . . into the state of marriage along with her" (*CS,* 445), corresponds to the "evil" aspect of Psyche's sisters. The impact of Beulah Renfro, who approves the family's force-feeding induction of Gloria into the clan in *Losing Battles,* is ambiguous. Beulah is certainly a candidate for the role of negative catalyst, but Gloria is already so determined to be independent that Beulah's action can only add a little fuel to her fire. Ironically, the two "good enough" mothers who preside over daughters' apparently successful escapes are Welty's only two "wicked stepmothers": Salome, in *The Robber Bridegroom,* and Fay, in *The Optimist's Daughter.*[6]

The daring act of waking the sleeping god and the acceptance of initiatory tasks represent the crucial elements in the myth in terms of its correspondence to Welty's feminist adaptations of mythic and gothic conventions: that is, the concept of the female protagonist as active and responsible agent. Welty's female characters who accept responsibility for their own development are the ones who escape—or show promise of escaping—from marriages of death. More than the simple physical escape from danger in Gothic fiction, their release results from a combination of physical and intellectual female energy, the archetypal pattern for which is found in the "labors" Psyche performs at the command of Aphrodite before she earns the right to love Eros as an equal. And central to Psyche's quest, and to that of all of Welty's female protagonists, is the ultimately feminist idea of escape from sexual bondages, most often in its feminine mode: *through* love toward more enlightened human rela-

6. Chodorow, *The Reproduction of Mothering,* 33, 88–89; Heilman, "Charlotte Brontë's 'New Gothic,'" 298; see also Susan V. Donaldson, "'Contradictors, Interferers, and Prevaricators': Opposing Modes of Discourse in Eudora Welty's *Losing Battles,*" in *Eudora Welty: The Eye of the Storyteller,* ed. Trouard, 32, 43, on the oral, community-oriented, and conservative mode of discourse of the Beecham-Renfro clan and the opposing mode associated with "writing, solitude, and change" of Julia Mortimer and those whom she influenced. As Donaldson points out, the brutal initiation scene in *Losing Battles* in which the family force-feeds watermelon to Gloria is directly related to this opposition.

tionships. Rosamond Musgrove, Welty's fairy-tale feminist in *The Robber Bridegroom*, brings "love in[to] the light" of knowledge with the magical ease appropriate to that genre; but the two ingredients are there: the practical and powerful help of the "good enough" mother, who gives Rosamond the recipe for removing the berry stains from Jamie's face so that she can truly know him, and Rosamond's own willingness to act publicly on that belief without regard for censure. When Jamie offers, "Shall I kill you with my little dirk, to save your name, or will you go home naked?" (*RB*, 50), Welty imagines an alternate end for this classic scene. By refusing to feel dishonored when Jamie has robbed her of her clothing, Rosamond shows that she is no sentimental heroine. "Why, sir, life is sweet," she declares, "and before I would die on the point of your sword, I would go home naked any day" (*RB*, 50); and she does.

Thus Welty deconstructs the conventional role of the dishonored heroine that Washington Irving's version of the story had followed. Not only does Welty's Rosamond refuse to submit to the heroine prescription, but her father, Clement, while often seen as weak, does not seem to think of disowning his "ruined" daughter. On the contrary, he proves to be a "good enough" father. He shows only mild amazement that she has come home "naked as a jay bird" and quickly covers her with his "planter's coat" (*RB*, 51), a covering symbolic of one who engenders life, not death, in spite of the narrator's humorous comment that the coat "doused her [nakedness] like a light" (37). By contrast, in Irving's "Story of the Young Robber," a ransom note to Rosetta's father brings only the cold reply, "My daughter has been dishonored by those wretches; let her be returned without ransom,—or let her die!"; and the young robber himself takes his "poignard [and] plunge[s] it in her bosom."[7]

In Welty's story, when Jamie has confined Rosamond in what is essentially a "marriage of death" in his hideout, where he comes to her only at night, Rosamond's call to conscience makes clear that we are not to read the story *only* as a fairy tale: "My husband was a robber and not a bridegroom," she complains. "He brought me his love under a mask, and kept all the truth hidden from me, and never called anything by its true name, even his name or mine, and what I would have given him he liked better to steal. And if I had no faith, he had little honor, to deprive a woman of giving her love freely" (*RB*, 146). And, of course, she takes the initiative in making an "honest" man of him.

Laurel McKelva Hand, in *The Optimist's Daughter*, escapes what has been effectively a marriage of death (to her dead husband) when her

---

7. Irving, *Tales of a Traveller*, 416–17.

stepmother, however unwittingly, helps her to emancipate herself from the memory of an ideal. Throughout the novel, the community of Mount Salus sees Becky, Laurel's actual mother, as good wife and mother. Fay, however, is seen as evil stepmother. But is she? Certainly, most critics think so; and even Welty herself has said that there is "evil" in Fay (*C*, 253). But just as we can see Salome and Clement's "good" first wife as two views of the same woman, if we follow Bruno Bettelheim's paradigm of the fairy tale's splitting of personalities to accommodate a child's inability to assimilate "good/bad" qualities in one's real mother, we can understand Fay as a character symbolic of Laurel's inability to deal with the bad memories of Becky's exasperating behavior during her fatal illness.

In fact, Welty has pointed to the use of such a split character as a narrative device in the work of D. H. Lawrence. In her essay "Looking at Short Stories," Welty discusses Lawrence's story "The Fox," in which, she says, Lawrence "is stating perfectly clearly within his story's terms the conventional separation at work in the two halves of the personality— the conscious and the unconscious, or the will and the passive susceptibility, what is 'ready' and what is submerged. March and Banford may well be the two halves of one woman, of woman herself in the presence of the male will" (*ES*, 98). In *The Optimist's Daughter*, where a similar narrative strategy is employed, Fay is not only Laurel's alter ego, as the strong daughter of a strong mother; she also doubles as the "good enough" mother who has given Laurel—explicitly in the breadboard scene—the long-needed impetus she has lacked to deal realistically with the world, including the world of memory.

In Fay's character, Welty has smoothly integrated many kinds of stock characters, some of which are female inversions: she is the vampire, preying on the judge in his bed and coffin, the aggressive prince who awakens a sleeping beauty, and the Terrible Mother who is the catalyst to a Psyche-character's self-actualization. But Fay alone could not have brought about change; her appropriation of Becky's place and Laurel's house are catalytic actions, but only that. Laurel's own more nebulous "labors" throughout the night in the attic of the house, and her will to power, which here is the power to relinquish the safety of stasis and to "join the feast of life," are also necessary for her complete maturation. Welty leaves the ending open, but Laurel's actions seem to promise a future in which she will enjoy more psychic integrity. Other female protagonists in Welty's fiction have more limited success, or even fail.

I have referred several times to Mary Anne Ferguson's analysis of "At the Landing," both because I value it and because I disagree with her conclusion that Jenny Lockhart "is armed with self-confidence and can survive, can even rejoice in life [and] can differentiate between the rapers' value of her only as a sexual object and her own sense of self-worth as a woman seeking love." Although Jenny has gone out into what Welty calls "the unsurrendering world," once she goes into the shantyboat to wait for Billy Floyd, she may persevere but she exhibits no initiative. She escapes from patriarchal confinement only because her father dies; and the brief "mothering" of Mag Lockhart has apparently provided too little in the way of feminine nurture to enable Jenny to escape from the symbolic "marriage of death" that is the result of her fascination with Billy Floyd. When, at the conclusion of "At the Landing," Jenny is gang-raped by the men on the houseboat, Ferguson sees it as "a grim but preferable alternative to the arrested development Jenny would have faced if she had stayed on at The Landing in her grandfather's house." In support of her thesis she cites the narrator's comment that the "rude laugh [that] covered her cry . . . *could* easily have been heard as rejoicing" (*CS*, 258, my emphasis). But I see as ominous both the ultimate image of the young boys throwing knives into the tree outside the boat and the fact that we see Jenny no more; nor do we hear from her except for the ambiguous cry. My reading has more in common with that of Peter Schmidt, who sees the story as "nightmarish" and who stresses the father-son knife throwing outside the boat where Jenny is under a "spell," which, he believes, suggests that "male violence toward women is passed down from one generation to the next." In addition, in view of the undisputed influence of Virginia Woolf on Welty, this use of the knife in "At the Landing" could be seen as a displaced symbol of Billy Floyd's essentially cruel effect on Jenny, as the knife is also the sign of Peter Walsh's "sexual and psychic colonization" of Clarissa in Woolf's *Mrs. Dalloway.* For surely Jenny, like Clarissa, has discovered that this possessive and intrusive kind of love is one of the "cruelest things in the world."[8]

Although Jenny has ventured out into the world, she is not experiencing "love in the light"; nor is there evidence of any awakening in Billy Floyd that would make such a relationship possible. Rather, she is suffering the same kind of torpor that Psyche does when she opens the box and is put to sleep by the powerful miasma it holds instead of beauty. The men who "come in to" Jenny may be symbolic of all men who exploit women, including women who await the homecoming of adventur-

8. Ferguson, "The Female Novel of Development and the Myth of Psyche," 64–65; Schmidt, *The Heart of the Story,* 128; Virginia Woolf, *Mrs. Dalloway* (New York, 1925), 10, 191.

ing males, from Homer's Penelope on. But Jenny is no Penelope, because she has no self-authority. Thus in view of its explicit depiction of the destructive nature of Jenny's rapists, including Billy Floyd, and of Jenny's passive state, and of the silent complicity of the old women outside the boat, on the landing, who are *not* "good enough" mothers, this story suggests neither escape nor enlightenment.

In developing the related themes of the female's enclosure by and escape from cultural betrayal, and of woman's emerging possibilities for individuation, Welty makes a place for herself among the most astute of contemporary feminist writers. Paula Snelling, the early reviewer of Welty's fiction who lamented her "failure to probe deeply and lay bare the realities of the South," did not perceive that Welty was about the business of laying bare the realities of the struggle with personal, as opposed to communal, identity and integrity, especially for women. Welty's essentially female literary imagination foregrounds the psychic essence of woman that yearns for liberation from physical and psychological confinement. And her spatial structures and stylistic patterns of containment and release deepen the impact of that theme. She prescribes no ideal scenario of female individuation; instead, she objectively demonstrates a spectrum of possibilities. Some of her protagonists perform "masculine" deeds that sever the bonds of intimacy, while others attempt, like Psyche, to "transcend, through suffering and struggle, the separation accomplished by [their] act[s]" of self-definition, to use Neumann's phrase. In *The Robber Bridegroom,* transcendence is accomplished, and Rosamond and Jamie live happily ever after. But in the stories that Welty says have "something to do with real life" (*C,* 152), woman's strong impulse toward union rather than separation places her in a jeopardy familiar to women who are, like Gloria in *Losing Battles,* "struck down by tender feelings" and, like Robbie Fairchild in *Delta Wedding,* lost in a virtual gothic wilderness of family and culture.[9]

The danger for women caught in such emotional and intellectual labyrinths has historically been, and is in Welty's fiction, the tragic loss of a fully realized humanity, resulting in personalities that often approach the grotesque, whether in a pathetic character like Clytie, a heroic character such as Julia Mortimer, or a comic one like Wanda Fay McKelva. Welty's fiction concerns the complex and vibrant human psyche as it does battle with the powerful ghosts of a patriarchal, matriarchal, and even a mythic, past. That the Gothic is a credible source of literary power for the ex-

9. Paula Snelling, Review of Eudora Welty's *A Curtain of Green,* in *South Today,* VII (1942), 61; Neumann, *Amor and Psyche,* 83.

pression of such powerful ghosts should come as no surprise to Welty readers, especially in terms of the modern Gothic's serious aim, as Judith Wilt states it: "to remind those caught in its plots of larger powers, of finer tremulations located in places outside (or inside) the scope of everyday life, located in places apparently abandoned but secretly tenanted, places apparently blank but secretly full of signals. . . . For [D. H.] Lawrence the places on the earth's body that once harbored powers still do, and the zone of human mind where live the great animating myths, Indian, Christian, Persian, Achaean, is a real place, and accessible through the hinterlands."[10] Such language is remarkably similar to that which Eudora Welty has used in describing how her own literary imagination operates. Moreover, Welty is, without question, aware of the contribution the Gothic novel has made since the nineteenth century, according to Devendra P. Varma, to "a certain spirit of curiosity and awe before the mystery of things . . . [as well as a] romantic spirit [that] was made to blend with the spirit of realism." Like the British novelists Judith Wilt writes about in *Ghosts of the Gothic,* Welty does what she can to "guard the mystery of life from the sanities of narrative."[11]

What she accomplishes is a richly suggestive corpus of fiction that is informed by a lifetime's reading across a wide spectrum of the world's literatures, especially Greek, Roman, English, Irish, and American. Much has already been written about Welty's relation to specific writers and to specific traditions. A few of Welty's stories have been identified as actually Gothic, including "Clytie," which has recently been included in *The Oxford Book of Gothic Tales*"; and Gothic influence has been suggested in others.[12] However, none has suggested it as the extensive and intensive shaping force in her work that I find it to be. The argument I make is many faceted, as are Welty's uses of the structures and conventions of Gothic tradition as components of the narrative techniques that support her pervasive theme of enclosure, exposure, and escape of women, and some men, in search of selfhood.

Her seamless creations from lyric and dramatic, realistic and romantic, epic, elegiac, and comic modes, as well as her dual perspectives of the community and the individual on its margins, result in modernist examples of the serious romance in American literature. The very nature of Welty's modernist detachment, her broad but ambivalent sympathies, precludes any one study of her work from a pretense to closure or to

---

10. Wilt, *Ghosts of the Gothic,* 295.
11. *Ibid.,* 302; Devendra P. Varma, *The Gothic Flame* (London, 1957), 199.
12. Chris Baldick, ed. *The Oxford Book of Gothic Tales* (New York, 1992).

definitive labels; yet a stylistic description that has haunted me throughout this study is one suggested by a painterly term to which I referred in Chapter II: Magic Realist. Welty may be said to write a verbal equivalent of the visual art of Magic Realism: a psychological realism imbued with unique perspective and an aura of mystery that is as haunting and real as Hawthorne's "moonlight in a familiar room, . . . showing all its figures so distinctly, . . . yet so unlike a morning or noontide visibility, . . . [that] [g]hosts might enter . . . without affrighting us." Gothic forms and figures provide such a clarifying "moonlight" in Welty's fiction, as an *ignis fatuus,* it might seem, that flickers in many narrative corners and flames up in unexpected turns of plots. However, here is no deceptive will-o'-the-wisp but rather the concrete presence of elements carefully selected by a meticulous crafter.[13] Such gothic elements are integral to many important shapes of Welty's imagination, for they are powerful conveyers of the mysterious energies of the world and of the human personality. Thus, a gothic reading lamp can illuminate unsuspected passageways through each of Welty's novels and stories—through the entire labyrinthine house of her fiction.

13. The technique is different only in degree from what has been recognized as Magic Realism in the fiction of African-American writers such as Alice Walker, Paul Laurence Dunbar, Langston Hughes, Paule Marshall, and Toni Morrison, and in Latin American writers such as Isabel Allende and Gabriel Garcia-Marquez. It was the subject of the first International Conference on Black Women Writers of Magic Realism, held at Jackson State University, Jackson, Miss., October 16–20, 1992.

Bibliography

Appel, Alfred, Jr. *A Season of Dreams: The Fiction of Eudora Welty.* Baton Rouge, 1965.

Aristotle. *Poetics.* Translated by Gerald F. Else. Ann Arbor, 1967.

Arnold, Marilyn. "Images of Memory in Eudora Welty's *The Optimist's Daughter.*" *Southern Literary Journal,* XIV (1982), 28–38.

Atwood, Margaret. *Lady Oracle.* New York, 1976.

Auerbach, Nina. *Communities of Women: An Idea in Fiction.* Cambridge, Mass., 1978.

———. *Romantic Imprisonment: Women and Other Glorified Outcasts.* New York, 1986.

Austen, Jane. *Emma.* 1816; rpr. New York, 1964.

———. *Sense and Sensibility.* 1811; rpr. New York, 1961.

Bakhtin, Mikhail M. *The Dialogic Imagination.* Translated by Caryl Emerson and Michael Holquist. Edited by Michael Holquist. Austin, 1981.

Baldeshwiler, Eileen. "The Lyric Short Story: The Sketch of a History." In *Short Story Theories,* edited by Charles E. May. Athens, Ohio, 1976.

Baldick, Chris, ed. *The Oxford Book of Gothic Tales.* New York, 1992.

Bank, Stanley. *American Romanticism: A Shape for Fiction.* New York, 1969.

Bell, Michael Davitt. "Arts of Deception: Hawthorne, 'Romance,' and *The Scarlet Letter.*" In *New Essays on "The Scarlet Letter,"* edited by Michael Colacurcio. Cambridge, Eng., 1985.

———. *The Development of American Romance: The Sacrifice of Relation.* Chicago, 1980.

Benton, Thomas Hart. *An American in Art: A Professional and Technical Autobiography.* Kansas City, Kans., 1969.

———. *Thomas Hart Benton: A Personal Commemorative.* Joplin, 1973.

Bettelheim, Bruno. *The Uses of Enchantment: The Meaning and Importance of Fairy Tales.* New York, 1977.

Bogan, Louise. "The Gothic South" (Review of Eudora Welty's *A Curtain of Green*). *Nation,* December 6, 1941, p. 572.

Bolsterli, Margaret. "'Bound' Characters in Porter, Welty, McCullers: The Prerevolutionary Status of Women in American Fiction." *Bucknell Review,* XXIV (1978), 95–105.

Borel, Émile. *Space and Time.* 1926; rpr. New York, 1960.

Bowen, Elizabeth. Introduction to *The Second Ghost Book*, edited by Cynthia Asquith. London, 1952.

Bowen Collection. Harry Ransom Humanities Research Center, University of Texas, Austin.

Brinkmeyer, Robert H., Jr. "An Openness to Otherness: The Imaginative Vision of Eudora Welty." *Southern Literary Journal*, XX (1988), 69–80.

Brodhead, Richard H. *The School of Hawthorne*. New York, 1986.

Brontë, Emily. *Wuthering Heights*. 1847; rpr. New York, 1959.

Brooks, Cleanth. *William Faulkner: The Yoknapatawpha Country*. New Haven, 1966.

Brooks, Cleanth, and Robert Penn Warren. *Understanding Fiction*. New York, 1943.

Brooks, Peter. *Reading for the Plot: Design and Intention in Narrative*. New York, 1984.

Brown, Charles Brockden. "To the Public." In *Edgar Huntly, or Memoirs of a Sleepwalker*, by Brown. 1799; rpr. New Haven, 1973.

Buber, Martin. *I and Thou*. Translated by Walter Kaufman. New York, 1970.

Butor, Michel. *Inventory*. Translated and edited by Richard Howard. New York, 1968.

Byrne, Bev. "A Return to the Source: Eudora Welty's *The Robber Bridegroom* and *The Optimist's Daughter*." *Southern Quarterly*, XXIV (1986), 74–85.

Carson, Barbara Harrell. *Eudora Welty: Two Pictures at Once in Her Frame*. Troy, N.Y., 1992.

———. "Eudora Welty's Tangled Bank." *South Atlantic Review*, XXXXVIII (1983), 1–18.

Carson, Gary. "The Romantic Tradition in Eudora Welty's *A Curtain of Green*." *Notes on Mississippi Writers*, IX (1976), 97–100.

Cash, W. J. *The Mind of the South*. New York, 1941.

Chamlee, Kenneth D. "Grimm and Apuleius: Myth-Blending in Eudora Welty's *The Robber Bridegroom*." *Notes on Mississippi Writers*, XXIII (1991), 37–45.

Chase, Richard V. *The American Novel and Its Tradition*. Garden City, 1957.

Chodorow, Nancy. *The Reproduction of Mothering: Psychoanalysis and the Sociology of Gender*. Berkeley, 1978.

Cirlot, J. E. *A Dictionary of Symbols*. Translated by Jack Sage. New York, 1962.

Coale, Samuel Chase. *In Hawthorne's Shadow: American Romance from Melville to Mailer*. Lexington, 1985.

Coates, Robert M. *The Outlaw Years: The History of the Land Pirates of the Natchez Trace*. New York, 1930.

Coleridge, Samuel Taylor. *Miscellaneous Criticism*. Edited by Thomas Middleton Raysor. Cambridge, Mass., 1936.

Cooper, James Fenimore. *The Spy: A Tale of the Neutral Ground*. Edited by James H. Pickering. 1821; rpr. New Haven, 1971.

Davidson, Abraham A. *The Story of American Painting*. New York, 1974.

Derrida, Jacques. *Of Grammatology*. Translated by Gayatri Chakravorty Spivak. Baltimore, 1976.

Desmond, John F., ed. *A Still Moment: Essays on the Art of Eudora Welty.* Metuchen, N.J., 1978.

Devlin, Albert J. *Eudora Welty's Chronicle: A Story of Mississippi Life.* Jackson, 1983.

Devlin, Albert J., and Peggy Whitman Prenshaw. "A Conversation with Eudora Welty, Jackson, 1986." *Mississippi Quarterly,* XXXIX (1986), 431–54.

Dollarhide, Louis, and Ann J. Abadie, eds. *Eudora Welty: A Form of Thanks.* Jackson, 1979.

Donovan, Josephine. *Feminist Theory: The Intellectual Traditions of American Feminism.* New York, 1990.

DuPlessis, Rachel Blau. *Writing Beyond the Ending: Narrative Strategies of Twentieth-Century Women Writers.* Bloomington, 1985.

Edel, Leon. *Henry James: The Conquest of London, 1870–1881.* New York, 1962.

Eliade, Mircea. *Rites and Symbols of Initiation: The Mysteries of Birth and Rebirth.* Translated by Willard R. Trask. New York, 1958.

———. *The Two and the One.* Translated by J. M. Cohen. Chicago, 1965.

Eliot, George. *Middlemarch.* 1872; rpr. Boston, 1956.

"Eudora Welty and Southern Literature in World Perspective: A Panel Discussion." *Southern Quarterly,* XXXII (1993), 31–39.

Evans, Elizabeth. *Eudora Welty.* New York, 1981.

Faulkner, William. *Go Down, Moses.* 1942; rpr. New York, 1973.

———. *Light in August.* 1932; rpr. New York, 1968.

———. *Requiem For a Nun.* 1951; rpr. New York, 1975.

———. *Sanctuary.* 1931; rpr. New York, 1958.

Ferguson, Mary Anne. "The Female Novel of Development and the Myth of Psyche." *Denver Quarterly,* XVII (1983), 58–74.

Ferris, Bill, dir. *Four Women Artists.* Interviews on videocassette with Eudora Welty, Ethel Mohammed, Theora Hamblett, and Pecolia Warner. Memphis, 1977.

———. *Images of the South: Visits with Eudora Welty and Walker Evans.* Memphis, 1977.

Fetterley, Judith. *The Resisting Reader: A Feminist Approach to American Fiction.* Bloomington, 1978.

Finlay, Marike. *The Romantic Irony of Semiotics: Frederich Schlegel and the Crisis of Representation.* Berlin, 1988.

Fleenor, Juliann E., ed. *The Female Gothic.* Montreal, 1983.

Fleishauer, John F. "The Focus of Mystery." *Southern Literary Journal,* V (1973), 64–79.

Fogel, Richard Harter. Introduction to *The House of the Seven Gables,* by Nathaniel Hawthorne. New York, 1979.

Forster, E. M. *Aspects of the Novel.* 1927; rpr. New York, 1954.

Foucault, Michel. *Discipline and Punish: The Birth of the Prison.* Translated by Alan Sheridan. New York, 1977.

Frank, Joseph. *The Widening Gyre: Crisis and Mastery in Modern Literature.* New Brunswick, 1963.

Frye, Northrop. *The Anatomy of Criticism.* New York, 1970.

Gardner, Helen. *Art Through the Ages.* Edited by Horst de la Croix and Richard G. Tansey. 2 vols. 6th ed. New York, 1975.

Gilbert, Sandra M., and Susan Gubar. *Madwoman in the Attic: The Woman Writer and the Nineteenth-Century Literary Imagination.* New Haven, 1979.

Gilligan, Carol. *In a Different Voice: Psychological Theory and Women's Development.* Cambridge, Mass., 1982.

Gohdes, Clarence. "An American Author as Democrat." In *Literary Romanticism in America,* edited by William L. Andrews. Baton Rouge, 1981.

Gray, Richard. *The Literature of Memory: Modern Writers of the American South.* Baltimore, 1977.

Gretlund, Jan Nordby. "Out of Life into Fiction: Eudora Welty and the City." *Notes on Mississippi Writers,* XIV (1982), 45–61.

Griffin, Dorothy. "The House as Container: Architecture and Myth in Eudora Welty's *Delta Wedding.* " *Mississippi Quarterly,* XXXIX (1986), 521–35.

Grimm, Jakob and Wilhelm. "The Robber Bridegroom." *Grimms' Tales for Young and Old: The Complete Stories.* Translated by Ralph Manheim. 1819; rpr. Garden City, 1977.

Gygax, Franziska. *Serious Daring from Within: Female Narrative Strategies in Eudora Welty's Novels.* Westport, Conn., 1990.

Haggerty, George E. *Gothic Fiction/Gothic Form.* University Park. Pa., 1989.

Hardy, John Edward. "*Delta Wedding* as Region and Symbol." *Sewanee Review,* LX (1952), 397–417.

Hawthorne, Nathaniel. *The Blithedale Romance.* 1852; rpr. New York, 1986.

———. *The Complete Short Stories of Nathaniel Hawthorne.* New York, 1959.

———. *The House of the Seven Gables.* Edited by Richard Harter Fogle. 1851; rpr. New York, 1962.

———. *The Scarlet Letter.* Edited by Sculley Bradley *et al.* 1850; rpr. New York. 1962.

Heilbrun, Carolyn G. *Toward a Recognition of Androgyny.* New York, 1973.

Heilman, Robert B. "Charlotte Brontë's 'New Gothic.'" In *The Brontës: A Collection,* edited by Ian Gregor. Englewood Cliffs, 1970.

———. "The Southern Temper." In *South: Modern Literature in Its Cultural Setting,* edited by Louis D. Rubin, Jr., and Robert D. Jacobs. Garden City, 1961.

Hobson, Fred. "The Rise of the Critical Temper." In *The History of Southern Literature,* ed. Louis D. Rubin, Jr., *et al.* Baton Rouge, 1985.

Hoffman, Frederick J. *The Art of Southern Fiction: A Study of Some Modern Novelists.* Carbondale, 1967.

Howard, Maureen, ed. *Seven American Women Writers of the Twentieth Century: An Introduction.* Minneapolis, 1977.

Hurston, Zora Neale. *Their Eyes Were Watching God.* Edited by Henry Louis Gates, Jr. 1937; rpr. New York, 1990.

Irving, Washington. "The Story of the Young Robber." In *The Works of Washington Irving.* 1824; rpr. Philadelphia, n.d.

Jacobs, Robert D. *Poe: Journalist and Critic.* Baton Rouge, 1969.

Bibliography

Jones, Alun R. "The World of Love: The Fiction of Eudora Welty." In *The Creative Present: Notes on Contemporary American Fiction,* edited by Nona Balakian and Charles Simmons. Garden City, 1963.

Jones, Anne Goodwyn. *Tomorrow Is Another Day: The Woman Writer in the South, 1859–1936.* Baton Rouge, 1981.

Jones, Howard Mumford. "Lord Byron." In *Atlantic Brief Lives: A Biographical Companion to the Arts.* Boston, 1973.

Jones, Louis C. *Things That Go Bump in the Night.* Syracuse, 1983.

Joyce, James. "A Portrait of the Artist." *Yale Review* (1960). Rpr. in Joyce, *A Portrait of the Artist as a Young Man,* edited by Chester G. Anderson. New York, 1977.

"Joyce Carol Oates: Writing as a Natural Reaction." *Time,* October 10, 1969, p. 108.

Jung, Carl G. *Man and His Symbols.* Edited by Carl G. Jung and M.-L. von Franz. New York, 1964.

Kahane, Claire. "The Gothic Mirror." In *The (M)other Tongue: Essays in Feminist Psychoanalytic Interpretation,* edited by Shirley Nelson Garner, Claire Kahane, and Madelon Sprengnether. Ithaca, N.Y., 1985.

Kayser, Wolfgang. *The Grotesque in Art and Literature.* Translated by Ulrich Weisstein. Bloomington, 1963.

Kazin, Alfred. *An American Procession: The Major Writers from 1830–1930—The Crucial Century.* New York, 1985.

Kestner, Joseph A. *The Spatiality of the Novel.* Detroit, 1978.

Kinnett, David. "Miss Kellogg's Quiet Passion." *Wisconsin Magazine of History,* LXII (1979), 267–99.

Kolbenschlag, Madonna. *Kiss Sleeping Beauty Good-Bye: Breaking the Spell of Feminine Myths and Models.* Garden City, 1979.

Kolmerten, Carol A., and Stephen Ross. "The Empty Locus of Desire: Woman as Familial Center in Modern American Fiction." *Denver Quarterly,* XVII (1985), 109–20.

Kreyling, Michael. *Author and Agent: Eudora Welty & Diarmuid Russell.* New York, 1991.

———. *Eudora Welty's Achievement of Order.* Baton Rouge, 1980.

———. *Figures of the Hero in Southern Narrative.* Baton Rouge, 1987.

———. "Myth and History: The Foes of *Losing Battles.*" *Mississippi Quarterly,* XXVI (1973), 639–49.

Kristeva, Julia. "Women's Time." *Signs,* VII (1981), 13–35.

Landess, Thomas. "The Function of Taste in the Fiction of Eudora Welty." *Mississippi Quarterly,* XXVI (1973), 543–57.

Landry, Donna E. "Genre and Revision: The Example of Welty's *The Optimist's Daughter.*" *Postscript,* I (1983), 90–98.

Lane, Suzette, and Paul d'Ambrosio. *A Shifting Wind: Views of American Folk Art.* Cooperstown, N.Y., 1986.

Lessing, Doris. *The Four-Gated City.* New York, 1976.

Levertov, Denise. *O Taste and See.* New York, 1964.

Lewis, R. W. B. *The American Adam: Innocence, Tragedy, and Tradition in the Nineteenth Century.* Chicago, 1955.

Lohafer, Susan, and Jo Ellyn Clarey, eds. *Short Story Theory at a Crossroads.* Baton Rouge, 1989.

Luraghi, Raimondo. *The Rise and Fall of the Plantation South.* New York, 1978.

Lytle, Andrew. *The Hero with the Private Parts.* Baton Rouge, 1966.

McAlpin, Sara. "Family in Eudora Welty's Fiction." *Southern Review,* XVIII (1982), 480–94.

McCullers, Carson. *The Mortgaged Heart.* Edited by Margarita G. Smith. Boston, 1971.

McDonald, W. U., Jr. "Postscript." *Eudora Welty Newsletter,* XII (1988), 15.

Magny, Claude Edmonde. *The Age of the American Novel: The Film Aesthetic of Fiction Between the Two Wars.* Translated by Eleanor Hochman. 1948; rpr. New York, 1972.

Mailer, Norman. *The Prisoner of Sex.* New York, 1971.

Malin, Irving. *The New American Gothic.* Carbondale, 1962.

Manning, Carol S. *With Ears Opening Like Morning Glories: Eudora Welty and the Love of Storytelling.* Westport, Conn., 1985.

Manz-Kunz, Marie-Antoinette. *Eudora Welty: Aspects of Fantasy in Her Short Fiction.* Bern, 1971.

Marrs, Suzanne. *The Welty Collection: A Guide to the Eudora Welty Manuscripts and Documents at the Mississippi Department of Archives and History.* Jackson, 1988.

Matore, Georges. *L'Espace humain.* Paris, 1962.

May, Charles E. "The Nature of Knowledge in Short Fiction." *Studies in Short Fiction,* XXI (1984), 327–338.

Matthiessen, F. O. *American Renaissance: Art and Expression in the Age of Emerson and Whitman.* London, 1941.

Miller, Lisa K. "The Dark Side of Our Frontier Heritage: Eudora Welty's Use of the Turner Thesis in *The Robber Bridegroom.*" *Notes on Mississippi Writers,* XIV (1981), 18–25.

Miller, Nancy. *The Heroine's Text: Readings in the French and English Novel, 1722–1782.* New York, 1980.

Moers, Ellen. *Literary Women.* New York, 1976.

Mortimer, Gail L. "Image and Myth in Eudora Welty's *The Optimist's Daughter.*" *American Literature,* LXII (1990), 617–633.

Muir, Edwin. *The Structure of the Novel.* London, 1928.

Natchez Literary Celebration Special Issue. *Southern Quarterly,* XXIX (Summer, 1991).

Neumann, Erich. *Amor and Psyche: The Psychic Development of the Feminine: A Commentary on the Tale by Apuleius.* Translated by Ralph Manheim. New York, 1962.

Oates, Joyce Carol. "The Art of Eudora Welty." *Shenandoah,* XX (1969), 54–57.

———. "Eudora's Web." In *Contemporary Women Novelists: A Collection of Critical Essays,* edited by Patricia Meyer Spacks. Englewood Cliffs, 1977.

O'Connor, Flannery. *Mystery and Manners: Occasional Prose.* Edited by Sally and Robert Fitzgerald. New York, 1969.

O'Doherty, Brian. "A Visit to Wyeth Country." In *The Art of Andrew Wyeth,* edited by Wanda M. Corn. Boston, 1973.

Opitz, Kurt. "The Order of a Captive Soul." *Critique,* VII (1964–65), 79–91.

Orr, Elaine. "'Unsettling Every Definition of Otherness': Another Reading of Eudora Welty's 'A Worn Path.'" *South Atlantic Review,* LVII (1992), 57–72.

Page, Walter Hines. *The Southerner.* New York, 1909.

Pickering, James H. Introduction to *The Spy: A Tale of the Neutral Ground,* by James Fenimore Cooper. New Haven, 1971.

Pitavy-Souques, Danièle. "'Shower of Gold,' ou les ambiguités de la narration." *Delta,* V (1977), 63–81.

Poe, Edgar Allan. *The Complete Works of Edgar Allan Poe.* Edited by James A. Harrison. 17 vols. 1902; rpr. New York, 1965.

Porte, Joel. *The Romance in America: Studies in Cooper, Poe, Hawthorne, Melville, and James.* Middletown, Conn., 1969.

Porter, Katherine Anne. Introduction to *Selected Stories of Eudora Welty.* New York, 1954.

Praz, Mario. Introduction to *Three Gothic Novels,* edited by Mario Praz. Hammondsworth, 1968.

Prenshaw, Peggy Whitman. "The Antiphonies of Eudora Welty's *One Writer's Beginnings* and Elizabeth Bowen's *Pictures and Conversations.*" *Mississippi Quarterly,* XXXIV (1986), 639–50.

———, ed. *Eudora Welty: Critical Essays.* Jackson, 1983.

———. "A Study of Setting in the Fiction of Eudora Welty." Ph.D. dissertation, University of Texas, 1970.

Proust, Marcel. *Remembrance of Things Past.* Translated by M. K. Scott Moncrief. Vol. II of 2 vols. New York, 1934.

Pryse, Marjorie. "Zora Neale Hurston, Alice Walker, and the 'Ancient Power' of Black Women." *Conjuring: Black Women, Fiction, and Literary Tradition,* edited by Marjorie Pryse and Hortense J. Spillars. Bloomington, 1985.

Randisi, Jennifer Lynn. *A Tissue of Lies: Eudora Welty and the Southern Romance.* Washington, D.C., 1982.

Reid-Petty, Jane, "The Town and the Writer: An Interview with Eudora Welty." *Jackson Magazine,* I (September, 1977), 34.

Rich, Adrienne. "When We Dead Awaken: Writing as Re-Vision." *College English,* XXXIV (1972), 18–25.

Richardson, Dorothy. *Backwater.* 1916; rpr. New York, 1979. Vol. I of Richardson, *Pilgrimage.* 4 vols.

———. *Deadlock.* 1921; rpr. New York, 1976. Vol. III of Richardson, *Pilgrimage.* 4 vols.

Ricoeur, Paul. "Narrative Time." In *On Narrative,* edited by W. J. T. Mitchell. Chicago, 1981.

Ringe, Donald A. *American Gothic: Imagination and Reason in Nineteenth-Century Fiction.* Lexington, 1982.

Rohrberger, Mary. *Hawthorne and the Modern Short Story: A Study in Genre.* The Hague, 1966.

Rosenblum, Joseph. "A New England Heron on the Natchez Trace: Sarah Orne Jewett's 'A White Heron' as Possible Source for Eudora Welty's 'A Still Moment.'" *Notes on Mississippi Writers,* XXII (1990), 69–73.

Rourke, Constance. *The Roots of American Culture and Other Essays.* Edited by Van Wyck Brooks. 1942; rpr. Westport, Conn., 1980.

Rubin, Louis D., Jr. "Art and Artistry in Morgana, Mississippi." In *A Gallery of Southerners,* by Louis D. Rubin, Jr. Baton Rouge, 1982.

———. *The Faraway Country: Writers of the Modern South.* Seattle, 1963.

Rubin, Louis D., Jr., *et al.,* eds. *The History of Southern Literature.* Baton Rouge, 1985.

Sartre, Jean-Paul. "La République du silence." In *Situations III,* by Jean-Paul Sartre. Paris, 1949.

Scholes, Robert. Introduction to *The Fantastic: A Structural Approach to a Literary Genre,* by Tzvetan Todorov, translated by Richard Howard. Ithaca, N.Y., 1975.

Scholes, Robert, and Robert Kellogg. *The Nature of Narrative.* New York, 1969.

Schmidt, Peter. *The Heart of the Story: Eudora Welty's Short Fiction.* Jackson, 1991.

Schulenberger, Arvid. *Cooper's Theory of Fiction: His Prefaces and Their Relation to His Novels.* New York, 1972.

Scott, Evelyn. *The Narrow House.* 1921; rpr. New York, 1977.

Sedgwick, Eve Kosofsky. *The Coherence of Gothic Convention.* New York, 1986.

Simonson, Harold P. *The Closed Frontier: Studies in American Literary Tragedy.* New York, 1970.

Simpson, Lewis P. "What Survivors Do." In *The Brazen Face of History: Studies in the Literary Consciousness of America,* by Lewis P. Simpson. Baton Rouge, 1980.

Smitten, Jeffrey R., and Ann Daghistany, eds. *Spatial Form in Narrative.* Ithaca, N.Y., 1981.

Snelling, Paula. Review of Eudora Welty's *A Curtain of Green. South Today,* VII (1942), 61.

Spacks, Patricia Meyer. Review of Eudora Welty's *The Optimist's Daughter. Hudson Review,* XXV (1972), 509.

Stapleton, Laurence. *The Elected Circle: Studies in the Art of Prose.* Princeton, 1973.

Steegmuller, Francis. "Small Town Life." *New York Times Book Review,* August 21, 1949. p. 5.

Sukenick, Ronald. "Twelve Digressions Toward a Study of Composition." *New Literary History,* VI (1975), 429–37.

———. *In Form: Digressions on the Art of Fiction.* Carbondale, 1985.

Tanner, Tony. *Adultery in the Novel: Contract and Transgression.* Baltimore, 1979.

Tate, Allen. "Techniques of Fiction." In *Essays of Four Decades,* by Allen Tate. Chicago, 1968.

Thompson, Harold. *Body, Boots and Britches.* Philadelphia, 1940.

Thomson, Philip John. *The Grotesque.* London, 1972.

Todorov, Tzvetan. *The Fantastic: A Structural Approach to a Literary Genre.* Translated by Richard Howard. Ithaca, N.Y., 1975.

———. *Mikhail Bakhtin: The Dialogical Principle.* Translated by Wlad Godzich. Minneapolis, 1984.

———. *The Poetics of Prose.* Translated by Richard Howard. Ithaca, N.Y., 1977.

Trilling, Diana. "Fiction in Review" (Review of Eudora Welty's *The Wide Net*). *Nation,* October 2, 1943, pp. 386–87.

Trouard, Dawn, ed. *Eudora Welty: The Eye of the Storyteller.* Kent, Ohio, 1989.

Vande Kieft, Ruth M. *Eudora Welty.* Boston, 1962.

———. *Eudora Welty.* Rev. ed. Boston, 1987.

———. "Eudora Welty: Visited and Revisited." *Mississippi Quarterly,* XXXIX (1986), 455–79.

———. "The Vision of Eudora Welty." *Mississippi Quarterly,* XXVI (1973), 517–42.

Varma, Devendra P. *The Gothic Flame.* London, 1957.

Vursell, H. D. Review of *The Best American Short Stories,* edited by Martha Foley. *Tomorrow,* III (November, 1943), 53.

Walpole, Horace. *The Castle of Otranto: A Gothic Story.* Edited by W. S. Lewis and Joseph W. Reed, Jr. 1764; rpr. new York, 1982.

Walzel, Oskar Franz. *German Romanticism.* Translated by Alma Elise Lussky. 1932; rpr. New York, 1965.

Warren, Robert Penn. "Love and Separateness in Eudora Welty." *Kenyon Review,* VI (1944), 245–59.

Watson, James G. "The American Short Story: 1930–1945." In *The American Short Story, 1900–1945: A Critical History,* edited by Philip Stevick. Boston, 1984.

Welty, Eudora. *Acrobats in a Park.* Northridge, Calif., 1980.

———. *The Collected Stories of Eudora Welty.* New York, 1980.

———. *Conversations with Eudora Welty.* Edited by Peggy Whitman Prenshaw. New York, 1984.

———. *Delta Wedding.* New York, 1946.

———. *The Eye of the Story: Selected Essays and Reviews.* New York, 1978.

———. *The Golden Apples.* New York, 1949.

———. Introduction to *Hanging by a Thread,* by Joan Kahn. Boston, 1969.

———. *Losing Battles.* New York, 1970.

———. "Magic." *Manuscript,* III (September/October, 1935), 3–7.

———. *One Writer's Beginnings.* Cambridge, Mass., 1984.

———. "The Optimist's Daughter." *New Yorker,* March 15, 1969.

———. *The Optimist's Daughter.* New York, 1972.

———. "The Physical World of Willa Cather." *New York Times Book Review,* January 27, 1974, p. 20.

———. *The Robber Bridegroom.* 1942; rpr. New York, 1978.

———. *Three Papers on Fiction.* Northampton, Mass., 1962.

Welty Collection. Mississippi Department of Archives and History, Jackson, Miss.

Westling, Louise. *Sacred Groves and Ravaged Gardens: The Fiction of Eudora Welty, Carson McCullers, and Flannery O'Connor.* Athens, Ga., 1985.

Weston, Ruth D. "The Feminine and Feminist Texts of Eudora Welty's *The Optimist's Daughter.*" *South Central Review,* IV (1987), 74–91.

———. "The Optimist in Hawthorne's Shadow: Eudora Welty's Gothic as Lyric Technique." *Short Story,* I (1991), 71–87.

Wiesenfarth, Joseph. *Gothic Manners and the Classic English Novel.* Madison, 1988.

Wilt, Judith. *Ghosts of the Gothic: Austen, Eliot and Lawrence.* Princeton, 1980.

Witt, Mary Ann Frese. *Existential Prisons: Captivity in Mid-Twentieth-Century French Literature.* Durham, N.C., 1985.

Wollstonecraft, Mary. *A Vindication of the Rights of Woman.* Edited by Charles W. Hagelman, Jr. 1792; rpr. New York, 1967.

Woolf, Virginia. *Mrs. Dalloway.* New York, 1925.

———. *A Room of One's Own.* New York, 1929.

———. *Three Guineas.* New York, 1938.

———. *The Waves.* 1921; rpr. New York, 1978.

Yaeger, Patricia S. "'Because a Fire Was in My Head': Eudora Welty and the Dialogic Imagination." *Mississippi Quarterly,* XXXIX (1986), 561–86.

———. "The Case of the Dangling Signifier: Phallic Imagery in Eudora Welty's 'Moon Lake.'" *Twentieth Century Literature,* XXVIII (1982), 431–52.

Young, Thomas Daniel. *The Past in the Present: A Thematic Study of Modern Southern Fiction.* Baton Rouge, 1981.

Zacharasiewicz, Waldemar. "The Sense of Place in Southern Fiction by Eudora Welty and Flannery O'Connor." *Arbeiten aus Anglistik und Amerikanistik,* X (1985), 189–206.

Index

Absurdist theater, 65, 73
Aeneas, 152
Alcatraz Island (California), 123
Alexander, Dr. Margaret Walker. *See* Walker, Margaret
Ali Baba, 37
Alienation, modern fiction of, 22
Allen, John Alexander, 92, 107, 111, 143, 155, 176
Allende, Isabel, 183*n*13
American Adam, 103
American dream, 27, 66, 96
American Revolution, 24–26
Anderson, Sherwood, 20, 137*n*8
Aphrodite, 13, 174–77
Appel, Alfred, Jr., 16, 137*n*8
Apuleius, 10
Archimedes, 145
Aristotle, 6
Arnold, Benedict, 24
Arnold, Marilyn, 161
Art: American folk, 63–66, 75, 168; architectural Gothic, 16, 21, 32; cubist, 69; Impressionist, 63; magic realist, 67; post-Impressionist, 63, 164; primitivist, 64–65, 71
Atwood, Margaret: *Lady Oracle,* 89
Audubon, John James, 36, 52, 55
Auerbach, Nina, 138, 142, 151, 156
Augustine, Saint, 90
Austen, Jane, 2, 4, 14, 20, 21, 31, 81, 93, 130, 134, 138, 142, 156, 162, 173

Bakhtin, Mikhail, 149
Baldeshwiler, Eileen, 56, 89
Baldick, Chris, 182*n*12
Bank, Stanley, 46

Barthes, Roland, 71
Beauty and the Beast, 156–58, 168
Beckett, Samuel, 65
Beethoven, Ludwig von, 117
Bell, Michael Davitt, 2, 50
Bentham, Jeremy, 93
Benton, Thomas Hart, 66, 71
Bergson, Henri, 78
Bettelheim, Bruno, 42, 157–58
Bildung, 12, 87
Black Women Writers of Magic Realism, conference on, 183*n*13
Blennerhassett, Harmon, 35, 39, 52
Bluebeard, 157
Boethius, 90
Bogan, Louise, 15, 16*n*2
Bolsterli, Margaret, 94
Bowen, Elizabeth, 14*n*15, 16*n*2, 17–18, 64, 125, 129
Bradford, M. E., 75*n*38
Breughel, Pieter, 64
Brinkmeyer, Robert H., Jr., 169
Broadway and off-Broadway stage, 34, 69
Brodhead, Richard, 55
Brontë, Charlotte, 4, 20, 93, 134, 156, 163
Brontë, Emily, 20, 21, 110, 130, 171
Brooks, Cleanth, 4, 54–55
Brooks, Peter, 6–7, 55–56, 61–62, 78–79, 124
Brown, Charles Brockden, 2, 4, 20, 26, 26*n*16, 27, 43
Bryant, J. A., Jr., 108
Buber, Martin, 6, 128
Burr, Aaron, 35, 39, 52
Butor, Michel, 78
Byrne, Bev, 155
Byron, Lord Percy, 138, 141, 153

The Cabinet of Dr. Caligari, 34, 168
Capote, Truman, 4, 5, 20, 31
Captivity narratives, American, 90
Carceral community, 90–132. *See also*
    Prison
Carden (Welty's grandmother), 150, 162
Carnival, 159–60
Carson, Barbara Harrell, 101, 129, 158
Carson, Gary, 50*n*3
Cash, W. J., 111
Cather, Willa, 66, 76, 86, 110, 142–43
Chamlee, Kenneth D., 10*n*11
Chaos, primordial, 128–29
Character types: Aphrodite, 13, 174–77;
    Argus, 118; Beauty and the Beast, 156–
    58, 168; "bound," 94; choral, 12, 69;
    Circe, 169; David and Goliath, 144;
    demi-god, 103–108, 121, 143, 171, 175;
    Dido, 152; Dionysian, 81, 103, 165; Dis,
    176; Eros, 13, 174–75; fairy, 156–57,
    166, 170; "flat," 61, 66, 69, 71, 74; ghost,
    159; Great Mother, 13, 176–77; Hansel
    and Gretel, 158; Helen of Troy, 108;
    Kore, 175; Leda, 121; maternal adminis-
    trators, 156; mysterious stranger, 160;
    orphan, 100, 104, 161; outcast/outsider/
    exile, 118, 122, 123, 125, 131, 138–39,
    150, 160–63; Pan, 122; Penelope, 116,
    181; Persephone, 175; Perseus, 118; pied
    piper, 122; *porte parole,* 113, 117; prin-
    cess, 157; prodigal son, 139; Psyche, 13,
    175, 177; Rapunzel, 154; Red Riding
    Hood, 32; sage, 147; sibyl/oracle, 141–
    42, 145; Sleeping Beauty, 13, 155, 168;
    sorceress, 169; split protagonist, 139,
    152–59, 171, 179; "two-faced," 155;
    warder, 122, 142; Welty's "third," 37–
    38, 57; Zeus, 114, 121
—hero: 132, 137, 141–42; Byronic, 138–
    41, 150, 153; female, 133–72; Gothic,
    138, 150; knight, 143–44, 147; mock-,
    131, 144; -monster, 150; Odysseus, 116;
    Percival, 141; Perseus, 118, 121, 141,
    168; picaresque, 133, 135, 149; Prince
    Charming/Handsome Prince, 13, 156,
    164, 168, 179; Romantic, 156; Saint
    George, 141; savior, 41, 104–105, 144;
    southern figural, 105, 109, 131, 139,
    143, 147; tragic, 142, 147; "Trojan," 108;

-victim, 138, 150; -villain, 118, 139–40,
    145, 153, 168
—villain: admirable, 141; beast-, 158; Blue-
    beard, 157; Byronic, 4; Gorgon, 160;
    gothic, 133, 157, 168; Medusa, 118, 142,
    160; wicked/evil/cruel stepmother, 13,
    46, 155–59, 179; Terrible Mother, 13,
    157, 176, 179; vampire, 164, 179; witch,
    156, 158; wolf-grandmother, 32. See also
    The Cabinet of Dr. Caligari
Chase, Richard, 20, 25, 46, 47, 48, 50
Chekhov, Anton, 52, 56, 63, 69, 88
Chodorov, Jerome (adapter of *The Ponder
    Heart* for the stage), 6*n*8
Chodorow, Nancy, 46, 177
Chopin, Kate, 20, 41
Choreography, 69
Chorus, Greek, 69
"Christ-haunted" South, 4
Cinema, French, 61
Cirlot, J. E., 106
Civil War, 4, 76–77, 88, 135, 145
Coale, Samuel Chase, 49
Coates, Robert M., 26
Codes, literary, 134, 174
Coleridge, Samuel T., 68
Collins, Carvel, 129
Columbia University, 69
Conger, Syndy McMillen, 22
Cooper, James Fenimore, 2, 3, 20, 24–28,
    40, 42, 46, 48, 59, 91
Cooper, Susan (daughter of J. Fenimore),
    25*n*16
Crane, Stephen: "The Bride Comes to
    Yellow-Sky," 66
Cubism, 69
Curley, Daniel, 120*n*39, 132*n*54
Currin, Brenda (star of *Sister and Miss
    Lexie*), 69

Daghistany, Ann, 62, 68
d'Ambrosio, Paul, 65*n*27
Dance, modern, 73
Davidson, Abraham, 64*n*25
Demmin, Julia L., 120*n*39, 132*n*54
Derrida, Jacques, 165
Devlin, Albert J., 91*n*2, 100, 119, 155
Dialogism. *See* Bakhtin, Mikhail
Dickens, Charles, 4, 22, 51, 173

Index

Dickinson, Emily, 3
Dido, 152
Dinesen, Isak, 110, 134
Dionysus, 103
Dis, 176
Discourse analysis, 113, 149
Doré, Gustave, 23
Dolson, Hildegard (Welty collaborator), 64
Donaldson, Susan V., 177*n*6
Donovan, Josephine, 11*n*12
Double natures, 46
Dow, Lorenzo, 36–37
Dragon: alligator as, 37; as image of ignorance, 141; as image of unfettered passions, 128
Dunbar, Paul Laurence, 183*n*13
DuPlessis, Rachel Blau, 12, 45, 74, 81, 92, 107, 136, 149, 152

Edel, Leon, 146
Eden, 103
Elegy, 141, 153
Eliade, Mircea, 129
Eliot, George, 4, 22, 31, 173
Eliot, T. S., 17, 140
Ellison, Ralph, 5
Emerson, Ralph Waldo, 3
Epic: comic, 152; heroic, 8, 133, 147, 153, 154; Homeric, 136
Eros, 13, 45, 174–77
Evans, Elizabeth, 64*n*26
Existentialism, 98, 104, 126

Fairy tale, 8, 13, 35, 42–46, 73, 133, 154, 156, 163, 171, 174, 178, 179
Faulkner, William: 9–10, 14, 20, 31, 66, 91, 97, 100, 104, 106, 111; *Absalom, Absalom!*, 4; *As I Lay Dying*, 4; "The Bear," 85, 95, 168; *Go Down, Moses*, 95; *Light in August*, 7–9, 131; "The Old People," 95; *Requiem for a Nun*, 17; "A Rose for Emily," 4, 31, 78, 113; *Sanctuary*, 130
Female physiology, Gothic male fear of, 130
Ferguson, Mary Anne, 136, 174–75, 179–80
Ferris, William, 15, 64
Fetterley, Judith, 123
Fields, Joe (adapter of *The Ponder Heart* for the stage), 6*n*8

Fink, Mike, 39, 42, 44
Finlay, Marike, 68
Flaubert, Gustave, 41, 58
Fleenor, Juliann E., 19, 46, 123
Fleishauer, John F., 58*n*15
Fogle, Richard Harter, 56
Folk art. *See* Art
Folklore, 55–56, 73, 96
Forster, E. M., 39, 61, 71
Foucault, Michel, 56, 75, 91, 93, 99, 105, 112
Fowles, John: *The French Lieutenant's Woman*, 21
Frank, Joseph, 61, 67, 71
Freudian psychology, 57, 165
Frye, Northrop, 52, 131
Fugitives, Vanderbilt, 135
Fuller, R. Buckminster, 43

Garcia-Marquez, Gabriel, 183*n*13
Gardner, Helen, 164*n*39
George, Saint, 141
Ghosts, 1, 4, 17, 24, 26–27, 30, 31, 33–34, 44
"Ghost sense": of Hawthorne, 17
Ghost stories, 17, 24, 33–34
Ghost town, 16–18
Gilbert, Sandra, 19, 22, 135, 154
Gilligan, Carol, 137, 175
Gilman, Charlotte Perkins, 20, 107, 134
Gohdes, Clarence, 3
Good-enough father, 178
Good-enough mother, 176–79, 181
Gorgon, 160
Gorky Institute (Russia), 63
Gothic: African-American, 5; American, 4, 10, 20–22, 24, 26–27, 43, 46, 50–51, 53, 55, 90, 92, 96, 173; architecture/houses, 16, 21, 24–47, 25*n*17, 53, 101; classic ("old"), 2–4, 20, 24, 39, 43, 46, 49–50, 55, 93, 96, 124, 133; dread, 19, 63, 77, 129, 173; European, 3, 16, 20–25, 46, 50, 90, 163, 173, 182; female, 2, 5, 19, 46, 133–35, 154; grotesque, 5, 19, 20, 62, 67, 137; horror, 16, 21, 26; melodramatic, 20; popular, 1; psychological, 4, 21, 134; novel of manners ("new"), 21, 50, 93; parody of, 29, 33, 44; realistic, 55, 134, 182; romance,

1, 4, 12, 22, 26–27, 31, 46, 50, 54–55,
89, 146, 173; and the serious aim of
modern, 182; shape of plot, 54; short
story, 51–54, 89, 182; Southern, 4–6,
20, 31, 63, 78, 137; space, 3, 6, 15,
18–20, 19n7, 24–47, 53, 54, 58–60,
75, 89, 92–93, 98, 101, 124, 130, 160,
182; sportive, 2; supernaturalistic, 20,
33, 133; terror, 16, 29, 36, 44, 93, 124,
142, 154; Welty's imagination as, 57
Gray, Richard, 79, 86, 99, 101
Great Depression, 15, 60
Great Mother, 13, 177
Greek chorus, 69
Gretlund, Jan Nordby, 119
Griffin, Dorothy, 100
Grimm, Brothers (Jakob and Wilhelm), 10,
35, 42
Gross, Seymour L., 151n24
Grotesque: art and architecture, 20, 23–
24; excessive sense or sensibility as, 162;
landscape, 24. See also Gothic
Gubar, Susan, 19, 22, 135, 154
Gygax, Franziska, 138

Hades, descent into, 105
Haggerty, George E., 19, 52, 91, 147, 171
Hamblett, Theora, 64
Hansel and Gretel, 158
Hardy, John Edward, 100, 102, 111, 157
Hardy, Thomas, 18, 125
Hare, Joseph Thompson, 44
Harpe Brothers, 42, 44
Hawthorne, Nathaniel: 2, 3, 17, 20, 27, 51,
52–57, 64, 89, 91, 95, 101, 130, 139,
160, 173; "Alice Doane's Appeal," 49n2,
52; "The Birth-Mark," 55; The Blithedale
Romance, 49; "The Custom House," 48;
The House of the Seven Gables, 31, 49,
49n2, 53, 56; "The Minister's Black
Veil," 147; "My Kinsman, Major Moli-
neux," 53; "Rappaccini's Garden," 53;
The Scarlet Letter, 28, 31, 49, 57; "Young
Goodman Brown," 28, 57, 102
Heilbrun, Carolyn, 39
Heilman, Robert, 5, 6, 15, 22, 51n5, 93,
143, 150, 177
Hemingway, Ernest, 18
Hero, female "traveling," 133, 149. See
also Character types

Hinton, Jane, 94
Hoffman, Frederick J., 96
Homer, 136, 169, 181
Howard, Maureen, 156
Howells, William Dean: realism of, 47n38
Hudson River/Hudson Highlands (New
York), 3, 25, 40
Hughes, Langston, 183n13
Huguenot Historical Association (New
York), 25n17
Hurston, Zora Neale, 12

Ibsen, Henrik, 72
Impressionism, 63
Inquisition, the, 90, 142
Irving, Washington: 2, 9, 43, 51, 52; "The
Legend of Sleepy Hollow," 24; "Story of
the Young Robber," 10, 45, 178

Jacobs, Robert D., 51
James, Henry: 3, 26, 27, 59, 64, 146; "The
Art of Fiction," 48; The Bostonians, 156;
The Turn of the Screw, 53
Jewett, Sarah Orne, 36
Johnson, J. J., 62, 68
Jones, Alun R., 60
Jones, Anne Goodwyn, 135
Jones, Howard, 141
Jones, Louis C., 25n17
Joyce, James, 53, 143, 153
Jung, Carl, 102, 155

Kafka, Franz, 62
Kahane, Claire, 19, 157
Kahn, Joan, 133n1
Kaplan, David (adapter of Welty's Sister
and Miss Lexie for the stage), 69
Kayser, Wolfgang, 24n14
Kazin, Alfred, 3
Kepler, Johannes, 113
Kestner, Joseph A., 67n29, 71n33
Klinkowitz, Jerome, 56
Kolbenschlag, Madonna, 154, 166
Kolmerten, Carol A., 97
Kore, 175
Kreyling, Michael, 39, 44, 49, 85, 105, 109,
111–12, 139, 143, 154, 159, 170
Kristeva, Julia, 170
Kuehl, Linda, 63

Landess, Thomas, 100
Landry, Donna, 154
Lane, Suzette, 65n27
Lawrence, D. H., 4, 31, 173, 179, 182
Legend. *See* Myth and legend
Lessing, Doris, 81–82
Levertov, Denise, 74
Lewis, Matthew G.: "Monk," 4, 20
Lewis, R. W. B., 96n11
Les Liaisons Dangereuses, 87
Lohafer, Susan, 56
Longwood Plantation (Mississippi): ruins of, 17
Luraghi, Raimondo, 97
Lytle, Andrew, 113

McAlpin, Sara, 112
McCullers, Carson: 4, 20, 67, 134, 139; *The Ballad of the Sad Cafe,* 5; *The Heart Is a Lonely Hunter,* 5; *Member of the Wedding,* 5, 137; *The Mortgaged Heart,* 63; *Reflections in a Golden Eye,* 5
McDonald, William, 1
McDonald Papers, 25n16
Madness, 29, 150, 158, 160, 163; as gothic topos, 19n7
Magic, 2, 20, 30, 39, 128
Magic realism: in painterly art, 67; in literary art, 183
Magny, Claude Edmond, 31
Mailer, Norman, 123, 130
Malin, Irving, 19
Manfred (heroic poem by Lord Byron), 153
Manning, Carol, 66, 144, 166, 168
Mansfield, Katherine, 53, 56
Manz-Kunz, Marie-Antoinette, 92, 131
Mardi Gras, 159–60
Marriage of death, 173–80
Marrs, Suzanne, 40
Marshall, Paule, 183n13
Mason, Thomas, 42
Mather, Cotton, 24, 52
Matore, Georges, 90n1
Matthiessen, F. O., 57
Maturin, C. R., 4, 138, 142
May, Charles E., 51n5, 52
Medusa, 121, 141, 168–69
Melville, Herman, 27, 52
Mickelsen, David, 71

Miller, Lisa K., 27
Miller, Nancy, 86
Miller, Perry, 50
Modernism, 22, 88. *See also* Welty, Eudora
Moers, Ellen, 5, 19, 110, 133
Mohammed, Ethel, 64, 71
Moore, Marianne, 48
Moral and ethical ideas: in Welty's fiction, 72
Morrison, Toni, 183n13
Mortimer, Gail, 8
Moses, Grandma, 64
Mother-child dyad, 107
Muir, Edwin, 71
Munch, Edvard, 164
Murder, 10, 32, 33, 36, 42, 44, 118, 120
Murrell, James, 36
Mystery, 2, 8, 15, 18, 19, 20, 23, 26, 28, 30, 31, 33, 34, 36, 38, 40, 43, 48, 50, 53, 58, 64, 76, 82–83, 89, 96, 98, 102, 106, 107, 109, 115, 121, 128, 129, 130, 137, 146, 182
Myth of concern, culture's, 22, 73, 88, 93
Myth and legend, 1, 28, 42, 49, 52–53, 75, 96, 111, 155, 174–75, 182

Narrative: spatial form in, 9, 61–89, 34–35, 164, 181
Narrative time, 6–7
Natchez Indian tribe, 18, 44
Natchez Trace, 3, 16–18, 26, 29, 33–36, 40, 42–43, 51, 96, 111, 155, 160
Natchez Trace Literary Celebration, 51n6, 58n15
Natives, returns of, 125
Naylor, Gloria, 5
Neumann, Erich, 175, 181
Neutral ground, 3, 26, 33, 36, 48, 58
Newton, Isaac, 113
New York State Historical Association, 25n16

Oates, Joyce Carol, 55, 130, 154, 173
O'Connor, Flannery, 4, 20, 67, 94n8, 100, 131
O'Doherty, Brian, 68n30
Odysseus, 116
Odyssey, The (of Homer), 116, 136
Oedipal syndrome, 107, 168
Oedipus, 11

O'Keeffe, Georgia, 63
Olson, Christina, 67
Opitz, Kurt, 98*n*14
Oral tradition, 24, 25*n*16, 65, 73, 141
Orr, Elaine, 169

Page, Walter Hines, 4
Parthenogenesis, 107
Penelope, 116, 181
Percival, 141
Persephone, 175
Perseus, 118, 121, 141, 168
Picaresque, female, 133
Pickering, James H., 25*n*16
Pissarro, Camille, 60
Pitavy-Souques, Danièle, 58*n*15, 114, 121, 168
Plantation ruins: Longwood (Mississippi), 17; Windsor (Mississippi), 40
Plato, 90–92
Poe, Edgar Allan: 4, 27, 51, 52, 64, 79, 147; "The Fall of the House of Usher," 23, 53, 101; "The Pit and the Pendulum," 92
Polk, Noel, 112
Porte, Joel, 27, 50
Porter, Katherine Anne, 10, 56, 75, 112, 157
Post-Impressionism, 63, 164
Praz, Mario, 19*n*7
Prenshaw, Peggy Whitman, 17, 42, 107, 138, 166, 171
Primitivism, 64, 71
Prince Charming, 13, 156, 164, 168, 179
Prison: existential, 99, 126, 132; as gothic topos, 19*n*7, 142; of memory, 7–8, 168; as metaphor for carceral society, 75, 90–94, 99, 112–13, 117, 122–23; self-induced, 157; tower of Rapunzel, 154
Propp, Vladimir, 55
Proust, Marcel, 61, 64
Pryse, Marjorie, 30*n*24
Psyche: myth of, 13, 45, 174–77, 180

Rabelais, François, 68
Radcliffe, Anne, 2, 4, 55, 133, 147
Randisi, Jennifer Lynn, 45
Rape, 41, 44–45, 76, 100, 104, 116, 121, 130, 136, 137, 142, 150–52, 165, 167, 170, 175, 180–81
Rapunzel, 154

Realism: Howellsian, 47*n*38. *See also* Magic realism
Red Riding Hood, 33
Reid-Petty, Jane, 64*n*27
Renaissance, southern, 135
Renoir, Jean, 61
Revolutionary War. *See* American Revolution
Rich, Adrienne, 31
Richardson, Dorothy, 12–13, 126
Ricoeur, Paul, 6–7
Ringe, Donald, 24, 26, 31
Ritual of the word, 162, 171
Robinson, Edwin Arlington, 137*n*8
Robinson, John, 10*n*11
Rodney's Landing (Mississippi), 16, 18, 40
Rohrberger, Mary, 51, 54
Roles. *See* Character types
Rosenblum, Joseph, 36*n*29
Ross, Stephen M., 97
Rourke, Constance, 65
Rubin, Louis D., Jr., 93, 94, 117*n*35
Russell, Diarmuid, 112*n*32
Russian formalists, 55
Russian view of Eudora Welty, 63

Sartre, Jean Paul, 31, 126
Savior characters, 41, 104, 144. *See also* Character types
Schlegel, August Wilhelm von, 68
Schmidt, Peter, 141–42, 180
Scholes, Robert, 8, 21, 134
Schorer, Mark, 173
Schulenberger, Arvid, 46
Scott, Evelyn, 5, 20, 134
Scott, Sir Walter, 4, 26, 46, 102
Sedgwick, Eve, 19, 92
Seurat, Georges Pierre, 60
Shakespeare, William, 72
Shelley, Mary: *Frankenstein,* 93, 124, 130, 138, 150
Sister and Miss Lexie (dramatic collage of Welty's fiction), 69
Simms, William Gilmore, 43
Simpson, Lewis P., 91*n*2
Simonson, Harold P., 91*n*2
Skaggs, Merrill Maguire, 114
Slavery: in Civil War, 76–78, 136; sexual bondage as, 136, 177, 180–81
Sleeping Beauty, 13, 155, 164

Smitten, Jeffrey, 71
Snelling, Paula, 181
Socrates, 90
Soviet-American Symposium on Eudora
    Welty, 63
Spacks, Patricia Meyer, 88
Spatiality. *See* Narrative
Stapleton, Laurence, 88
Steegmuller, Francis, 60*n*19
Stein, Karen F., 46
Stepmother, wicked, 13, 46, 155–58, 179
Sterne, Lawrence, 68
Sukenick, Ronald, 42, 61
Surrealism and the surreal, 5, 32, 34, 39,
    120, 160
Swift, Jonathan, 68

Tanner, Tony, 22, 126
Tate, Allen, 46
Tatler, The, 68
Terrible Mother, 13, 157, 176, 179
"Third character": Welty's, 37–39, 57
Thomson, Philip, 23
Thompson, Harold, 25*n*16
Todorov, Tzvetan, 8*n*10, 21, 147
Trilling, Diana, 59*n*17
Turgenev, Ivan Sergeyevich, 56
Turner, Frederick, 27
Twain, Mark, 40

Utopia, female, 107

Vande Kieft, Ruth M., 1, 15, 17, 28, 64,
    69*n*32, 74, 98*n*14, 102, 103, 148, 151
Varma, Devendra P., 182
Victorian marriage customs, 126
Villain, Byronic, 4. *See also* Character types
Villon, François, 60
Virgil, 152, 153
Vursell, H. D., 59*n*17

Walker, Alice, 22, 171, 183*n*13
Walker, Margaret, 57
Wall, Carey, 113
Walpole, Hugh, 4, 20, 55, 91
Walzel, Oskar Franz, 62*n*22
Warner, Pecolia, 64
Warren, Robert Penn, 36, 54, 55
Washington, George, 26

Wasteland, image of, 19, 29, 93, 118,
    139–41
Watson, James Gray, 118
Welty, Eudora: as comic writer, 9, 68, 73,
    94, 130; dramatic modifications from,
    34, 69; dramatic musical by ("What Year
    Is This?"), 64; as feminist, 11–13, 111,
    170–71, 174–81; as magic realist, 183;
    as modernist, 54, 65, 73, 74, 77, 88, 111,
    143, 182; as painter, 65; as playwright,
    64; as postmodernist, 77; as realist, 38,
    65, 67, 112, 129, 133, 138, 182
—fiction by: "Acrobats in a Park," 97; "As-
    phodel," 40, 69*n*32, 176; "At the Land-
    ing," 13, 40–42, 53, 83, 84, 92, 104,
    120, 136–37, 175, 177, 179–81; "The
    Bride of the Innisfallen," 14*n*15, 74,
    171–72; *The Bride of the Innisfallen
    and Other Stories,* 14, 74, 76, 77; "The
    Burning," 9, 56, 76–78, 79, 87, 95, 127,
    135, 167; "Circe," 15, 169; "Clytie," 13,
    30–33, 62, 66, 92, 136, 181, 182; *Col-
    lected Stories,* 123; "A Curtain of Green,"
    16, 29, 34; *A Curtain of Green and
    Other Stories,* 15, 33, 62, 112, 118;
    "Death of a Traveling Salesman," 16,
    28–29, 34, 53, 119; "The Delta Cous-
    ins," 49; *Delta Wedding,* 57, 74, 82, 86,
    94–112, 120, 121, 130–31, 137, 143,
    148, 155, 158–59, 176, 181; "The Dem-
    onstrators," 9, 126; "First Love," 34–36,
    42, 52; "Flowers for Marjorie," 13, 118;
    "Going to Naples," 56, 79–88, 94, 97,
    110, 122, 128, 143; *The Golden Apples,*
    14, 32, 60, 74, 94–95, 112–28, 131,
    149, 154, 156, 166, 168, 176, 177; "The
    Hitchhikers," 119; "June Recital," 55,
    88, 113–18, 131, 138; "Keela, the Out-
    cast Indian Maiden," 66; "Lily Daw and
    the Three Ladies," 56, 62, 65, 68–76,
    69*n*32, 77, 79, 82, 84, 97, 102, 128;
    "Livvie," 136, 176; *Losing Battles,*
    11, 60, 64, 105, 111, 130, 133, 136,
    138–56, 170–71, 181; "Magic," 148; "A
    Memory," 59, 94, 101, 106, 118, 157;
    "Moon Lake," 104, 110, 118, 128, 137,
    177; "Music from Spain," 9, 77, 94, 106,
    116–17, 119, 121–24, 130; "No Place
    For You, My Love," 9, 37–39, 84, 102,
    120, 129, 160; "Old Mr. Marblehall,"

30, 32–33, 150, 158; "The Optimist's Daughter" (*New Yorker* story), 148, 154; *The Optimist's Daughter,* 11, 14, 53, 64, 74, 82, 110, 111, 117, 119, 136, 138–39, 148, 153–72, 177, 178–79, 181; "Petrified Man," 62; *The Ponder Heart,* 6, 156; "The Purple Hat," 33–34, 39; *The Robber Bridegroom,* 9–11, 25, 27, 33, 40, 42–46, 49, 52, 112, 136, 155–56, 160, 163, 174–79, 181; "Shower of Gold," 58*n*15, 113–14; "Sir Rabbit," 57, 131; "A Still Moment," 9, 34, 36–37, 42, 52, 55; "A Visit of Charity," 32–33; "The Wanderers," 9, 66, 72, 77, 78, 87, 94, 116, 118, 124–28, 167, 177; "Where Is the Voice Coming From?" 58*n*15; "The Whole World Knows," 119–20, 136; "Why I Live at the P.O.," 13, 69, 138; *The Wide Net,* 33, 34, 59, 62; "A Worn Path," 29–30, 62, 68
—nonfiction by: "Fairy Tale of the Natchez Trace," 42; Introduction to *Hanging by a Thread,* by Joan Kahn, 133*n*1; "Is Phoenix Jackson's Grandson Really Dead?" 30; "Looking at Short Stories," 179; "The Physical World of Willa Cather," 143*n*15; "Place in Fiction," 18, 58; "The Radiance of Jane Austen," 93; "Some Notes on River Country," 1, 17, 40

West, Benjamin, 63
Westling, Louise, 4, 100
Weston, Ruth D., 11*n*12, 171*n*46
West Point, New York, 25
Wharton, Edith, 41
Whistler, James A. McNeill, 66
Wicked stepmother. *See* Character types
Wiesenfarth, Joseph, 21–22, 93
Wilderness: as gothic topos, 182
Wilt, Judith, 3, 19, 31, 81, 173, 182
Windsor ruin. *See* Plantation ruins
Witch, 24, 32, 72, 156
Witt, Mary Ann Frese, 90*n*1, 99, 126
Wollstonecraft, Mary, 151
Wood, Grant, 66
Woolf, Virginia, 11, 56, 108, 180
Works Progress Administration (WPA), 15, 65
World War II, 90
Wright, Richard, 5
Wyeth, Andrew, 63, 67–68, 70

Yaeger, Patricia, 137, 149
Yeats, W. B., 121, 149
Young, Thomas Daniel, 159

Zacharasiewicz, Waldemar, 23*n*13